Identity *and* Self-Respect

Identity *and* Self-Respect

The Great Books Foundation

A nonprofit educational organization

Published and distributed by

 The Great Books Foundation
A nonprofit educational organization

35 East Wacker Drive, Suite 2300
Chicago, IL 60601-2298

Copyright © 1997 by The Great Books Foundation
Chicago, Illinois
All rights reserved
ISBN 1-880323-79-6

First Printing
9 8 7 6 5 4 3 2 1 0

Library of Congress Cataloging-in-Publication Data
Identity and self-respect.
    p.   cm. — (50th anniversary series)
    Contents: The fire next time / James Baldwin — Apology / Plato — A real life /
Alice Munro — A room of one's own / Virginia Woolf — A dull story / Anton
Chekhov — Poetry / T. S. Eliot — Questions for Emma (Jane Austen) — Questions
for Invisible man (Ralph Ellison)
    ISBN 1-880323-79-6
    1. Literature — Collections. 2. Group reading. 3. Reader-response criticism.
I. Great Books Foundation (U.S.)   II. Series: Great Books Foundation 50th
anniversary series.
PN6014.I34   1997
808.8—DC21   97-42325

CONTENTS

PREFACE

"Why does Ellison have the black activist Tod Clifton fall out of history and sell Sambo dolls?" "So that's what Baldwin means when he says that denial of the fact of death is at the root of white America's racial fears!" "Why does the intelligent and principled Emma imagine everything wrong when it comes to love?"

Anyone who has been in a book discussion group has experienced the joy of new insight. Sometimes an idea or question occurs to us during the group meeting. Often, it is afterward—sometimes much later—that an idea we had overlooked unexpectedly strikes us with new force. A good group becomes a community of minds. We share perspectives, questions, insights, and surprises. Our fellow readers challenge and broaden our thinking as we probe deeply into characters and ideas. They help us resolve questions, and raise new ones, in a creative process that connects literature with life.

It is this kind of experience that makes book discussion groups worthwhile, and that the Great Books Foundation fosters for thousands of readers around the world.

The Great Books Foundation is a pioneer of book discussion groups that bring together dedicated readers who wish to continue to learn throughout their lives. The literature anthologies published by the Foundation have been the focus of many enlightening discussions among people of all educational backgrounds and walks of life. And the *shared inquiry* method practiced by Great Books groups has proven to be a powerful approach to literature that solves many practical concerns of new discussion groups: How can we maintain a flow of ideas? What kinds of questions should we discuss? How can we keep the discussion focused on the reading so that we use our time together to really get at the heart of a work—to learn from it and each other?

With the publication of its 50th Anniversary Series, the Great Books Foundation continues and expands upon its tradition of helping all readers engage in a meaningful exchange of ideas about outstanding works of literature.

ABOUT *IDENTITY AND SELF-RESPECT*

The reading selections in *Identity and Self-Respect* have been chosen to stimulate lively shared inquiry discussions. This collection brings together works from around the world that speak to each other on a theme of universal human significance. In this volume you will find classic statements on identity and self-respect from Plato, James Baldwin, and Virginia Woolf; fiction by Anton Chekhov and the contemporary Canadian writer Alice Munro; and poetry by T. S. Eliot.

These are carefully crafted works that readers will interpret in different ways. They portray characters whose lives and motivations are complex, embody concepts that go beyond simple analysis, and raise many questions to inspire extended reflection.

As an aid to reading and discussion, open-ended *interpretive questions* are included with each selection in the volume, and also for the recommended novels *Emma* by Jane Austen and *Invisible Man* by Ralph Ellison. A fundamental or *basic* interpretive question about the meaning of the selection is printed in boldface, followed by a list of related questions that will help you fully discuss the issue raised by the basic question. Passages for *textual analysis* that you may want to look at closely during discussion are suggested for each set of questions. Questions under the heading "For Further Reflection" can be used at the end of discussion to help your group consider the reading selection in a broader context.

ABOUT SHARED INQUIRY

The success of Great Books discussions depends not only on thought-provoking literature, but also on the shared inquiry method of discussion. A shared inquiry discussion begins with a basic interpretive question—a genuine question about the meaning of the selection that continues to be puzzling even after careful reading. As participants offer different possible answers to this question, the discussion leader or members of the group follow up on the ideas that are voiced, asking questions about how responses relate to the original question or to new ideas, and probing what specifically in the text prompted the response.

In shared inquiry discussion, readers think for themselves about the selection, and do not rely on critical or biographical sources outside the text for ideas about its meaning. Discussion remains focused on the text. Evidence for opinions is found in the selection. Because interpretive questions have no single "correct answer," participants are encouraged to entertain a range of ideas. The exchange of ideas is open and spontaneous, a common search for understanding that leads to closer, more illuminating reading.

Shared inquiry fosters a habit of critical questioning and thinking. It encourages patience in the face of complexity, and a respect for the opinions of others. As participants explore the work in depth, they try out ideas, reconsider simple answers, and synthesize interpretations. Over time, shared inquiry engenders a profound experience of intellectual intimacy as your group searches together for meaning in literature.

IMPROVING YOUR DISCUSSIONS

The selections in *Identity and Self-Respect* will support six meetings of your discussion group, with each selection being the focus of a single meeting. Discussions usually last about two hours, and are guided by a member of the group who acts as leader. Since the leader has no special knowledge or qualification beyond a genuine curiosity about the text, any member of the group may lead discussion. The leader carefully prepares the interpretive questions that he or she wants to explore with the group, and is primarily responsible for continuing the process of questioning that maintains the flow of ideas.

To ensure a successful discussion, we encourage you to make it a policy to read the selection twice. A first reading will familiarize you with the plot and ideas of a selection; on a second reading you will read more reflectively and discover many aspects of the work that deepen your thinking about it. Allowing a few days to pass between your readings will also help you approach a second reading with greater insight.

Read the selection actively. Make marginal comments that you might want to refer to in discussion. While our interpretive questions can help you think about different aspects of the work, jotting down your own questions as you read is the best way to engage with the selection and bring a wealth of ideas and meaningful questions to discussion.

During discussion, expect a variety of answers to the basic question. Follow up carefully on these different ideas. Refer to and read from the text often—by way of explaining your answer, and to see if the rest of the group understands the author's words the same way you do. (You will often be surprised!) As your group looks closely at the text, many new ideas will arise.

While leaders in shared inquiry discussion strive to keep comments focused on the text and on the basic interpretive question the group is discussing, the entire group can share responsibility for politely refocusing comments that wander from the text into personal anecdotes or issues that begin to sidetrack discussion.

Remember that during shared inquiry discussion you are investigating differing perspectives on the reading, not on social issues. Talk should be about characters in the story, not about participants' own lives. By maintaining this focus, each discussion will be new and interesting, with each participant bringing a different perspective to bear on the text. After the work has been explored thoroughly on its own terms, your thinking about important issues of the day or in your own life will be enhanced. We have found that it is best to formally set aside a time—perhaps the last half-hour of discussion or over coffee afterward—for members of the group to share personal experiences and opinions that go beyond a discussion of the selection.

DISCUSSING THE POETRY SELECTION

Many book groups shy away from the challenge of discussing poetry, but the shared inquiry method will enable you to make poetry a very satisfying part of your discussion group. Poetry, by its very nature, communicates ideas through suggestion, allusion, and resonance. Because meaning in poetry resides in the interaction between author and reader, and is brought to light through the pooling of different perspectives and readers' responses, poems are ideal for shared inquiry discussion.

It is helpful to read the poem aloud before beginning discussion. Because poetry is usually more densely constructed than prose and highly selective in detail, it often lends itself to what we call *textual analysis*—looking closely at particular lines, words, and images as an entryway to discussing the whole work. Having readers share their different associations with a word or image can often help broaden interpretations.

DISCUSSING THE NOVELS

Many novels might come to mind that relate to the theme of identity and self-respect. We have recommended *Emma* and *Invisible Man* as particularly enriching novels on this theme, and have provided interpretive questions that can be a significant aid to the reader. Even readers familiar with these novels will find a shared inquiry discussion of them a fresh and rewarding experience.

Most shared inquiry groups discuss a novel at a single discussion; some prefer to spread the discussion over more than one session, especially for longer novels. Since it is usually not realistic to expect participants to read a novel twice in full before discussion, we recommend that you at least reread parts of the novel that seemed especially important to you or that raised a number of questions in your mind. Our passages for textual analysis suggest parts of the novel where reading twice might be most valuable. You might even begin your discussion, after posing a basic question, by looking closely at one or two short passages to get people talking about central ideas and offering a variety of opinions that can be probed and expanded into a discussion of the whole work.

How the Great Books Foundation Can Help You

The Great Books Foundation can be a significant resource for you and your discussion group. Our staff conducts shared inquiry workshops throughout the country that will help you or your entire group conduct better discussions. Thousands of people—from elementary school teachers and college professors to those who just love books and ideas—have found our workshops to be an enjoyable experience that changes forever how they approach literature.

The Foundation publishes a variety of reading series that might interest you. We invite you to call us at 1-800-222-5870 or visit our Web site at http://www.greatbooks.org. We can help you start a book group, put you in touch with established Great Books groups in your area, or give you information about many special events—such as poetry weekends or week-long discussion institutes—sponsored by Great Books groups around the country.

Finally, we invite you to inquire about Junior Great Books for students in kindergarten through high school, to learn how you can help develop the next generation of book lovers and shared inquiry participants.

We hope you enjoy *Identity and Self-Respect* and that it inaugurates many years of exciting discussions for your group. Great Books programs—for children as well as adults—are founded on the idea that readers discussing together can achieve insight and great pleasure from literature. We look forward, with you, to cultivating this idea through the next century.

*Footnotes by the author are not bracketed; footnotes by
the Great Books Foundation, an editor,
or a translator are [bracketed].*

THE FIRE NEXT TIME

(selection)

James Baldwin

JAMES BALDWIN (1924–1987), novelist, essayist, short story writer, and dramatist, was born in Harlem, the oldest of nine children. He left home at the age of nineteen, after the death of his stepfather, to live in Greenwich Village and pursue his ambition to be a writer. After five years, and many ill-paid jobs, he was awarded a Rosenwald Fellowship, which allowed him to move to Paris and concentrate on his writing in a less racist environment. It was during this period that he rose to prominence with his semiautobiographical novel *Go Tell It on the Mountain* (1953), and with his eloquent exploration of black-white relations in essays published in such magazines as *Harper's* and the *Reporter*. These essays and others— collected in *Notes of a Native Son* (1955), *Nobody Knows My Name* (1961), and *The Fire Next Time* (1963)—are perhaps Baldwin's greatest artistic achievement.

My Dungeon Shook

Letter to My Nephew on the One Hundredth Anniversary of the Emancipation

D EAR JAMES:

I have begun this letter five times and torn it up five times. I keep seeing your face, which is also the face of your father and my brother. Like him, you are tough, dark, vulnerable, moody—with a very definite tendency to sound truculent because you want no one to think you are soft. You may be like your grandfather in this, I don't know, but certainly both you and your father resemble him very much physically. Well, he is dead, he never saw you, and he had a terrible life; he was defeated long before he died because, at the bottom of his heart, he really believed what white people said about him. This is one of the reasons that he became so holy. I am sure that your father has told you something about all that. Neither you nor your father exhibit any tendency towards holiness: you really *are* of another era, part of what happened when the Negro left the land and came into what the late E. Franklin Frazier called "the cities of destruction." You can only be destroyed by believing that you really are what the white world calls a *nigger*. I tell you this because I love you, and please don't you ever forget it.

I have known both of you all your lives, have carried your daddy in my arms and on my shoulders, kissed and spanked him and watched him learn to walk. I don't know if you've known anybody from that far back; if you've loved anybody that long, first as an infant, then as a child, then as a man, you gain a strange perspective on time and human pain and effort. Other people cannot see what I see whenever I look into your father's face, for behind your father's face as it is today are all those other faces which were his. Let him laugh and I see a cellar your father does not remember and a house he does not remember and I hear in his present laughter his laughter as a child. Let him curse and I remember him falling down the cellar steps, and howling, and I remember, with pain, his tears, which my hand or your grandmother's so easily wiped away. But no one's hand can wipe away those tears he sheds invisibly today, which one hears in his laughter and in his speech and in his songs. I know what the world has done to my brother and how narrowly he has survived it. And I know, which is much worse, and this is the crime of which I accuse my country and my countrymen, and for which neither I nor time nor history will ever forgive them, that they have destroyed and are destroying hundreds of thousands of lives and do not know it and do not want to know it. One can be, indeed one must strive to become, tough and philosophical concerning destruction and death, for this is what most of mankind has been best at since we have heard of man. (But remember: *most* of mankind is not *all* of mankind.) But it is not permissible that the authors of devastation should also be innocent. It is the innocence which constitutes the crime.

Now, my dear namesake, these innocent and well-meaning people, your countrymen, have caused you to be born under conditions not very far removed from those described for us by Charles Dickens in the London of more than a hundred years ago. (I hear the chorus of the innocents screaming, "No! This is not true! How *bitter* you are!"—but I am writing this letter to *you,* to try to tell you something about how to handle *them,* for most of them do not yet really know that you exist. I *know* the conditions under which you were born, for I was there. Your countrymen were *not* there, and haven't made it yet. Your grandmother was also there, and no one has ever accused her of being bitter. I suggest that the innocents check with her. She isn't hard to find. Your countrymen don't know that *she* exists, either, though she has been working for them all their lives.)

Well, you were born, here you came, something like fifteen years ago; and though your father and mother and grand-mother, looking about the streets through which they were carrying you, staring at the walls into which they brought you, had every reason to be heavy-hearted, yet they were not. For here you were, Big James, named for me—you were a big baby, I was not—here you were: to be loved. To be loved, baby, hard, at once, and forever, to strengthen you against the loveless world. Remember that: I know how black it looks today, for you. It looked bad that day, too, yes, we were trembling. We have not stopped trembling yet, but if we had not loved each other none of us would have survived. And now you must survive because we love you, and for the sake of your children and your children's children.

This innocent country set you down in a ghetto in which, in fact, it intended that you should perish. Let me spell out precisely what I mean by that, for the heart of the matter is here, and the root of my dispute with my country. You were born where you were born and faced the future that you faced because you were black and *for no other reason.* The limits of your ambition were, thus, expected to be set forever. You were born into a society which spelled out with brutal clarity, and in as many ways as possible, that you were a worthless human being. You were not expected to aspire to excellence: you were expected to make peace with mediocrity. Wherever you have turned, James, in your short time on this earth, you have been told where you could go and what you could do (and *how* you could do it) and where you could live and whom you could marry. I know your countrymen do not agree with me about this, and I hear them saying, "You exaggerate." They do not know Harlem, and I do. So do you. Take no one's word for anything, including mine—but trust your experience. Know whence you came. If you know whence you came, there is really no limit to where you can go. The details and symbols of your life have been deliberately constructed to make you believe what white people say about you. Please try to remember that what they believe, as well as what they do and cause you to endure, does not testify to your inferiority but to their inhumanity and fear. Please try to be clear, dear James, through the storm which rages about your youthful head today, about the reality which lies behind the words *acceptance* and *integration*. There is no reason for you to try to become like white people and there is no basis whatever for their impertinent assumption that *they* must accept *you*. The really terrible thing, old buddy, is that *you* must accept *them*. And I mean that very seriously. You must accept them and accept them with love. For these innocent people have no other hope. They are, in effect, still trapped in a history which they do not understand; and until they understand it, they cannot be released from it. They have had to believe for many years, and for innumerable reasons, that black men are inferior to white men. Many of them, indeed, know better, but, as you will discover, people find it very difficult to act on what they know. To act is to be committed, and to be committed is to be in danger. In this case, the danger, in the minds of most white Americans, is the loss of their identity. Try to imagine how you would feel if you woke up one morning to find the sun shining and all the stars aflame. You would be frightened because it is out of the order of nature. Any upheaval in the universe is terrifying because it so profoundly attacks one's sense of one's own reality. Well, the black man has functioned in the white man's world as a fixed star, as an immovable pillar: and as he moves out of his place, heaven and earth are shaken to their foundations. You, don't be afraid. I said that it was intended that you should perish in the ghetto, perish by never being allowed to go behind the white man's definitions, by never being allowed to spell your proper name. You have, and many of us have, defeated this intention; and, by a terrible law, a terrible paradox, those innocents who believed that your imprisonment made them safe are losing their grasp of reality. But these men are your brothers—your lost, younger brothers. And if the word *integration* means anything, this is what it means: that we, with love, shall force our brothers to see themselves as they are, to cease fleeing from reality and begin to change it. For this is your home, my friend, do not be driven from it; great men have done great things here, and will again, and we can make America what America must become. It will be hard, James, but you come from sturdy, peasant stock, men who picked cotton and dammed rivers and built railroads, and, in the teeth of the most terrifying odds, achieved an unassailable and monumental dignity. You come from a long line of great poets, some of the greatest poets since Homer. One of them said, *The very time I thought I was lost, My dungeon shook and my chains fell off.*

You know, and I know, that the country is celebrating one hundred years of freedom one hundred years too soon. We cannot be free until they are free. God bless you, James, and Godspeed.

Your uncle,
James

DOWN AT THE CROSS
Letter from a Region in My Mind

Take up the White Man's burden—
Ye dare not stoop to less—
Nor call too loud on Freedom
To cloak your weariness;
By all ye cry or whisper,
By all ye leave or do,
The silent, sullen peoples
Shall weigh your Gods and you.
                    —Kipling

Down at the cross where my Saviour died,
Down where for cleansing from sin I cried,
There to my heart was the blood applied,
Singing glory to His name!
                    —Hymn

I underwent, during the summer that I became fourteen, a pro-longed religious crisis. I use the word "religious" in the common, and arbitrary, sense, meaning that I then discovered God, His saints and angels, and His blazing Hell. And since I had been born in a Christian nation, I accepted this Deity as the only one. I supposed Him to exist only within the walls of a church—in fact, of *our* church—and I also supposed that God and safety were synonymous. The word "safety" brings us to the real meaning of the word "religious" as we use it. Therefore, to state it in another, more accurate way, I became, during my fourteenth year, for the first time in my life, afraid—afraid of the evil within me and afraid of the evil without. What I saw around me that summer in Harlem was what I had always seen; nothing had changed. But now, without any warning, the whores and pimps and racketeers on the Avenue had become a personal menace. It had not before occurred to me that I could become one of them, but now I realized that we had been produced by the same circumstances. Many of my comrades were clearly headed for the Avenue, and my father said that I was headed that way, too. My friends began to drink and smoke, and embarked—at first avid, then groaning—on their sexual careers. Girls, only slightly older than I was, who sang in the choir or taught Sunday school, the children of holy parents, underwent, before my eyes, their incredible metamorphosis, of which the most bewildering aspect was not their budding breasts or their rounding behinds but something deeper and more subtle, in their eyes, their heat, their odor, and the inflection of their voices. Like the strangers on the Avenue, they became, in the twinkling of an eye, unutterably different and fantastically *present*. Owing to the way I had been raised, the abrupt discomfort that all this aroused in me and the fact that I had no idea what my voice or my mind or my body was likely to do next caused me to consider myself one of the most depraved people on earth. Matters were not helped by the fact that these holy girls seemed rather to enjoy my terrified lapses, our grim, guilty, tormented experiments, which were at once as chill and joyless as the Russian steppes and hotter by far than all the fires of Hell.

Yet there was something deeper than these changes, and less definable, that frightened me. It was real in both the boys and the girls, but it was, somehow, more vivid in the boys. In the case of the girls, one watched them turning into matrons before they had become women. They began to manifest a curious and really rather terrifying single-mindedness. It is hard to say exactly how this was conveyed: something implacable in the set of the lips, something farseeing (seeing what?) in the eyes, some new and crushing determination in the walk, something peremptory in the voice. They did not tease us, the boys, any more; they reprimanded us sharply, saying, "You better be thinking about your soul!" For the girls also saw the evidence on the Avenue, knew what the price would be, for them, of one misstep, knew that they had to be protected and that we were the only protection there was. They understood that they must act as God's decoys, saving the souls of the boys for Jesus and binding the bodies of the boys in marriage. For this was the beginning of our burning time, and "It is better," said St. Paul— who elsewhere, with a most unusual and stunning exactness, described himself as a "wretched man"—"to marry than to burn." And I began to feel in the boys a curious, wary, bewildered despair, as though they were now settling in for the long, hard winter of life. I did not know then what it was that I was reacting to; I put it to myself that they were letting themselves go. In the same way that the girls were destined to gain as much weight as their mothers, the boys, it was clear, would rise no higher than their fathers. School began to reveal itself, therefore, as a child's game that one could not win, and boys dropped out of school and went to work. My father wanted me to do the same. I refused, even though I no longer had any illusions about what an education could do for me; I had already encountered too many college-graduate handymen. My friends were now "downtown," busy, as they put it, "fighting the man." They began to care less about the way they looked, the way they dressed, the things they did; presently, one found them in twos and threes and fours, in a hallway, sharing a jug of wine or a bottle of whiskey, talking, cursing, fighting, sometimes weeping: lost, and unable to say what it was that oppressed them, except that they knew it was "the man"—the white man. And there seemed to be no way whatever to remove this cloud that stood between them and the sun, between them and love and life and power, between them and whatever it was that they wanted. One did not have to be very bright to realize how little one could do to change one's situation; one did not have to be abnormally sensitive to be worn down to a cutting edge by the incessant and gratuitous humiliation and danger one encountered every working day, all day long. The humiliation did not apply merely to working days, or workers; I was thirteen and was crossing Fifth Avenue on my way to the Forty-second Street library, and the cop in the middle of the street muttered as I passed him, "Why don't you niggers stay uptown where you belong?" When I was ten, and didn't look, certainly, any older, two policemen amused themselves with me by frisking me, making comic (and terrifying) speculations concerning my ancestry and probable sexual prowess, and for good measure, leaving me flat on my back in one of Harlem's empty lots. Just before and then during the Second World War, many of my friends fled into the service, all to be changed there, and rarely for the better, many to be ruined, and many to die. Others fled to other states and cities—that is, to other ghettos. Some went on wine or whiskey or the needle, and are still on it. And others, like me, fled into the church.

For the wages of sin were visible everywhere, in every wine-stained and urine-splashed hallway, in every clanging ambulance bell, in every scar on the faces of the pimps and their whores, in every helpless, newborn baby being brought into this danger, in every knife and pistol fight on the Avenue, and in every disastrous bulletin: a cousin, mother of six, suddenly gone mad, the children parceled out here and there; an indestructible aunt rewarded for years of hard labor by a slow, agonizing death in a terrible small room; someone's bright son blown into eternity by his own hand; another turned robber and carried off to jail. It was a summer of dreadful speculations and discoveries, of which these were not the worst. Crime became real, for example—for the first time—not as *a* possibility but as *the* possibility. One would never defeat one's circumstances by working and saving one's pennies; one would never, by working, acquire that many pennies, and, besides, the social treatment accorded even the most successful Negroes proved that one needed, in order to be free, something more than a bank account. One needed a handle, a lever, a means of inspiring fear. It was absolutely clear that the police would whip you and take you in as long as they could get away with it, and that everyone else—housewives, taxi-drivers, elevator boys, dishwashers, bartenders, lawyers, judges, doctors, and grocers—would never, by the operation of any generous human feeling, cease to use you as an outlet for his frustrations and hostilities. Neither civilized reason nor Christian love would cause any of those people to treat you as they presumably wanted to be treated; only the fear of your power to retaliate would cause them to do that, or to seem to do it, which was (and is) good enough. There appears to be a vast amount of confusion on this point, but I do not know many Negroes who are eager to be "accepted" by white people, still less to be loved by them; they, the blacks, simply don't wish to be beaten over the head by the whites every instant of our brief passage on this planet. White people in this country will have quite enough to do in learning how to accept and love themselves and each other, and when they have achieved this—which will not be tomorrow and may very well be never—the Negro problem will no longer exist, for it will no longer be needed.

People more advantageously placed than we in Harlem were, and are, will no doubt find the psychology and the view of human nature sketched above dismal and shocking in the extreme. But the Negro's experience of the white world cannot possibly create in him any respect for the standards by which the white world claims to live. His own condition is over-whelming proof that white people do not live by these standards. Negro servants have been smuggling odds and ends out of white homes for generations, and white people have been delighted to have them do it, because it has assuaged a dim guilt and testified to the intrinsic superiority of white people. Even the most doltish and servile Negro could scarcely fail to be impressed by the disparity between his situation and that of the people for whom he worked; Negroes who were neither doltish nor servile did not feel that they were doing anything wrong when they robbed white people. In spite of the Puritan-Yankee equation of virtue with well-being, Negroes had excellent reasons for doubting that money was made or kept by any very striking adherence to the Christian virtues; it certainly did not work that way for black Christians. In any case, white people, who had robbed black people of their liberty and who profited by this theft every hour that they lived, had no moral ground on which to stand. They had the judges, the juries, the shotguns, the law—in a word, power. But it was a criminal power, to be feared but not respected, and to be outwitted in any way whatever. And those virtues preached but not practiced by the white world were merely another means of holding Negroes in subjection.

It turned out, then, that summer, that the moral barriers that I had supposed to exist between me and the dangers of a criminal career were so tenuous as to be nearly nonexistent. I certainly could not discover any principled reason for not becoming a criminal, and it is not my poor, God-fearing parents who are to be indicted for the lack but this society. I was icily determined—more determined, really, than I then knew—never to make my peace with the ghetto but to die and go to Hell before I would let any white man spit on me, before I would accept my "place" in this republic. I did not intend to allow the white people of this country to tell me who I was, and limit me that way, and polish me off that way. And yet, of course, at the same time, I *was* being spat on and defined and described and limited, and could have been polished off with no effort whatever. Every Negro boy—in my situation during those years, at least—who reaches this point realizes, at once, profoundly, because he wants to live, that he stands in great peril and must find, with speed, a "thing," a gimmick, to lift him out, to start him on his way. *And it does not matter what the gimmick is.* It was this last realization that terrified me and—since it revealed that the door opened on so many dangers—helped to hurl me into the church. And, by an unforeseeable paradox, it was my career in the church that turned out, precisely, to be my gimmick.

For when I tried to assess my capabilities, I realized that I had almost none. In order to achieve the life I wanted, I had been dealt, it seemed to me, the worst possible hand. I could not become a prizefighter—many of us tried but very few succeeded. I could not sing. I could not dance. I had been well conditioned by the world in which I grew up, so I did not yet dare take the idea of becoming a writer seriously. The only other possibility seemed to involve my becoming one of the sordid people on the Avenue, who were not really as sordid as I then imagined but who frightened me terribly, both because I did not want to live that life and because of what they made me feel. Everything inflamed me, and that was bad enough, but I myself had also become a source of fire and temptation. I had been far too well raised, alas, to suppose that any of the extremely explicit overtures made to me that summer, sometimes by boys and girls but also, more alarmingly, by older men and women, had anything to do with my attractiveness. On the contrary, since the Harlem idea of seduction is, to put it mildly, blunt, whatever these people saw in me merely confirmed my sense of my depravity.

It is certainly sad that the awakening of one's senses should lead to such a merciless judgment of oneself—to say nothing of the time and anguish one spends in the effort to arrive at any other—but it is also inevitable that a literal attempt to mortify the flesh should be made among black people like those with whom I grew up. Negroes in this country—and Negroes do not, strictly or legally speaking, exist in any other—are taught really to despise themselves from the moment their eyes open on the world. This world is white and they are black. White people hold the power, which means that they are superior to blacks (intrinsically, that is: God decreed it so), and the world has innumerable ways of making this difference known and felt and feared. Long before the Negro child perceives this difference, and even longer before he understands it, he has begun to react to it, he has begun to be controlled by it. Every effort made by the child's elders to prepare him for a fate from which they cannot protect him causes him secretly, in terror, to begin to await, without knowing that he is doing so, his mysterious and inexorable punishment. He must be "good" not only in order to please his parents and not only to avoid being punished by them; behind their authority stands another, nameless and impersonal, infinitely harder to please, and bottomlessly cruel. And this filters into the child's consciousness through his parents' tone of voice as he is being exhorted, punished, or loved; in the sudden, uncontrollable note of fear heard in his mother's or his father's voice when he has strayed beyond some particular boundary. He does not know what the boundary is, and he can get no explanation of it, which is frightening enough, but the fear he hears in the voices of his elders is more frightening still. The fear that I heard in my father's voice, for example, when he realized that I really *believed* I could do anything a white boy could do, and had every intention of proving it, was not at all like the fear I heard when one of us was ill or had fallen down the stairs or strayed too far from the house. It was another fear, a fear that the child, in challenging the white world's assumptions, was putting himself in the path of destruction. A child cannot, thank Heaven, know how vast and how merciless is the nature of power, with what unbelievable cruelty people treat each other. He reacts to the fear in his parents' voices because his parents hold up the world for him and he has no protection without them. I defended myself, as I imagined, against the fear my father made me feel by remembering that he was very old-fashioned. Also, I prided myself on the fact that I already knew how to outwit him. To defend oneself against a fear is simply to insure that one will, one day, be conquered by it; fears must be faced. As for one's wits, it is just not true that one can live by them—not, that is, if one wishes really to live. That summer, in any case, all the fears with which I had grown up, and which were now a part of me and controlled my vision of the world, rose up like a wall between the world and me, and drove me into the church.

As I look back, everything I did seems curiously deliberate, though it certainly did not seem deliberate then. For example, I did not join the church of which my father was a member and in which he preached. My best friend in school, who attended a different church, had already "surrendered his life to the Lord," and he was very anxious about my soul's salvation. (I wasn't, but any human attention was better than none.) One Saturday afternoon, he took me to his church. There were no services that day, and the church was empty, except for some women cleaning and some other women praying. My friend took me into the back room to meet his pastor—a woman. There she sat, in her robes, smiling, an extremely proud and handsome woman, with Africa, Europe, and the America of the American Indian blended in her face. She was perhaps forty-five or fifty at this time, and in our world she was a very celebrated woman. My friend was about to introduce me when she looked at me and smiled and said, "Whose little boy are you?" Now this, unbelievably, was precisely the phrase used by pimps and racketeers on the Avenue when they suggested, both humorously and intensely, that I "hang out" with them. Perhaps part of the terror they had caused me to feel came from the fact that I unquestionably wanted to be *somebody's* little boy. I was so frightened, and at the mercy of so many conundrums, that inevitably, that summer, *someone* would have taken me over; one doesn't, in Harlem, long remain standing on any auction block. It was my good luck—perhaps—that I found myself in the church racket instead of some other, and surrendered to a spiritual seduction long before I came to any carnal knowledge. For when the pastor asked me, with that marvelous smile, "Whose little boy are you?" my heart replied at once, "Why, yours."

The summer wore on, and things got worse. I became more guilty and more frightened, and kept all this bottled up inside me, and naturally, inescapably, one night, when this woman had finished preaching, everything came roaring, screaming, crying out, and I fell to the ground before the altar. It was the strangest sensation I have ever had in my life—up to that time, or since. I had not known that it was going to happen, or that it could happen. One moment I was on my feet, singing and clapping and, at the same time, working out in my head the plot of a play I was working on then; the next moment, with no transition, no sensation of falling, I was on my back, with the lights beating down into my face and all the vertical saints above me. I did not know what I was doing down so low, or how I had got there. And the anguish that filled me cannot be described. It moved in me like one of those floods that devastate counties, tearing everything down, tearing children from their parents and lovers from each other, and making everything an unrecognizable waste. All I really remember is the pain, the unspeakable pain; it was as though I were yelling up to Heaven and Heaven would not hear me. And if Heaven would not hear me, if love could not descend from Heaven—to wash me, to make me clean—then utter disaster was my portion. Yes, it does indeed mean something—something unspeakable—to be born, in a white country, an Anglo-Teutonic, antisexual country, black. You very soon, without knowing it, give up all hope of communion. Black people, mainly, look down or look up but do not look at each other, not at you, and white people, mainly, look away. And the universe is simply a sounding drum; there is no way, no way whatever, so it seemed then and has sometimes seemed since, to get through a life, to love your wife and children, or your friends, or your mother and father, or to be loved. The universe, which is not merely the stars and the moon and the planets, flowers, grass, and trees, but *other people,* has evolved no terms for your existence, has made no room for you, and if love will not swing wide the gates, no other power will or can. And if one despairs—as who has not?—of human love, God's love alone is left. But God—and I felt this even then, so long ago, on that tremendous floor, unwillingly—is white. And if His love was so great, and if He loved all His children, why were we, the blacks, cast down so far? Why? In spite of all I said thereafter, I found no answer on the floor—not *that* answer, anyway—and I was on the floor all night. Over me, to bring me "through," the saints sang and rejoiced and prayed. And in the morning, when they raised me, they told me that I was "saved."

Well, indeed I was, in a way, for I was utterly drained and exhausted, and released, for the first time, from all my guilty torment. I was aware then only of my relief. For many years, I could not ask myself why human relief had to be achieved in a fashion at once so pagan and so desperate—in a fashion at once

so unspeakably old and so unutterably new. And by the time I
was able to ask myself this question, I was also able to see that
the principles governing the rites and customs of the churches in
which I grew up did not differ from the principles governing the
rites and customs of other churches, white. The principles were
Blindness, Loneliness, and Terror, the first principle necessarily
and actively cultivated in order to deny the two others. I would
love to believe that the principles were Faith, Hope, and
Charity, but this is clearly not so for most Christians, or for
what we call the Christian world.

I was saved. But at the same time, out of a deep, adolescent
cunning I do not pretend to understand, I realized immediately
that I could not remain in the church merely as another wor-
shipper. I would have to give myself something to do, in order
not to be too bored and find myself among all the wretched
unsaved of the Avenue. And I don't doubt that I also intended
to best my father on his own ground. Anyway, very shortly after
I joined the church, I became a preacher—a Young Minister—
and I remained in the pulpit for more than three years. My
youth quickly made me a much bigger drawing card than my
father. I pushed this advantage ruthlessly, for it was the most
effective means I had found of breaking his hold over me. That
was the most frightening time of my life, and quite the most dishonest, and the resulting hysteria lent great passion to my
sermons—for a while. I relished the attention and the relative
immunity from punishment that my new status gave me, and
I relished, above all, the sudden right to privacy. It had to be
recognized, after all, that I was still a schoolboy, with my
schoolwork to do, and I was also expected to prepare at least
one sermon a week. During what we may call my heyday, I
preached much more often than that. This meant that there were
hours and even whole days when I could not be interrupted—
not even by my father. I had immobilized him. It took rather
more time for me to realize that I had also immobilized myself,
and had escaped from nothing whatever.

The church was very exciting. It took a long time for me to disengage myself from this excitement, and on the blindest, most visceral level, I never really have, and never will. There is no music like that music, no drama like the drama of the saints rejoicing, the sinners moaning, the tambourines racing, and all those voices coming together and crying holy unto the Lord. There is still, for me, no pathos quite like the pathos of those multicolored, worn, somehow triumphant and transfigured faces, speaking from the depths of a visible, tangible, continuing despair of the goodness of the Lord. I have never seen anything to equal the fire and excitement that sometimes, without warning, fill a church, causing the church, as Leadbelly and so many others have testified, to "rock." Nothing that has happened to me since equals the power and the glory that I sometimes felt when, in the middle of a sermon, I knew that I was somehow, by some miracle, really carrying, as they said, "the Word"— when the church and I were one. Their pain and their joy were mine, and mine were theirs—they surrendered their pain and joy to me, I surrendered mine to them—and their cries of "Amen!" and "Hallelujah!" and "Yes, Lord!" and "Praise His name!" and "Preach it, brother!" sustained and whipped on my solos until we all became equal, wringing wet, singing and dancing, in anguish and rejoicing, at the foot of the altar. It was, for a long time, in spite of—or, not inconceivably, because of— the shabbiness of my motives, my only sustenance, my meat and drink. I rushed home from school, to the church, to the altar, to be alone there, to commune with Jesus, my dearest Friend, who would never fail me, who knew all the secrets of my heart. Perhaps He did, but I didn't, and the bargain we struck, actually, down there at the foot of the cross, was that He would never let me find out.

He failed His bargain. He was a much better Man than I took Him for. It happened, as things do, imperceptibly, in many ways at once. I date it—the slow crumbling of my faith, the pulverization of my fortress—from the time, about a year after I had

begun to preach, when I began to read again. I justified this
desire by the fact that I was still in school, and I began, fatally,
with Dostoevsky. By this time, I was in a high school that was
predominantly Jewish. This meant that I was surrounded by
people who were, by definition, beyond any hope of salvation,
who laughed at the tracts and leaflets I brought to school, and
who pointed out that the Gospels had been written long after
the death of Christ. This might not have been so distressing if it
had not forced me to read the tracts and leaflets myself, for they
were indeed, unless one believed their message already, impossible to believe. I remember feeling dimly that there was a kind of
blackmail in it. People, I felt, ought to love the Lord *because*
they loved Him, and not because they were afraid of going to
Hell. I was forced, reluctantly, to realize that the Bible itself had
been written by men, and translated by men out of languages I
could not read, and I was already, without quite admitting it to
myself, terribly involved with the effort of putting words on
paper. Of course, I had the rebuttal ready: These men had all
been operating under divine inspiration. *Had* they? *All* of them?
And I also knew by now, alas, far more about divine inspiration
than I dared admit, for I knew how I worked myself up into my
own visions, and how frequently—indeed, incessantly—the
visions God granted to me differed from the visions He granted
to my father. I did not understand the dreams I had at night, but
I knew that they were not holy. For that matter, I knew that my
waking hours were far from holy. I spent most of my time in a
state of repentance for things I had vividly desired to do but had
not done. The fact that I was dealing with Jews brought the
whole question of color, which I had been desperately avoiding,
into the terrified center of my mind. I realized that the Bible had
been written by white men. I knew that, according to many
Christians, I was a descendant of Ham, who had been cursed,
and that I was therefore predestined to be a slave. This had
nothing to do with anything I was, or contained, or could
become; my fate had been sealed forever, from the beginning of
time. And it seemed, indeed, when one looked out over

Christendom, that this was what Christendom effectively believed. It was certainly the way it behaved. I remembered the Italian priests and bishops blessing Italian boys who were on their way to Ethiopia.

Again, the Jewish boys in high school were troubling because I could find no point of connection between them and the Jewish pawnbrokers and landlords and grocery-store owners in Harlem. I knew that these people were Jews—God knows I was told it often enough—but I thought of them only as white. Jews, as such, until I got to high school, were all incarcerated in the Old Testament, and their names were Abraham, Moses, Daniel, Ezekiel, and Job, and Shadrach, Meshach, and Abednego. It was bewildering to find them so many miles and centuries out of Egypt, and so far from the fiery furnace. My best friend in high school was a Jew. He came to our house once, and afterward my father asked, as he asked about everyone, "Is he a Christian?"—by which he meant "Is he saved?" I really do not know whether my answer came out of innocence or venom, but I said coldly, "No. He's Jewish." My father slammed me across the face with his great palm, and in that moment everything flooded back—all the hatred and all the fear, and the depth of a merciless resolve to kill my father rather than allow my father to kill me—and I knew that all those sermons and tears and all that repentance and rejoicing had changed nothing. I wondered if I was expected to be glad that a friend of mine, or anyone, was to be tormented forever in Hell, and I also thought, suddenly, of the Jews in another Christian nation, Germany. They were not so far from the fiery furnace after all, and my best friend might have been one of them. I told my father, "He's a better Christian than you are," and walked out of the house. The battle between us was in the open, but that was all right; it was almost a relief. A more deadly struggle had begun.

Being in the pulpit was like being in the theatre; I was behind the scenes and knew how the illusion was worked. I knew the other ministers and knew the quality of their lives. And I don't mean to suggest by this the "Elmer Gantry" sort of hypocrisy

concerning sensuality; it was a deeper, deadlier, and more subtle
hypocrisy than that, and a little honest sensuality, or a lot, would
have been like water in an extremely bitter desert. I knew how
to work on a congregation until the last dime was surrendered—
it was not very hard to do—and I knew where the money for
"the Lord's work" went. I knew, though I did not wish to know
it, that I had no respect for the people with whom I worked. I
would not have said it then, but I also knew that if I continued
I would soon have no respect for myself. And the fact that I was
"the young Brother Baldwin" increased my value with those
same pimps and racketeers who had helped to stampede me into
the church in the first place. They still saw the little boy they
intended to take over. They were waiting for me to come to my
senses and realize that I was in a very lucrative business. They
knew that I did not yet realize this, and also that I had not yet
begun to suspect where my own needs, *coming up* (they were
very patient), could drive me. They themselves did know the
score, and they knew that the odds were in their favor. And,
really, I knew it, too. I was even lonelier and more vulnerable
than I had been before. And the blood of the Lamb had not
cleansed me in any way whatever. I was just as black as I had
been the day that I was born. Therefore, when I faced a congregation, it began to take all the strength I had not to stammer,
not to curse, not to tell them to throw away their Bibles and get
off their knees and go home and organize, for example, a rent
strike. When I watched all the children, their copper, brown,
and beige faces staring up at me as I taught Sunday school, I felt
that I was committing a crime in talking about the gentle Jesus,
in telling them to reconcile themselves to their misery on earth
in order to gain the crown of eternal life. Were only Negroes
to gain this crown? Was Heaven, then, to be merely another
ghetto? Perhaps I might have been able to reconcile myself even
to this if I had been able to believe that there was any loving-
kindness to be found in the haven I represented. But I had been
in the pulpit too long and I had seen too many monstrous
things. I don't refer merely to the glaring fact that the minister

eventually acquires houses and Cadillacs while the faithful continue to scrub floors and drop their dimes and quarters and dollars into the plate. I really mean that there was no love in the church. It was a mask for hatred and self-hatred and despair. The transfiguring power of the Holy Ghost ended when the service ended, and salvation stopped at the church door. When we were told to love everybody, I had thought that that meant *everybody*. But no. It applied only to those who believed as we did, and it did not apply to white people at all. I was told by a minister, for example, that I should never, on any public conveyance, under any circumstances, rise and give my seat to a white woman. White men never rose for Negro women. Well, that was true enough, in the main—I saw his point. But what was the point, the purpose, of *my* salvation if it did not permit me to behave with love toward others, no matter how they behaved toward me? What others did was their responsibility, for which they would answer when the judgment trumpet sounded. But what *I* did was *my* responsibility, and I would have to answer, too—unless, of course, there was also in Heaven a special dispensation for the benighted black, who was not to be judged in the same way as other human beings, or angels. It probably occurred to me around this time that the vision people hold of the world to come is but a reflection, with predictable wishful distortions, of the world in which they live. And this did not apply only to Negroes, who were no more "simple" or "spontaneous" or "Christian" than anybody else—who were merely more oppressed. In the same way that we, for white people, were the descendants of Ham, and were cursed forever, white people were, for us, the descendants of Cain. And the passion with which we loved the Lord was a measure of how deeply we feared and distrusted and, in the end, hated almost all strangers, always, and avoided and despised ourselves.

But I cannot leave it at that; there is more to it than that. In spite of everything, there was in the life I fled a zest and a joy and a capacity for facing and surviving disaster that are very moving and very rare. Perhaps we were, all of us—pimps, whores, racketeers, church members, and children—bound together by the nature of our oppression, the specific and peculiar complex of risks we had to run; if so, within these limits we sometimes achieved with each other a freedom that was close to love. I remember, anyway, church suppers and outings, and, later, after I left the church, rent and waistline parties where rage and sorrow sat in the darkness and did not stir, and we ate and drank and talked and laughed and danced and forgot all about "the man." We had the liquor, the chicken, the music, and each other, and had no need to pretend to be what we were not. This is the freedom that one hears in some gospel songs, for example, and in jazz. In all jazz, and especially in the blues, there is something tart and ironic, authoritative and double-edged. White Americans seem to feel that happy songs are *happy* and sad songs are *sad,* and that, God help us, is exactly the way most white Americans sing them—sounding, in both cases, so helplessly, defenselessly fatuous that one dare not speculate on the temperature of the deep freeze from which issue their brave and sexless little voices. Only people who have been "down the line," as the song puts it, know what this music is about. I think it was Big Bill Broonzy who used to sing "I Feel So Good," a really joyful song about a man who is on his way to the railroad station to meet his girl. She's coming home. It is the singer's incredibly moving exuberance that makes one realize how leaden the time must have been while she was gone. There is no guarantee that she will stay this time, either, as the singer clearly knows, and, in fact, she has not yet actually arrived. Tonight, or tomorrow, or within the next five minutes, he may very well be singing "Lonesome in My Bedroom," or insisting, "Ain't we, ain't we, going to make it all right? Well, if we don't today, we will tomorrow night." White Americans do not understand the depths out of which such an ironic tenacity comes, but they suspect that the force is sensual, and they are terrified of sensuality and do not any longer understand it. The word "sensual" is not intended to bring to mind quivering dusky maidens or priapic black studs. I am referring to something much simpler and much less fanciful. To be sensual, I think, is to respect and rejoice in the force of life, of life itself, and to be *present* in all that one does, from the effort of loving to the breaking of bread. It will be a great day for America, incidentally, when we begin to eat bread again, instead of the blasphemous and tasteless foam rubber that we have substituted for it. And I am not being frivolous now, either. Something very sinister happens to the people of a country when they begin to distrust their own reactions as deeply as they do here, and become as joyless as they have become. It is this individual uncertainty on the part of white American men and women, this inability to renew themselves at the fountain of their own lives, that makes the discussion, let alone elucidation, of any conundrum—that is, any reality—so supremely difficult. The person who distrusts himself has no touchstone for reality—for this touchstone can be only oneself. Such a person interposes between himself and reality nothing less than a labyrinth of attitudes. And these attitudes, furthermore, though the person is usually unaware of it (is unaware of so much!), are historical and public attitudes. They do not relate to the present any more than they relate to the person. Therefore, whatever white people do not know about Negroes reveals, precisely and inexorably, what they do not know about themselves.

White Christians have also forgotten several elementary historical details. They have forgotten that the religion that is now identified with their virtue and their power—"God is on our side," says Dr. Verwoerd—came out of a rocky piece of ground in what is now known as the Middle East before color was invented, and that in order for the Christian church to be established, Christ had to be put to death, by Rome, and that the real architect of the Christian church was not the disreputable, sunbaked Hebrew who gave it his name but the mercilessly fanatical and self-righteous St. Paul. The energy that was buried with the rise of the Christian nations must come back into the world; nothing can prevent it. Many of us, I think, both long to see this happen and are terrified of it, for though this transformation contains the hope of liberation, it also imposes a necessity for great change. But in order to deal with the untapped and dormant force of the previously subjugated, in order to survive as a human, moving, moral weight in the world, America and all the Western nations will be forced to reexamine themselves and release themselves from many things that are now taken to be sacred, and to discard nearly all the assumptions that have been used to justify their lives and their anguish and their crimes so long.

"The white man's Heaven," sings a Black Muslim minister, "is the black man's Hell." One may object—possibly—that this puts the matter somewhat too simply, but the song is true, and it has been true for as long as white men have ruled the world. The Africans put it another way: When the white man came to Africa, the white man had the Bible and the African had the land, but now it is the white man who is being, reluctantly and bloodily, separated from the land, and the African who is still attempting to digest or to vomit up the Bible. The struggle, therefore, that now begins in the world is extremely complex, involving the historical role of Christianity in the realm of power—that is, politics—and in the realm of morals. In the realm of power, Christianity has operated with an unmitigated arrogance and cruelty—necessarily, since a religion ordinarily imposes on those who have discovered the true faith the spiritual duty of liberating the infidels. This particular true faith, moreover, is more deeply concerned about the soul than it is about the body, to which fact the flesh (and the corpses) of countless infidels bears witness. It goes without saying, then, that whoever questions the authority of the true faith also contests the right of the nations that hold this faith to rule over him—contests, in short, their title to his land. The spreading of the Gospel, regardless of the motives or the integrity or the heroism of some of the missionaries, was an absolutely indispensable justification for the planting of the flag. Priests and nuns and schoolteachers helped to protect and sanctify the power that was so ruthlessly being used by people who were indeed seeking a city, but not one in the heavens, and one to be made, very definitely, by captive hands. The Christian church itself—again, as distinguished from some of its ministers—sanctified and rejoiced in the conquests of the flag, and encouraged, if it did not formulate, the belief that conquest, with the resulting relative well-being of the Western populations, was proof of the favor of God. God had come a long way from the desert—but then so had Allah, though in a very different direction. God, going north, and rising on the wings of power, had become white, and Allah, out of power, and on the dark side of Heaven, had become—for all practical purposes, anyway—black. Thus, in the realm of morals the role of Christianity has been, at best, ambivalent. Even leaving out of account the remarkable arrogance that assumed that the ways and morals of others were inferior to those of Christians, and that they therefore had every right, and could use any means, to change them, the collision between cultures—and the schizophrenia in the mind of Christendom—had rendered the domain of morals as chartless as the sea once was, and as treacherous as the sea still is. It is not too much to say that whoever wishes to become a truly moral human being (and let us not ask whether or not this is possible; I think we must believe that it is possible) must first divorce himself from all the prohibitions, crimes, and hypocrisies of the Christian church. If the concept of God has any validity or any use, it can only be to make us larger, freer, and more loving. If God cannot do this, then it is time we got rid of Him.

Now, it is extremely unlikely that Negroes will ever rise to power in the United States, because they are only approximately a ninth of this nation. They are not in the position of the Africans, who are attempting to reclaim their land and break the colonial yoke and recover from the colonial experience. The Negro situation is dangerous in a different way, both for the Negro qua Negro and for the country of which he forms so troubled and troubling a part. The American Negro is a unique creation; he has no counterpart anywhere, and no predecessors. The Muslims react to this fact by referring to the Negro as "the so-called American Negro" and substituting for the names inherited from slavery the letter "X." It is a fact that every American Negro bears a name that originally belonged to the white man whose chattel he was. I am called Baldwin because I was either sold by my African tribe or kidnapped out of it into the hands of a white Christian named Baldwin, who forced me to kneel at the foot of the cross. I am, then, both visibly and legally the descendant of slaves in a white, Protestant country, and this is what it means to be an American Negro, this is who he is—a kidnapped pagan, who was sold like an animal and treated like one, who was once defined by the American Constitution as "three-fifths" of a man, and who, according to the Dred Scott decision, had no rights that a white man was bound to respect. And today, a hundred years after his technical emancipation, he remains—with the possible exception of the American Indian—the most despised creature in his country. Now, there is simply no possibility of a real change in the Negro's situation without the most radical and far-reaching changes in the American political and social structure. And it is clear that white Americans are not simply unwilling to effect these changes; they are, in the main, so slothful have they become, unable even to envision them. It must be added that the Negro himself no longer believes in the good faith of white Americans—if, indeed, he ever could have. What the Negro *has* discovered, and on an international level, is that power to intimidate which he has always had privately but hitherto could manipulate only privately—for private ends often, for limited ends always. And therefore when the country speaks of a "new" Negro, which it has been doing every hour on the hour for decades, it is not really referring to a change in the Negro, which, in any case, it is quite incapable of assessing, but only to a new difficulty in keeping him in his place, to the fact that it encounters him (again! again!) barring yet another door to its spiritual and social ease. This is probably, hard and odd as it may sound, the most important thing that one human being can do for another—it is certainly *one* of the most important things; hence the torment and necessity of love—and this is the enormous contribution that the Negro has made to this otherwise shapeless and undiscovered country. Consequently, white Americans are in nothing more deluded than in supposing that Negroes could ever have imagined that white people would "give" them anything. It is rare indeed that people give. Most people guard and keep; they suppose that it is they themselves and what they identify with themselves that they are guarding and keeping, whereas what they are actually guarding and keeping is their system of reality and what they assume themselves to be. One can give nothing whatever without giving oneself—that is to say, risking oneself. If one cannot risk oneself, then one is simply incapable of giving. And, after all, one can give freedom only by setting someone free. This, in the case of the Negro, the American republic has never become sufficiently mature to do. White Americans have contented themselves with gestures that are now described as "tokenism." For hard example, white Americans congratulate themselves on the 1954 Supreme Court decision outlawing segregation in the schools; they suppose, in spite of the mountain of evidence that has since accumulated to the contrary, that this was proof of a change of heart—or, as they like to say, progress. Perhaps. It all depends on how one reads the word "progress." Most of the Negroes I know do not believe that this immense concession would ever have been made if it had not been for the competition of the Cold War, and the fact that Africa was clearly liberating herself and therefore had, for political reasons, to be wooed by the descendants of her former masters. Had it been a matter of love or justice, the 1954 decision would surely have occurred sooner; were it not for the realities of power in this difficult era, it might very well not have occurred yet. This seems an extremely harsh way of stating the case—ungrateful, as it were—but the evidence that supports this way of stating it is not easily refuted. I myself do not think that it can be refuted at all. In any event, the sloppy and fatuous nature of American good will can never be relied upon to deal with hard problems. These have been dealt with, when they have been dealt with at all, out of necessity—and in political terms, anyway, necessity means concessions made in order to stay on top. I think this is a fact, which it serves no purpose to deny, *but, whether it is a fact or not, this is what the black population of the world, including black Americans, really believe.* The word "independence" in Africa and the word "integration" here are almost equally meaningless; that is, Europe has not yet left Africa, and black men here are not yet free. And both of these last statements are undeniable facts, related facts, containing the gravest implications for us all. The Negroes of this country may never be able to rise to power, but they are very well placed indeed to precipitate chaos and ring down the curtain on the American dream.

This has everything to do, of course, with the nature of that dream and with the fact that we Americans, of whatever color, do not dare examine it and are far from having made it a reality. There are too many things we do not wish to know about ourselves. People are not, for example, terribly anxious to be equal (equal, after all, to what and to whom?) but they love the idea of being superior. And this human truth has an especially grinding force here, where identity is almost impossible to achieve and people are perpetually attempting to find their feet on the shifting sands of status. (Consider the history of labor in a country in which, spiritually speaking, there are no workers, only candidates for the hand of the boss's daughter.) Furthermore, I have met only a very few people—and most of these were not Americans—who had any real desire to be free. Freedom is hard to bear. It can be objected that I am speaking of political freedom in spiritual terms, but the political institutions of any nation are always menaced and are ultimately controlled by the spiritual state of that nation. We are controlled here by our confusion, far more than we know, and the American dream has therefore become something much more closely resembling a nightmare, on the private, domestic, and international levels. Privately, we cannot stand our lives and dare not examine them; domestically, we take no responsibility for (and no pride in) what goes on in our country; and, internationally, for many millions of people, we are an unmitigated disaster. Whoever doubts this last statement has only to open his ears, his heart, his mind, to the testimony of—for example—any Cuban peasant or any Spanish poet, and ask himself what *he* would feel about us if *he* were the victim of our performance in pre-Castro Cuba or in Spain. We defend our curious role in Spain by referring to the Russian menace and the necessity of protecting the free world. It has not occurred to us that we have simply been mesmerized by Russia, and that the only real advantage Russia has in what we think of as a struggle between the East and the West is the moral history of the Western world. Russia's secret weapon is the bewilderment and despair and hunger of millions of people of whose existence we are scarcely aware. The Russian Communists are not in the least concerned about these people. But our ignorance and indecision have had the effect, if not of delivering them into Russian hands, of plunging them very deeply in the Russian shadow, for which effect—and it is hard to blame them—the most articulate among them, and the most oppressed as well, distrust us all the more. Our power and our fear of change help bind these people to their misery and bewilderment, and insofar as they find this state intolerable we are intolerably menaced. For if they find their state intolerable, but are too heavily oppressed to change it, they are simply pawns in the hands of larger powers, which, in such a context, are always unscrupulous, and when, eventually, they do change their situation—as in Cuba—we are menaced more than ever by the vacuum that succeeds all violent upheavals. We should certainly know by now that it is one thing to overthrow a dictator or repel an invader and quite another thing really to achieve a revolution. Time and time and time again, the people discover that they have merely betrayed themselves into the hands of yet another Pharaoh, who, since he was necessary to put the broken country together, will not let them go. Perhaps, people being the conundrums that they are, and

having so little desire to shoulder the burden of their lives, this
is what will always happen. But at the bottom of my heart I do
not believe this. I think that people can be better than that, and
I know that people can be better than they are. We are capable
of bearing a great burden, once we discover that the burden is
reality and arrive where reality is. Anyway, the point here is that
we are living in an age of revolution, whether we will or no, and
that America is the only Western nation with both the power
and, as I hope to suggest, the experience that may help to make
these revolutions real and minimize the human damage. Any
attempt we make to oppose these outbursts of energy is tantamount to signing our death warrant.

Behind what we think of as the Russian menace lies what we
do not wish to face, and what white Americans do not face
when they regard a Negro: reality—the fact that life is tragic.
Life is tragic simply because the earth turns and the sun inexorably rises and sets, and one day, for each of us, the sun will go
down for the last, last time. Perhaps the whole root of our trouble, the human trouble, is that we will sacrifice all the beauty of
our lives, will imprison ourselves in totems, taboos, crosses,
blood sacrifices, steeples, mosques, races, armies, flags, nations,
in order to deny the fact of death, which is the only fact we
have. It seems to me that one ought to rejoice in the *fact* of
death—ought to decide, indeed, to *earn* one's death by con-
fronting with passion the conundrum of life. One is responsible
to life: It is the small beacon in that terrifying darkness from
which we come and to which we shall return. One must negotiate this passage as nobly as possible, for the sake of those who
are coming after us. But white Americans do not believe in
death, and this is why the darkness of my skin so intimidates
them. And this is also why the presence of the Negro in this
country can bring about its destruction. It is the responsibility
of free men to trust and to celebrate what is constant—birth,
struggle, and death are constant, and so is love, though we may
not always think so—and to apprehend the nature of change, to
be able and willing to change. I speak of change not on the sur-

face but in the depths—change in the sense of renewal. But renewal becomes impossible if one supposes things to be constant that are not—safety, for example, or money, or power. One clings then to chimeras, by which one can only be betrayed, and the entire hope—the entire possibility—of freedom disappears. And by destruction I mean precisely the abdication by Americans of any effort really to be free. The Negro can precipitate this abdication because white Americans have never, in all their long history, been able to look on him as a man like themselves. This point need not be labored; it is proved over and over again by the Negro's continuing position here, and his indescribable struggle to defeat the stratagems that white Americans have used, and use, to deny him his humanity. America could have used in other ways the energy that both groups have expended in this conflict. America, of all the Western nations, has been best placed to prove the uselessness and the obsolescence of the concept of color. But it has not dared to accept this opportunity, or even to conceive of it as an opportunity. White Americans have thought of it as their shame, and have envied those more civilized and elegant European nations that were untroubled by the presence of black men on their shores. This is because white Americans have supposed "Europe" and "civilization" to be synonyms—which they are not—and have been distrustful of other standards and other sources of vitality, especially those produced in America itself, and have attempted to behave in all matters as though what was east for Europe was also east for them. What it comes to is that if we, who can scarcely be considered a white nation, persist in thinking of ourselves as one, we condemn ourselves, with the truly white nations, to sterility and decay, whereas if we could accept ourselves as we are, we might bring new life to the Western achievements, and transform them. The price of this transformation is the unconditional freedom of the Negro; it is not too much to say that he, who has been so long rejected, must now be embraced, and at no matter what psychic or social risk. He is *the* key figure in his country, and the American future is precisely as bright or as dark as his. And the Negro recognizes this, in a negative way. Hence the question: Do I really *want* to be integrated into a burning house?

White Americans find it as difficult as white people elsewhere do to divest themselves of the notion that they are in possession of some intrinsic value that black people need, or want. And this assumption—which, for example, makes the solution to the Negro problem depend on the speed with which Negroes accept and adopt white standards—is revealed in all kinds of striking ways, from Bobby Kennedy's assurance that a Negro can become President in forty years to the unfortunate tone of warm congratulation with which so many liberals address their Negro equals. It is the Negro, of course, who is presumed to have become equal—an achievement that not only proves the comforting fact that perseverance has no color but also overwhelmingly corroborates the white man's sense of his own value. Alas, this value can scarcely be corroborated in any other way; there is certainly little enough in the white man's public or private life that one should desire to imitate. White men, at the bottom of their hearts, know this. Therefore, a vast amount of the energy that goes into what we call the Negro problem is produced by the white man's profound desire not to be judged by those who are not white, not to be seen as he is, and at the same time a vast amount of the white anguish is rooted in the white man's equally profound need to be seen as he is, to be released from the tyranny of his mirror. All of us know, whether or not we are able to admit it, that mirrors can only lie, that death by drowning is all that awaits one there. It is for this reason that love is so desperately sought and so cunningly avoided. Love takes off the masks that we fear we cannot live without and know we cannot live within. I use the word "love" here not merely in the personal sense but as a state of being, or a state of grace—not in the infantile American sense of being made happy but in the tough and universal sense of quest and daring and growth. And I submit, then, that the racial tensions that menace Americans today have little to do with real antipathy—on the contrary, indeed—and are involved only symbolically with color. These tensions are rooted in the very same depths as those from which love springs, or murder. The white man's unadmitted— and apparently, to him, unspeakable—private fears and longings are projected onto the Negro. The only way he can be released from the Negro's tyrannical power over him is to con- sent, in effect, to become black himself, to become a part of that suffering and dancing country that he now watches wistfully from the heights of his lonely power and, armed with spiritual traveler's checks, visits surreptitiously after dark. How can one respect, let alone adopt, the values of a people who do not, on any level whatever, live the way they say they do, or the way they say they should? I cannot accept the proposition that the four-hundred-year travail of the American Negro should result merely in his attainment of the present level of the American civ- ilization. I am far from convinced that being released from the African witch doctor was worthwhile if I am now—in order to support the moral contradictions and the spiritual aridity of my life—expected to become dependent on the American psychia- trist. It is a bargain I refuse. The only thing white people have that black people need, or should want, is power—and no one holds power forever. White people cannot, in the generality, be taken as models of how to live. Rather, the white man is himself in sore need of new standards, which will release him from his confusion and place him once again in fruitful communion with the depths of his own being. And I repeat: The price of the lib- eration of the white people is the liberation of the blacks—the total liberation, in the cities, in the towns, before the law, and in the mind. Why, for example—especially knowing the family as I do—I should *want* to marry your sister is a great mystery to me. But your sister and I have every right to marry if we wish to, and no one has the right to stop us. If she cannot raise me to her level, perhaps I can raise her to mine.

In short, we, the black and the white, deeply need each other here if we are really to become a nation—if we are really, that is, to achieve our identity, our maturity, as men and women. To create one nation has proved to be a hideously difficult task; there is certainly no need now to create two, one black and one white. But white men with far more political power than that possessed by the Nation of Islam movement have been advocating exactly this, in effect, for generations. If this sentiment is honored when it falls from the lips of Senator Byrd, then there is no reason it should not be honored when it falls from the lips of Malcolm X. And any Congressional committee wishing to investigate the latter must also be willing to investigate the former. They are expressing exactly the same sentiments and represent exactly the same danger. There is absolutely no reason to suppose that white people are better equipped to frame the laws by which I am to be governed than I am. It is entirely unacceptable that I should have no voice in the political affairs of my own country, for I am not a ward of America; I am one of the first Americans to arrive on these shores.

This past, the Negro's past, of rope, fire, torture, castration, infanticide, rape; death and humiliation; fear by day and night, fear as deep as the marrow of the bone; doubt that he was worthy of life, since everyone around him denied it; sorrow for his women, for his kinfolk, for his children, who needed his protection, and whom he could not protect; rage, hatred, and murder, hatred for white men so deep that it often turned against him and his own, and made all love, all trust, all joy impossible—this past, this endless struggle to achieve and reveal and confirm a human identity, human authority, yet contains, for all its horror, something very beautiful. I do not mean to be sentimental about suffering—enough is certainly as good as a feast—but people who cannot suffer can never grow up, can never discover who they are. That man who is forced each day to snatch his manhood, his identity, out of the fire of human cruelty that rages to destroy it knows, if he survives his effort, and even if he does not survive it, something about self and human life that no school on earth—and, indeed, no church—can teach. He achieves his own authority, and that is unshakable. This is because, in order to save his life, he is forced to look beneath appearances, to take nothing for granted, to hear the meaning behind the words. If one is continually surviving the worst that life can bring, one eventually ceases to be controlled by a fear of what life can bring; whatever it brings must be borne. And at this level of experience one's bitterness begins to be palatable, and hatred becomes too heavy a sack to carry. The apprehension of life here so briefly and inadequately sketched has been the experience of generations of Negroes, and it helps to explain how they have endured and how they have been able to produce children of kindergarten age who can walk through mobs to get to school. It demands great force and great cunning continually to assault the mighty and indifferent fortress of white supremacy, as Negroes in this country have done so long. It demands great spiritual resilience not to hate the hater whose foot is on your neck, and an even greater miracle of perception and charity not to teach your child to hate. The Negro boys and girls who are facing mobs today come out of a long line of improbable aristocrats—the only genuine aristocrats this country has produced. I say "this country" because their frame of reference was totally American. They were hewing out of the mountain of white supremacy the stone of their individuality. I have great respect for that unsung army of black men and women who trudged down back lanes and entered back doors, saying "Yes, sir" and "No, ma'am" in order to acquire a new roof for the schoolhouse, new books, a new chemistry lab, more beds for the dormitories, more dormitories. They did not like saying "Yes, sir" and "No, ma'am," but the country was in no hurry to educate Negroes, these black men and women knew that the job had to be done, and they put their pride in their pockets in order to do it. It is very hard to believe that they were in any way inferior to the white men and women who opened those back doors. It is very hard to believe that those men and women, raising their children, eating their greens, crying their curses, weeping their tears, singing their songs, making their love, as the sun rose, as the sun set, were in any way inferior to the white men and women who crept over to share these splendors after the sun went down. But we must avoid the European error; we must not suppose that, because the situation, the ways, the perceptions of black people so radically differed from those of whites, they were racially superior. I am proud of these people not because of their color but because of their intelligence and their spiritual force and their beauty. The country should be proud of them, too, but, alas, not many people in this country even know of their existence. And the reason for this ignorance is that a knowledge of the role these people played—and play—in American life would reveal more about America to Americans than Americans wish to know.

The American Negro has the great advantage of having never believed that collection of myths to which white Americans cling: that their ancestors were all freedom-loving heroes, that they were born in the greatest country the world has ever seen, or that Americans are invincible in battle and wise in peace, that Americans have always dealt honorably with Mexicans and Indians and all other neighbors or inferiors, that American men are the world's most direct and virile, that American women are pure. Negroes know far more about white Americans than that; it can almost be said, in fact, that they know about white Americans what parents—or, anyway, mothers— know about their children, and that they very often regard white Americans that way. And perhaps this attitude, held in spite of what they know and have endured, helps to explain why Negroes, on the whole, and until lately, have allowed themselves to feel so little hatred. The tendency has really been, insofar as this was possible, to dismiss white people as the slightly mad victims of their own brainwashing. One watched the lives they led. One could not be fooled about that; one watched the things they did and the excuses that they gave themselves, and if a white man was really in trouble, deep trouble, it was to the Negro's door that he came. And one felt that if one had had that white man's worldly advantages, one would never have become as bewildered and as joyless and as thought-

lessly cruel as he. The Negro came to the white man for a roof
or for five dollars or for a letter to the judge; the white man
came to the Negro for love. But he was not often able to give
what he came seeking. The price was too high; he had too much
to lose. And the Negro knew this, too. When one knows this
about a man, it is impossible for one to hate him, but unless he
becomes a man—becomes equal—it is also impossible for one
to love him. Ultimately, one tends to avoid him, for the universal characteristic of children is to assume that they have a
monopoly on trouble, and therefore a monopoly on *you*. (Ask
any Negro what he knows about the white people with whom
he works. And then ask the white people with whom he works
what they know about *him*.)

How can the American Negro past be used? It is entirely possible that this dishonored past will rise up soon to smite all of
us. There are some wars, for example (if anyone on the globe is
still mad enough to go to war) that the American Negro will not
support, however many of his people may be coerced—and
there is a limit to the number of people any government can put
in prison, and a rigid limit indeed to the practicality of such a
course. A bill is coming in that I fear America is not prepared
to pay. "The problem of the twentieth century," wrote W. E. B.
Du Bois around sixty years ago, "is the problem of the color
line." A fearful and delicate problem, which compromises,
when it does not corrupt, all the American efforts to build a better world—here, there, or anywhere. It is for this reason that
everything white Americans think they believe in must now be
reexamined. What one would not like to see again is the con-
solidation of peoples on the basis of their color. But as long as
we in the West place on color the value that we do, we make it
impossible for the great unwashed to consolidate themselves
according to any other principle. Color is not a human or a personal reality; it is a political reality. But this is a distinction so
extremely hard to make that the West has not been able to make
it yet. And at the center of this dreadful storm, this vast confusion, stand the black people of this nation, who must now share

the fate of a nation that has never accepted them, to which they were brought in chains. Well, if this is so, one has no choice but to do all in one's power to change that fate, and at no matter what risk—eviction, imprisonment, torture, death. For the sake of one's children, in order to minimize the bill that *they* must pay, one must be careful not to take refuge in any delusion—and the value placed on the color of the skin is always and everywhere and forever a delusion. I know that what I am asking is impossible. But in our time, as in every time, the impossible is the least that one can demand—and one is, after all, emboldened by the spectacle of human history in general, and American Negro history in particular, for it testifies to nothing less than the perpetual achievement of the impossible.

When I was very young, and was dealing with my buddies in those wine- and urine-stained hallways, something in me wondered, *What will happen to all that beauty?* For black people, though I am aware that some of us, black and white, do not know it yet, are very beautiful. And when I sat at Elijah's[1] table and watched the baby, the women, and the men, and we talked about God's—or Allah's—vengeance, I wondered, when that vengeance was achieved, *What will happen to all that beauty then?* I could also see that the intransigence and ignorance of the white world might make that vengeance inevitable—a vengeance that does not really depend on, and cannot really be executed by, any person or organization, and that cannot be prevented by any police force or army: historical vengeance, a cosmic vengeance, based on the law that we recognize when we say, "Whatever goes up must come down." And here we are, at the center of the arc, trapped in the gaudiest, most valuable, and most improbable water wheel the world has ever seen. Everything now, we must assume, is in our hands; we have no right to assume otherwise. If we—and now I mean the relatively conscious whites and the relatively conscious blacks, who must, like lovers, insist on, or create, the consciousness of the

---

1. [Elijah Muhammad, U.S. leader of the Nation of Islam, 1934–1975.]

others—do not falter in our duty now, we may be able, handful that we are, to end the racial nightmare, and achieve our country, and change the history of the world. If we do not now dare everything, the fulfillment of that prophecy, re-created from the Bible in song by a slave, is upon us: *God gave Noah the rainbow sign, No more water, the fire next time!* ∽

INTERPRETIVE QUESTIONS
FOR DISCUSSION

Why is Baldwin's participation in the Christian church as preacher and penitent merely a defense against—rather than a cure for—all of his hatred and fear?

1. Why does Baldwin's sexual awakening make him suddenly aware of the dangers that surround him in the ghetto? Why does he say, "I became . . . for the first time in my life . . . afraid of the evil within me and afraid of the evil without"? (8–9)

2. Why does Baldwin say that his fears were what drove him into the church? (15)

3. Why does Baldwin's night of anguish on the church floor bring release from all his "guilty torment" but provide no answers? (17)

4. What is the "hold" that Baldwin implies his father has over him? Why is it the author's preaching and his newfound right to privacy that immobilize his father? (18)

5. Why is the battle between Baldwin and his father brought into the open when his father strikes him across the face? (21)

6. Why does Baldwin see the battle with his father as distinct from the "deadly struggle" of separating himself from the "prohibitions, crimes, and hypocrisies of the Christian church"? (21, 27)

7. Why does Baldwin's reading eventually cause the "slow crumbling" of the fortress of his faith? (19–20)

8. If Baldwin ultimately rejects the Christian God as white, why is he so moved by the pathos of the "triumphant and transfigured faces" of black Christians speaking from the depths of their despair of the "goodness of the Lord"? (17, 19)

9. Does Baldwin's essay offer an answer to his question about why, if God's "love was so great, and if He loved all His children," black people were cast down so far? (17)

Suggested textual analysis
Pages 16–21: beginning, "The summer wore on," and ending, "A more deadly struggle had begun."

Why does Baldwin believe that white Americans' denial of the fact of death is at the root of their racial fears?

1. According to Baldwin, why have white Americans lost individual certainty? What does he mean when he says that they are unable to "renew themselves at the fountain of their own lives"? (25)

2. What does Baldwin mean when he says that white Americans do not believe in death? (32)

3. Why is Baldwin adamant that a failure on the part of whites to face reality—"the fact that life is tragic"—will result in the destruction of America? (32)

4. What, in Baldwin's view, is the connection between white Americans' failure to face reality and their propensity for projecting their unconscious "private fears and longings . . . onto the Negro"? (35)

5. What does Baldwin mean when he says that the only way the white man can be released "from the Negro's tyrannical power over him is to consent, in effect, to become black himself"? (35)

6. Why does Baldwin believe that the liberation of America's whites depends on the absolute liberation of its blacks? (35)

7. What values does Baldwin envision for American civilization when he says that white society is sorely in need of "new standards"? (35) What does he mean when he says that these new standards will place the white man "once again in fruitful communion with the depths of his own being"? (35)

8. Why does Baldwin reject absolutely the notion that white Americans "are in possession of some intrinsic value that black people need, or want"? (34)

9. Why does Baldwin end his essay with the quotation: "*God gave Noah the rainbow sign, / No more water, the fire next time!*"? (41)

Suggested textual analysis
Pages 32–35: beginning, "Behind what we think of as the Russian menace," and ending, "I can raise her to mine."

Why does Baldwin insist that we, the black and the white, deeply need each other if we are to "achieve our identity, our maturity, as men and women"?

1. Why does Baldwin say that identity is almost impossible to achieve in America? (30)

2. Why does Baldwin value social unrest and unease? Why does he say that barring the door to a person's spiritual and social ease is "the most important thing that one human being can do for another"? (28–29)

3. What does the author mean when he says that black people cannot be free until white people are released from "a history which they do not understand"? (6, 7)

4. Why does Baldwin believe that when whites learn to love and accept themselves the "Negro problem will no longer exist, for it will no longer be needed"? (12)

5. Why does Baldwin insist that it is *black* Americans who must, with love, force their white brothers and sisters to "see themselves as they are"? (7) Why can't whites do this for themselves?

6. Why does the author believe that the identity of white people is dependent upon the image of themselves as superior to the black man? (6)

7. Why does Baldwin hold out the hope that positive change for blacks in America will come not only out of political necessity, but also through a voluntary desire on the part of whites to divest themselves of the attitude of racial superiority? (29–30, 34, 35)

8. Why does Baldwin believe that it will depend on a handful of "relatively conscious" whites and blacks to end America's racial nightmare? (40–41)

9. What does Baldwin mean when he says that blacks and whites "must, like lovers, insist on, or create, the consciousness of the others"? (40–41)

Suggested textual analyses
Pages 28–31: beginning, "Now, there is simply no possibility of a real change," and ending, "for many millions of people, we are an unmitigated disaster."

Pages 39–41: from "Color is not a human or a personal reality;" to the end of the selection.

FOR FURTHER REFLECTION

1. Is the identity of American whites threatened when they can't feel superior to blacks?

2. Do you agree that it is not real antipathy that separates blacks and whites, but white people's propensity for projecting their unadmitted "private fears and longings . . . onto the Negro"?

3. Does America persist in thinking of itself as a white nation? Does America today—or did it ever—envy a Europe envisioned as white, civilized, and elegant?

4. Is Baldwin right when he says that white Americans do not believe in death?

5. Do you agree with Baldwin that "people who cannot suffer can never grow up, can never discover who they are"?

6. Does Baldwin's statement, made in the early 1960s, that "domestically, we take no responsibility for (and no pride in) what goes on in our country" hold true today?

APOLOGY

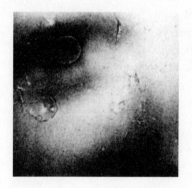

Plato

PLATO (427?–347? B.C.) was born in Athens,
Greece, of a family prominent in Athenian
affairs. His association with the followers
of Socrates led Plato to found the Academy,
a school dedicated to philosophical and
scientific research in Athens that survived
for more than 900 years. He taught and
officiated there—while also writing his
thirty-five dialogues—until his death. In his
dialogues, Plato portrayed his master,
Socrates, in a leading role. Socrates himself
did not leave any writings.

To what degree, Gentlemen of Athens, you have been affected by my accusers, I do not know. I, at any rate, was almost led to forget who I am—so convincingly did they speak. Yet hardly anything they have said is true. Among their many falsehoods, I was especially surprised by one; they said you must be on guard lest I deceive you, since I am a clever speaker. To have no shame at being directly refuted by facts when I show myself in no way clever with words—that, I think, is the very height of shamelessness. Unless, of course, they call a man a clever speaker if he speaks the truth. If that is what they mean, why, I would even admit to being an orator—though not after *their* fashion.

These men, I claim, have said little or nothing true. But from me, Gentlemen, you will hear the whole truth. It will not be prettily tricked out in elegant speeches like theirs, words and phrases all nicely arranged. To the contrary: you will hear me speak naturally in the words which happen to occur to me. For I believe what I say to be just, and let no one of you expect otherwise. Besides, it would hardly be appropriate in a man of my age, Gentlemen, to come before you making up speeches like a boy. So I must specifically ask one thing of you, Gentlemen. If you hear me make my defense in the same words I customarily use at the tables in the Agora, and other places where many of you have heard me, please do not be surprised or make a disturbance because of it. For things stand thus: I am now come into court for the first time; I am seventy years old; and I am an utter stranger to this place. If I were a foreigner, you would unquestionably make allowances if I spoke in the dialect and manner in which I was raised. In just the same way, I specifically ask you now, and justly so, I think, to pay no attention to my manner of speech—it may perhaps be poor, but then perhaps an improvement—and look strictly to this one thing, whether or not I speak justly. For that is the virtue of a judge, and the virtue of an orator is to speak the truth.

First of all, Gentlemen, it is right for me to defend myself against the first false accusations lodged against me, and my first accusers; and next, against later accusations and later accusers. For the fact is that many accusers have risen before you against me; at this point they have been making accusations for many years, and they have told no truth. Yet I fear them more than I fear Anytus and those around him—though they too are dangerous. Still, the others are more dangerous. They took hold of most of you in childhood, persuading you of the truth of accusations which were in fact quite false: "There is a certain Socrates . . . Wise man . . . Thinker on things in the Heavens . . . Inquirer into all things beneath Earth . . . Making the weaker argument stronger. . . ." Those men, Gentlemen of Athens, the men who spread that report, are my dangerous accusers; for their hearers believe that those who inquire into such things acknowledge no gods.

Again, there have been many such accusers, and they have now been at work for a long time; they spoke to you at a time when you were especially trusting—some of you children, some only a little older—and they lodged their accusations quite by default, no one appearing in defense. But the most absurd thing is that one cannot even know or tell their names—unless perhaps in the case of a comic poet. But those who use malicious slander to persuade you, and those who, themselves persuaded, persuade others—all are most difficult to deal with. For it is impossible to bring any one of them forward as a witness and cross-examine him. I must rather, as it were, fight with shadows in making my defense, and question where no one answers.

Please grant, then, as I say, that two sets of accusers have risen against me: those who now lodge their accusations, and those who lodged accusations long since. And please accept the fact that I must defend myself against the latter first. For in fact, you heard their accusations earlier, and with far greater effect than those which came later.

Very well then. A defense is to be made, Gentlemen of Athens. I am to attempt to remove from you in this short time that prejudice which you have been long in acquiring. I might wish that this should come to pass, if it were in some way better for you and for me, wish that I might succeed in my defense. But I think the thing difficult, and its nature hardly escapes me. Still, let that go as pleases the God; the law must be obeyed, and a defense conducted.

Let us then take up from the beginning the charges which have given rise to the prejudice—the charges on which Meletus in fact relied in lodging his indictment. Very well, what do those who slander me say? It is necessary to read, as it were, their sworn indictment: "Socrates is guilty of needless curiosity and meddling interference, inquiring into things beneath Earth and in the Sky, making the weaker argument stronger, and teaching others the same." The charge is something like that. Indeed, you have seen it for yourselves in a comedy by Aristophanes—a certain Socrates being carried around on the stage, talking about walking on air and babbling a great deal of other nonsense, of which I understand neither much nor little. Mark you, I do not mean to disparage such knowledge, if anyone in fact has it—let me not be brought to trial by Meletus on such a charge as that!

But Gentlemen, I have no share of it. Once again, I offer the majority of you as witnesses, and ask those of you who have heard me in conversation—there are many among you—inform each other, please, whether any of you ever heard anything of the sort. From that you will recognize the nature of the other things the multitude says about me.

The fact is that there is nothing in these accusations. And if you have heard from anyone that I undertake to educate men, and make money doing it, that is false too. Once again, I think it would be a fine thing to be able to educate men, as Gorgias of Leontini does, or Prodicus of Ceos, or Hippias of Elis. For each of them, Gentlemen, can enter any given city and convince the youth—who might freely associate with any of their fellow citizens they please—to drop those associations and associate with them, to pay money for it, and give thanks in the bargain. As a matter of fact, there is a man here right now, a Parian, and a wise one, who as I learn has just come to town. For I happened to meet a person who has spent more money on Sophists than everyone else put together, Callias, son of Hipponicus. So I asked him—for he has two sons—"Callias," I said, "if your two sons were colts or calves, we could get an overseer for them and hire him, and his business would be to make them excellent in their appropriate virtue. He would be either a horse trainer or a farmer. But as it is, since the two of them are men, whom do you intend to get as an overseer? Who has knowledge of that virtue which belongs to a man and a citizen? Since you have sons, I'm sure you have considered this. Is there such a person," I said, "or not?"

"To be sure," he said.

"Who is he?" I said. "Where is he from, and how much does he charge to teach?"

"Evenus, Socrates," he said. "A Parian. Five minas."

And I count Evenus fortunate indeed, if he really possesses that art, and teaches it so modestly. For my own part, at any rate, I would be puffed up with vanity and pride if I had such knowledge. But I do not, Gentlemen.

Perhaps one of you will ask, "But Socrates, what is this all about? Whence have these slanders against you arisen? You must surely have been busying yourself with something out of the ordinary; so grave a report and rumor would not have arisen had you not been doing something rather different from most folk. Tell us what it is, so that we may not take action in your case unadvisedly." That, I think, is a fair request, and I shall try to indicate what it is that has given me the name I have. Hear me, then. Perhaps some of you will think I joke; be well assured that I shall be telling the whole truth.

Gentlemen of Athens, I got this name through nothing but a kind of wisdom. What kind? The kind which is perhaps peculiarly human, for it may be I am really wise in that. And perhaps the men I just mentioned are wise with a wisdom greater than human—either that, or I cannot say what. In any case, I have no knowledge of it, and whoever says I do is lying and speaks to my slander.

Please, Gentlemen of Athens. Do not make a disturbance, even if I seem to you to boast. For it will not be my own words I utter; I shall refer you to the speaker, as one worthy of credit. For as witness to you of my wisdom—whether it is wisdom of a kind, and what kind of wisdom it is—I shall call the God at Delphi.

You surely knew Chaerephon. He was my friend from youth, and a friend of your democratic majority. He went into exile with you, and with you he returned. And you know what kind of a man he was, how eager and impetuous in whatever he rushed into. Well, he once went to Delphi and boldly asked the oracle—as I say, Gentlemen, please do not make a disturbance—he asked whether anyone is wiser than I. Now, the Pythia replied that no one is wiser. And to this his brother here will testify, since Chaerephon is dead.

Why do I mention this? I mention it because I intend to inform you whence the slander against me has arisen. For when I heard it, I reflected: "What does the God mean? What is the sense of this riddling utterance? I know that I am not wise at all;

what then does the God mean by saying I am wisest? Surely he does not speak falsehood; it is not permitted to him." So I puzzled for a long time over what was meant, and then, with great reluctance, I turned to inquire into the matter in some such way as this.

I went to someone with a reputation for wisdom, in the belief that there if anywhere I might test the meaning of the utterance and declare to the oracle, "This man is wiser than I am, and you said I was wisest." So I examined him—there is no need to mention a name, but it was someone in political life who produced this effect on me in discussion, Gentlemen of Athens—and I concluded that though he seemed wise to many other men, and most especially to himself, he was not. I tried to show him this; and thence I became hated, by him and by many who were present. But I left thinking to myself, "I am wiser than that man. Neither of us probably knows anything worthwhile; but he thinks he does and does not, and I do not and do not think I do. So it seems at any rate that I am wiser in this one small respect: I do not think I know what I do not." I then went to another man who was reputed to be even wiser, and the same thing seemed true again; there too I became hated, by him and by many others.

Nevertheless, I went on, perceiving with grief and fear that I was becoming hated, but still, it seemed necessary to put the God first—so I had to go on, examining what the oracle meant by testing everyone with a reputation for knowledge. And by the Dog, Gentlemen—I must tell you the truth—I swear that I had some such experience as this: it seemed to me that those most highly esteemed for wisdom fell little short of being most deficient, as I carried on inquiry in behalf of the God, and that others reputedly inferior were men of more discernment.

But really, I must display my wanderings to you; they were like those of a man performing labors—all to the end that I might not leave the oracle untested. From the politicians I went to the poets—tragic, dithyrambic, and the rest—thinking that there I would discover myself manifestly less wise by comparison. So I took up poems over which I thought they had taken special pains, and asked them what they meant, so as also at the same time to learn from them. Now, I am ashamed to tell you the truth, Gentlemen, but still, it must be told. There was hardly anyone present who could not give a better account than they of what they had themselves produced. So presently I came to realize that poets do not make what they make by wisdom, but by a kind of native disposition or divine inspiration, exactly like seers and prophets. For the latter also utter many fine things, but know nothing of the things of which they speak. That is how the poets also appeared to me, while at the same time I realized that because of their poetry they thought themselves the wisest of men in other matters—and were not. Once again, I left thinking myself superior to them in just the way I was to the politicians.

Finally I went to the craftsmen. I was aware that although I knew scarcely anything, I would find that they knew many things, and fine ones. In this I was not mistaken: they knew things that I did not, and in that respect were wiser. But Gentlemen of Athens, it seemed to me that the poets and our capable public craftsmen had exactly the same failing: because they practiced their own arts well, each deemed himself wise in other things, things of great importance. This mistake quite obscured their wisdom. The result was that I asked myself on behalf of the oracle whether I would accept being such as I am, neither wise with their wisdom nor foolish with their folly, or whether I would accept wisdom and folly together and become such as they are. I answered, both for myself and the oracle, that it was better to be as I am.

From this examination, Gentlemen of Athens, much enmity has risen against me, of a sort most harsh and heavy to endure, so that many slanders have arisen, and the name is put abroad that I am "wise." For on each occasion those present think I am wise in the things in which I test others. But very likely, Gentlemen, it is really the God who is wise, and by his oracle he means to say, "Human nature is a thing of little worth, or none." It appears that he does not mean this fellow Socrates, but uses my name to offer an example, as if he were saying, "He among you, Gentlemen, is wisest who, like Socrates, realizes that he is truly worth nothing in respect to wisdom." That is why I still go about even now on behalf of the God, searching and inquiring among both citizens and strangers, should I think some one of them is wise; and when it seems he is not, I help the God and prove it. Due to this pursuit, I have no leisure worth mentioning either for the affairs of the City or for my own estate; I dwell in utter poverty because of my service to God.

Then too the young men follow after me—especially the ones with leisure, namely, the richest. They follow of their own initiative, rejoicing to hear men tested, and often they imitate me and undertake to test others; and next, I think, they find an ungrudging plenty of people who think they have some knowledge but know little or nothing. As a result, those whom they test become angry at me, not at themselves, and say, "This fellow Socrates is utterly polluted, and corrupts the youth." And when someone asks them what it is he does, what it is he teaches, they cannot say because they do not know; but so as not to seem at a loss, they mutter the kind of thing that lies ready to hand against anyone who pursues wisdom: "Things in the Heavens and beneath the Earth," or, "Not acknowledging gods," or, "Making the weaker argument stronger." The truth, I suppose, they would not wish to state, namely, that it is become quite clear that they pretend to knowledge and know nothing. And because they are concerned for their pride, I think, and zealous, and numerous, and speak vehemently and persuasively about me, they have long filled your ears with zealous slander. It was on the strength of this that Meletus attacked me, along with Anytus and Lycon—Meletus angered on behalf of the poets, Anytus on behalf of the public craftsmen and the politicians, Lycon on behalf of the orators. So the result is, as I said to begin with, that I should be most surprised were I able to remove from you in this short time a slander which has grown so great. There, Gentlemen of Athens, you have the truth, and I have concealed or misrepresented nothing in speaking it, great or small. Yet I know quite well that it is just for this that I have become hated—which is in fact an indication of the truth of what I say, and that this is the basis of the slander and charges against me. Whether you inquire into it now or hereafter you will find it to be so.

Against the charges lodged by my first accusers, let this defense suffice. But for Meletus—the good man who loves his City, so he says—and for my later accusers, I shall attempt a further defense. Once more then, as before a different set of accusers, let us take up their sworn indictment. It runs something like this: it says that Socrates is guilty of corrupting the youth, and of not acknowledging the gods the City acknowledges, but other new divinities. Such is the charge. Let us examine its particulars.

It claims I am guilty of corrupting the youth. But I claim, Gentlemen of Athens, that it is Meletus who is guilty—guilty of jesting in earnest, guilty of lightly bringing men to trial, guilty of pretending a zealous concern for things he never cared about at all. I shall try to show you that this is true.

Come here, Meletus. Now tell me. Do you count it of great importance that the young should be as good as possible?

"I do."

Then come and tell the jurors this: who improves them? Clearly you know, since it is a matter of concern to you. Having discovered, so you say, that I am the man who is corrupting them, you bring me before these judges to accuse me. But now come and say who makes them better. Inform the judges who he is.

You see, Meletus. You are silent. You cannot say. And yet, does this not seem shameful to you, and a sufficient indication of what I say, namely, that you never cared at all? Tell us, my friend. Who improves them?

"The laws."

But I did not ask you that, dear friend. I asked you what man improves them—whoever it is who in the first place knows just that very thing, the laws.

"These men, Socrates. The judges."

Really, Meletus? These men here are able to educate the youth and improve them?

"Especially they."

All of them? Or only some?

"All."

By Hera, you bring good news. An ungrudging plenty of benefactors! But what about the audience here. Do they improve them, or not?

"They too."

And members of the Council?

"The Councillors too."

Well then, Meletus, do the members of the Assembly, the Ecclesiasts, corrupt the young? Or do they all improve them too?

"They too."

So it seems that every Athenian makes them excellent except me, and I alone corrupt them. Is that what you are saying?

"That is exactly what I am saying."

You condemn me to great misfortune. But tell me, do you think it is so with horses? Do all men improve them, while some one man corrupts them? Or quite to the contrary, is it some one man or a very few, namely horse trainers, who are able to improve them, while the majority of people, if they handle horses and use them, corrupt them? Is that not true, Meletus, both of horses and all other animals? Of course it is, whether you and Anytus affirm or deny it. It would be good fortune indeed for the youth if only one man corrupted them and the rest benefited. But the fact is, Meletus, that you sufficiently show that you never gave thought to the youth; you clearly indicate your own lack of concern, indicate that you never cared at all about the matters in which you bring action against me.

But again, dear Meletus, tell us this: is it better to dwell among fellow citizens who are good, or wicked? Do answer, dear friend; surely I ask nothing hard. Do not wicked men do evil things to those around them, and good men good things?

"Of course."

Now, is there anyone who wishes to be harmed rather than benefited by those with whom he associates? Answer me, dear friend, for the law requires you to answer. Is there anyone who wishes to be harmed?

"Of course not."

Very well then, are you bringing action against me here because I corrupt the youth intentionally, or unintentionally?

"Intentionally, I say."

How can that be, Meletus? Are you at your age so much wiser than I at mine that you recognize that evil men always do evil things to those around them, and good men do good, while I have reached such a pitch of folly that I am unaware that if I do some evil to those with whom I associate, I shall very likely receive some evil at their hands, with the result that I do such great evil intentionally, as you claim? I do not believe you, Meletus, and I do not think anyone else does either. On the contrary: either I do not corrupt the youth, or if I do, I do so unintentionally. In either case, you lie. And if I corrupt them unintentionally, it is not the law to bring action here for that sort of mistake, but rather to instruct and admonish in private; for clearly, if I once learn, I shall stop what I unintentionally do. You, however, were unwilling to associate with me and teach me; instead, you brought action here, where it is law to bring those in need of punishment rather than instruction.

Gentlemen of Athens, what I said is surely now clear: Meletus was never concerned about these matters, much or little. Still, Meletus, tell us this: how do you say I corrupt the youth? Or is it clear from your indictment that I teach them not to acknowledge gods the City acknowledges, but other new divinities? Is this what you mean by saying I corrupt by teaching?

"Certainly. That is exactly what I mean."

Then in the name of these same gods we are now discussing, Meletus, please speak a little more plainly still, both for me and for these gentlemen here. Do you mean that I teach the youth to acknowledge that there are gods, and thus do not myself wholly deny gods, and am not in that respect guilty—though the gods are not those the City acknowledges, but different ones? Or are you claiming that I do not myself acknowledge any gods at all, and teach this to others?

"I mean that. You acknowledge no gods at all."

Ah, my dear Meletus, why do you say such things? Do I not at least acknowledge Sun and Moon as gods, as other men do?

"No, no, Gentlemen and Judges, not when he says the Sun is a stone and the Moon earth."

My dear Meletus! Do you think it is Anaxagoras you are accusing? Do you so despise these judges here and think them so unlettered that they do not know it is the books of Anaxagoras of Clazomenae which teem with such statements? Are young men to learn these things specifically from me, when they can buy them sometimes in the Orchestra for a drachma, if the price is high, and laugh at Socrates if he pretends they are his own—especially since they are so absurd? Well, dear friend, is that what you think? I acknowledge no gods at all?

"No, none whatever."

You cannot be believed, Meletus—even, I think, by yourself. Gentlemen of Athens, I think this man who stands here before you is insolent and unchastened, and has brought this suit precisely out of insolence and unchastened youth. He seems to be conducting a test by propounding a riddle: "Will Socrates, the wise man, realize how neatly I contradict myself, or will I deceive him and the rest of the audience?" For certainly it seems clear that he is contradicting himself in his indictment. It is as though he were saying, "Socrates is guilty of not acknowledging gods, and acknowledges gods." Yet surely this is to jest.

Please join me, Gentlemen, in examining why it appears to me that this is what he is saying. And you answer us, Meletus.

The rest of you will please remember what I asked you at the beginning, and make no disturbance if I fashion arguments in my accustomed way.

Is there any man, Meletus, who acknowledges that there are things pertaining to men, but does not acknowledge that there are men? Let him answer for himself, Gentlemen—and let him stop interrupting. Is there any man who does not acknowledge that there are horses, but acknowledges things pertaining to horsemanship? Or does not acknowledge that there are flutes, but acknowledges things pertaining to flute playing? There is not, my good friend. If you do not wish to answer, I'll answer for you and for the rest of these people here. But do please answer my next question, at least: Is there any man who acknowledges that there are things pertaining to divinities, but does not acknowledge that there are divinities?

"There is not."

How obliging of you to answer—reluctantly, and under compulsion from these gentlemen here. Now, you say that I acknowledge and teach things pertaining to divinities—whether new or old, still at least I acknowledge them, by your account; indeed, you swore to that in your indictment. But if I acknowledge that there are things pertaining to divinities, must I surely not also acknowledge that there are divinities? Isn't that so? Of course it is—since you do not answer, I count you as agreeing. And divinities, we surely believe, are either gods or children of gods? Correct?

"Of course."

So if I believe in divinities, as you say, and if divinities are a kind of god, there is the jesting riddle I attributed to you: you are saying that I do not believe in gods, and again that I do believe in gods because I believe in divinities. On the other hand, if divinities are children of gods, some born illegitimately of nymphs, or others of whom this is also told, who could possibly believe that there are children of gods, but not gods? It would be as absurd as believing that there are children of horses and asses, namely mules, without believing there are horses and asses. Meletus, you could not have brought this indictment except in an attempt to test us—or because you were at a loss for any true basis of prosecution. But as to how you are to convince anyone of even the slightest intelligence that one and the same man can believe that there are things pertaining to divinities and gods, and yet believe that there are neither divinities nor heroes—there is no way.

Gentlemen of Athens, I do not think further defense is needed to show that, by the very terms of Meletus' indictment, I am not guilty; this, surely, is sufficient. But as I said before, a great deal of enmity has risen against me among many people, and you may rest assured this is true. And that is what will convict me, if I am convicted—not Meletus, not Anytus, but the grudging slander of the multitude. It has convicted many another good and decent man; I think it will convict me; nor is there reason to fear that with me it will come to a stand.

Perhaps someone may say, "Are you not ashamed, Socrates, at having pursued such a course that you now stand in danger of being put to death?" To him I would make a just reply: You are wrong, Sir, if you think that a man worth anything at all should take thought for danger in living or dying. He should look when he acts to one thing: whether what he does is just or unjust, the work of a good man or a bad one. By your account, those demigods and heroes who laid down their lives at Troy would be of little worth—the rest of them, and the son of Thetis too; Achilles so much despised danger instead of submitting to disgrace that when he was intent on killing Hector his goddess mother told him, as I recall, "My son, if you avenge the slaying of your comrade Patroclus with the death of Hector, you yourself shall die; for straightway with Hector is his fate prepared for you." Achilles heard, and thought little of the death and danger. He was more afraid to live as a bad man, with friends left unavenged. "Straightway let me die," he said, "exacting right from him who did the wrong, that I may not remain here as a butt of mockery beside the crook-beaked ships, a burden to the earth." Do you suppose that he gave thought to death and danger?

Gentlemen of Athens, truly it is so: wherever a man stations himself in belief that it is best, wherever he is stationed by his commander, there he must I think remain and run the risks, giving thought to neither death nor any other thing except disgrace. I should indeed have wrought a fearful thing, Gentlemen of Athens, if, when the commanders you chose stationed me at Potidaea and Amphipolis and Delium, I there remained as others did, and ran the risk of death; but then, when the God stationed me, as I thought and believed, obliging me to live in the pursuit of wisdom, examining myself and others—if then, at that point, through fear of death or any other thing, I left my post. That would have been dreadful indeed, and then in truth might I be justly brought to court for not acknowledging the existence of gods, for willful disobedience to the oracle, for fearing death, for thinking myself wise when I am not.

For to fear death, Gentlemen, is nothing but to think one is wise when one is not; for it is to think one knows what one does not. No man knows death, nor whether it is not the greatest of all goods; and yet men fear it as though they well knew it to be the worst of evils. Yet how is this not folly most to be reproached, the folly of believing one knows what one does not? I, at least, Gentlemen, am perhaps superior to most men here and just in this, and if I were to claim to be wiser than anyone else it would be in this: that as I have no satisfactory knowledge of things in the Place of the Dead, I do not think I do. I do know that to be guilty of disobedience to a superior, be he god or man, is shameful evil.

So as against evils I know to be evils, I shall never fear or flee from things which for aught I know may be good. Thus, even if you now dismiss me, refusing to do as Anytus bids—Anytus, who said that either I should not have been brought to trial to begin with or, since brought, must be put to death, testifying before you that if I were once acquitted your sons would pursue what Socrates teaches and all be thoroughly corrupted—if with this in view you were to say to me, "Socrates, we shall not at this time be persuaded by Meletus, and we dismiss you. But on this condition: that you no longer pass time in that inquiry of yours, or pursue philosophy. And if you are again taken doing it, you die." If, as I say, you were to dismiss me on that condition, I would reply that I hold you in friendship and regard, Gentlemen of Athens, but I shall obey the God rather than you, and while I have breath and am able I shall not cease to pursue wisdom or to exhort you, charging any of you I happen to meet in my accustomed manner. "You are the best of men, being an Athenian, citizen of a city honored for wisdom and power beyond all others. Are you then not ashamed to care for the getting of money, and reputation, and public honor, while yet having no thought or concern for truth and understanding and the greatest possible excellence of your soul?" And if some one of you disputes this, and says he does care, I shall not immediately dismiss him and go away. I shall question him and examine him and test him, and if he does not seem to me to possess virtue, and yet says he does, I shall rebuke him for counting of more importance things which by comparison are worthless. I shall do this to young and old, citizen and stranger, whomever I happen to meet, but I shall do it especially to citizens, inasmuch as they are more nearly related to me. For the God commands this, be well assured, and I believe that you have yet to gain in this City a greater good than my service to the God. I go about doing nothing but persuading you, young and old, to care not for body or money in place of, or so much as, excellence of soul. I tell you that virtue does not come from money, but money and all other human goods both public and private from virtue. If in saying this I corrupt the youth, that would be harm indeed. But anyone who claims I say other than this speaks falsehood. In these matters, Gentlemen of Athens, believe Anytus, or do not. Dismiss me, or do not. For I will not do otherwise, even if I am to die for it many times over.

Please do not make a disturbance, Gentlemen. Abide in my request and do not interrupt what I have to say, but listen. Indeed, I think you will benefit by listening. I am going to tell you certain things at which you may perhaps cry out; please do not do it. Be well assured that if you kill me, and if I am the sort of man I claim, you will harm me less than you harm yourselves. There is no harm a Meletus or Anytus can do me; it is not possible, for it does not, I think, accord with divine law that a better man be harmed by a worse. Meletus perhaps can kill me, or exile me, or disenfranchise me; and perhaps he and others too think those things great evils. I do not. I think it a far greater evil to do what he is now doing, attempting to kill a man unjustly. And so, Gentlemen of Athens, I am far from making a defense for my own sake, as some might think; I make it for yours, lest you mistake the gift the God has given you and cast your votes against me. If you kill me, you will not easily find such another man as I, a man who—if I may put it a bit absurdly—has been fastened as it were to the City by the God as to a large and well-bred horse, a horse grown sluggish because of its size, and in need of being roused by a kind of gadfly. Just so, I think, the God has fastened me to the City. I rouse you. I persuade you. I upbraid you. I never stop lighting on each one of you, everywhere, all day long. Such another will not easily come to you again, Gentlemen, and if you are persuaded by me, you will spare me. But perhaps you are angry, as men roused from sleep are angry, and perhaps you will swat me, persuaded by Meletus that you may lightly kill. Then will you continue to sleep out your lives, unless the God sends someone else to look after you.

That I am just that, a gift from the God to the City, you may recognize from this: it scarcely seems a human matter merely, that I should take no thought for anything of my own and endure the neglect of my house and its affairs for these long years now, and ever attend to yours, going to each of you in private like a father or elder brother, persuading you to care for virtue. If I got something from it, if I took pay for this kind of exhortation, that would explain it. But as things are, you can see for yourselves that even my accusers, who have accused me so shamefully, of everything else, could not summon shamelessness enough to provide witnesses to testify that I ever took pay or asked for it. For it is enough, I think, to provide my poverty as witness to the truth of what I say.

Perhaps it may seem peculiar that I go about in private advising men and busily inquiring, and yet do not enter your Assembly in public to advise the City. The reason is a thing you have heard me mention many times in many places, that something divine and godlike comes to me—which Meletus, indeed, mocked in his indictment. I have had it from childhood. It comes as a kind of voice, and when it comes, it always turns me away from what I am about to do, but never toward it. That is what opposed my entering political life, and I think it did well to oppose. For be well assured, Gentlemen of Athens, that had I attempted long since to enter political affairs, I should long since have been destroyed—to the benefit of neither you nor myself.

Please do not be angry at me for telling the simple truth. It is impossible for any man to be spared if he legitimately opposes you or any other democratic majority, and prevents many unjust and illegal things from occurring in his city. He who intends to fight for what is just, if he is to be spared even for a little time, must of necessity live a private rather than a public life.

I shall offer you a convincing indication of this—not words, but what you respect, deeds. Hear, then, what befell me, so that you may know that I will not through fear of death give way to any man contrary to what is right, even if I am destroyed for it. I shall tell you a thing which is tedious—it smacks of the law courts—but true. Gentlemen of Athens, I never held other office in the City, but I was once a member of the Council. And it happened that our Tribe, Antiochis, held the Prytanate when you decided to judge as a group the cases of the ten generals who had failed to gather up the bodies of the slain in the naval battle—illegally, as later it seemed to all of you. But at that time, I alone of the Prytanies opposed doing a thing contrary to law, and cast my vote against it. And when the orators were ready to impeach me and have me arrested—you urging them on with your shouts—I thought that with law and justice on my side I must run the risk, rather than concur with you in an unjust decision through fear of bonds or death. Those things happened while the City was still under the Democracy. But when Oligarchy came, the Thirty in turn summoned me along with four others to the Rotunda and ordered us to bring back Leon the Salamanian from Salamis so that he might be executed, just as they ordered many others to do such things, planning to implicate as many people as possible in their own guilt. But I then showed again, not by words but deeds, that death, if I may be rather blunt, was of no concern whatever to me; to do nothing unjust or unholy—that was my concern. Strong as it was, that oligarchy did not so frighten me as to do a thing unjust, and when we departed the Rotunda, the other four went into Salamis and brought back Leon, and I left and went home. I might have been killed for that, if the oligarchy had not shortly afterward been overthrown. And of these things you will have many witnesses.

Now, do you think I would have lived so many years if I had been in public life and acted in a manner worthy of a good man, defending what is just and counting it, as is necessary, of first importance? Far from it, Gentlemen of Athens. Not I, and not any other man. But through my whole life I have shown myself to be that sort of man in public affairs, the few I've engaged in; and I have shown myself the same man in private. I never gave way to anyone contrary to what is just—not to others, and certainly not to those slanderously said to be my pupils. In fact, I have never been teacher to anyone. If, in speaking and tending my own affairs, anyone wished to hear me, young or old, I never begrudged him; nor do I discuss for a fee and not otherwise. To rich and poor alike I offer myself as a questioner, and if anyone wishes to answer, he may hear what I have to say. And if any of them turned out to be useful men, or any did not, I cannot justly be held responsible. To none did I promise instruction, and none did I teach; if anyone says that he learned from me or heard in private what others did not, you may rest assured he is not telling the truth.

Why is it, then, that some people enjoy spending so much time with me? You have heard, Gentlemen of Athens: I told you the whole truth. It is because they enjoy hearing people tested who think they are wise and are not. After all, it is not unamusing. But for my own part, as I say, I have been ordered to do this by God—in oracles, in dreams, in every way in which other divine apportionment ever ordered a man to do anything.

These things, Gentlemen of Athens, are both true and easily tested. For if I am corrupting some of the youth, and have corrupted others, it must surely be that some among them, grown older, if they realize that I counseled them toward evil while young, would now come forward to accuse me and exact a penalty. And if they were unwilling, then some of their relatives—fathers, brothers, other kinsmen—if their own relatives had suffered evil at my hands, would now remember, and exact a penalty. Certainly there are many such men I see present. Here is Crito, first, of my own age and deme, father of Critobulus; then there is Lysanias of Sphettos, father of Aeschines here. Next there is Antiphon of Cephisus, father of Epigenes. Then there are others whose brothers engaged in this pastime. There is Nicostratus, son of Theozotides, brother of Theodotus—and Theodotus is dead, so he could not have swayed him—and Paralus here, son of Demodocus, whose brother was Theages. And here is Adeimantus, son of Ariston, whose brother is Plato there; and Aeantodorus, whose brother is Apollodorus here. I could name many others, some of whom at least Meletus ought certainly have provided in his speech as witnesses. If he forgot it then, let him do it now—I yield the floor—and let him say whether he has any witnesses of the sort. You will find that quite to the contrary, Gentlemen, every one of these men is ready to help me—I, who corrupt their relatives, as Meletus and

Anytus claim. Those who are themselves corrupted might perhaps have reason to help me; but their relatives are older men
who have not been corrupted. What reason could they have for
supporting me except that it is right and just, because they know
Meletus is lying and I am telling the truth?

Very well then, Gentlemen. This, and perhaps a few other
things like it, is what I have to say in my defense. Perhaps some
of you will remember his own conduct and be offended, if when
brought to trial on a lesser charge than this, he begged his
judges with tearful supplication, and caused his children to
come forward so that he might be the more pitied, along with
other relatives and a host of friends; whereas I shall do none of
these things, even though I am, as it would seem at least, in the
extremity of danger. Perhaps someone with this in mind may
become hardened against me; angered by it, he may cast his vote
in anger. If this is true of any of you—not that I expect it, but if
it is—I think it might be appropriate to say, "I too have relatives, my friend; for as Homer puts it, I am not 'of oak and
rock,' but born of man, so I have relatives—yes, and sons too,
Gentlemen of Athens, three of them, one already a lad and two
of them children. Yet not one of them have I caused to come forward here, and I shall not beg you to acquit me." Why not? Not
out of stubbornness, Gentlemen of Athens, nor disrespect for
you. Whether or not I am confident in the face of death is
another story; but I think that my own honor, and yours, and
that of the whole City would suffer, if I were to behave in this
way, I being of the age I am and having the name I have—truly
or falsely, it being thought that Socrates is in some way superior
to most men. If those of you reputed to be superior in wisdom
or courage or any other virtue whatever are to be men of this
sort, it would be disgraceful; I have often seen such people
behave surprisingly when put on trial, even though they had a
reputation to uphold, because they were persuaded that they
would suffer a terrible thing if they were put to death—as
though they would be immortal if you did not kill them. I think
they cloak the City in shame, so that a stranger might think that

those among the Athenians who are superior in virtue, and whom the Athenians themselves judge worthy of office and other honors, are no better than women. These are things, Gentlemen of Athens, which those of you who have a reputation to uphold ought not to do; nor if we defendants do them, ought you permit it. You ought rather make it clear that you would far rather cast your vote against a man who stages these pitiful scenes, and makes the City a butt of mockery, than against a man who shows quiet restraint.

But apart from the matter of reputation, Gentlemen, it does not seem to me just to beg a judge, or to be acquitted by begging; it is rather just to teach and persuade. The judge does not sit to grant justice as a favor, but to render judgment; he has sworn no oath to gratify those whom he sees fit, but to judge according to law. We ought not accustom you, nor ought you become accustomed, to forswear yourselves; it is pious in neither of us. So do not expect me, Gentlemen of Athens, to do such things in your presence as I believe to be neither honorable nor just nor holy, especially since, by Zeus, it is for impiety that I am being prosecuted by this fellow Meletus here. For clearly, if I were to persuade and compel you by supplication, you being sworn as judges, I would teach you then indeed not to believe that there are gods, and in making my defense I would in effect accuse myself of not acknowledging them. But that is far from so; I do acknowledge them, Gentlemen of Athens, as no one of my accusers does, and to you and to the God I now commit my case, to judge in whatever way shall be best both for me and for you.

I am not distressed, Gentlemen of Athens, at what has happened, nor angered that you have cast your votes against me. Many things contribute to this, among them the fact that I expected it. I am much more surprised at the number of votes either way: I did not think it would be by so little, but by more. As it is, it seems, if only thirty votes had fallen otherwise,

I would have been acquitted. And so far as Meletus at least is concerned, it seems to me, I am already acquitted—and more than acquitted, since it is clear that if Anytus and Lycon had not come forward to accuse me, Meletus would have been fined a thousand drachmas for not obtaining a fifth part of the vote.

The man demands death for me. Very well. Then what counterpenalty shall I propose to you, Gentlemen of Athens? Clearly something I deserve, but what? What do I deserve to pay or suffer because I did not through life keep quiet, and yet did not concern myself, as the multitude do, with money or property or military and public honors and other office, or the secret societies and political clubs which keep cropping up in the City, believing that I was really too reasonable and temperate a man to enter upon these things and survive. I did not go where I could benefit neither you nor myself; instead, I went to each of you in private, where I might perform the greatest service. I undertook to persuade each of you not to care for anything which belongs to you before first caring for yourselves, nor to care for anything which belongs to the City before caring for the City itself, and so too with everything else. Now, what do I deserve to suffer for being this sort of man? Some good thing, Gentlemen of Athens, if penalty is really to be assessed according to desert. What then is fitting for a poor man who has served his City well, and needs leisure to exhort you? Why, Gentlemen of Athens, nothing is more fitting for such a man than to be fed in the Prytaneum, at the common table of the City—yes, and far more fitting than for one of you who has been an Olympic victor in the single-horse or two- or four-horse chariot races. For he makes you seem happy, whereas I make you happy in truth, and he does not need subsistence, and I do. If then I must propose a penalty I justly deserve, I propose that, public subsistence in the Prytaneum.

Perhaps some of you will think that in saying this I speak much as I spoke of tears and pleading, out of stubborn pride. That is not so, Gentlemen of Athens, though something of this sort is: I am persuaded that I have not intentionally wronged any man, but I cannot persuade you of it; we have talked so short a time. Now, I believe if you had a law, as other people do, that cases involving death shall not be decided in a single day, that you would be persuaded; but as things are, it is not easy in so short a time to do away with slanders grown so great. Being persuaded, however, that I have wronged no one, I am quite unwilling to wrong myself, or claim that I deserve some evil and propose any penalty of the kind. What is there to fear? That I may suffer the penalty Meletus proposes, when as I say, I do not know whether it is good or evil? Shall I choose instead a penalty I know very well to be evil? Imprisonment, perhaps? But why should I live in prison, a slave to men who happen to occupy office as the Eleven? A fine, then, and imprisonment till I pay it? But that comes to the same thing, since I have no money to pay it. Shall I then propose exile? Perhaps you would accept that. But I must indeed love life and cling to it dearly, Gentlemen, if I were so foolish as to think that, although you, my own fellow citizens, cannot bear my pursuits and discussions, which have become so burdensome and hateful that you now seek to be rid of them, others will bear them lightly. No, Gentlemen. My life would be fine indeed, if at my age I went to live in exile, always moving from city to city, always driven out. For be well assured that wherever I go, the young men will listen to what I say as they do here; if I turn them away they will themselves drive me out, appealing to their elders; if I do not turn them away, their fathers and relations will drive me out in their behalf.

Perhaps someone may say, "Would it not be possible for you to live in exile, Socrates, if you were silent and kept quiet?" But this is the hardest thing of all to make some of you believe. If I say that to do so would be to disobey the God, and therefore I cannot do it, you will not believe me because you will think that I am being sly and dishonest. If on the other hand I say that the greatest good for man is to fashion arguments each day about virtue and the other things you hear me discussing, when I examine myself and others, and that the unexamined life is not for man worth living, you will believe what I say still less. I claim these things are so, Gentlemen; but it is not easy to convince you. At the same time, I am not accustomed to think myself deserving of any evil. If I had money, I would propose a fine as great as I could pay—there would be no harm in that. But as things stand, I have no money, unless the amount I can pay is the amount you are willing to exact of me. I might perhaps be able to pay a mina of silver. So I propose a penalty in that amount. But Plato here, Gentlemen of Athens, and Crito and Critobulus and Apollodorus bid me propose thirty minas, and they will stand surety. So I propose that amount. You have guarantors sufficient for the sum.

For the sake of only a little time, Gentlemen of Athens, you are to be accused by those who wish to revile the City of having killed Socrates, a wise man—for those who wish to reproach you will say I am wise even if I am not. And if you had only waited a little, the thing would have come of its own initiative. You see my age. You see how far spent my life already is, how near to death.

I say this, not to all of you, but to those of you who voted to condemn me. To them I also say this. Perhaps you think, Gentlemen of Athens, that I have been convicted for lack of words to persuade you, had I thought it right to do and say anything to be acquitted. Not so. It is true I have been convicted for a lack; not a lack of words, but lack of bold shamelessness, unwillingness to say the things you would find it pleasant to hear—weeping and wailing, saying and doing many things I claim to be unworthy of me, but things of the sort you are accustomed to hear from others. I did not then think it necessary to do anything unworthy of a free man because of danger; I do not now regret so having conducted my defense; and I would far rather die with that defense than live with the other. Neither in court of law nor in war ought I or any man contrive to escape death by any means possible. Often in battle it becomes clear that a man may escape death by throwing down his arms and turning in supplication to his pursuers; and there are many other devices for each of war's dangers, so that one can avoid dying if he is bold enough to say and do anything at all. It is not difficult to escape death, Gentlemen; it is more difficult to escape wickedness, for wickedness runs faster than death. And now I am old and slow, and I have been caught by the slower runner. But my accusers are clever and quick, and they have been caught by the faster runner, namely Evil. I now take my leave, sentenced by you to death; they depart convicted by Truth for injustice and wickedness. I abide in my penalty, and they in theirs. That is no doubt as it should be, and I think it is fit.

I desire next to prophesy to you who condemned me. For I have now reached that point where men are especially prophetic, when they are about to die. I say to you who have decreed my death that to you there will come hard on my dying a thing far more difficult to bear than the death you have visited upon me. You have done this thing in the belief that you would be released from submitting to an examination of your lives. I say that it will turn out otherwise. Those who come to examine you will be more numerous, and I have up to now restrained them, though you perceived it not. They will be more harsh inasmuch as they are younger, and you will be the more troubled. If you think by killing to hold back the reproach due you for not living rightly, you are profoundly mistaken. That release is neither possible nor honorable. The release which is both most honorable and most easy is not to cut down others, but to so prepare yourselves that you will be as good as possible. This I utter as prophecy to you who voted for my condemnation, and take my leave.

But with you who voted for my acquittal, I should be glad to discuss the nature of what has happened, now, while the authorities are busy and I am not yet gone where, going, I must die. Abide with me, Gentlemen, this space of time; nothing prevents our talking with each other while we still can. To you, as my friends, I wish to display the meaning of what has now fallen to my lot. A remarkable thing has occurred, Gentlemen and Judges—and I am correct in calling you Judges. My accustomed oracle, which is divine, always came quite frequently before in everything, opposing me even in trivial matters if I was about to err. And now a thing has fallen to my lot which you also see yourselves, a thing which some might think, and do in fact believe, to be ultimate among evils. But the sign of the God did not oppose me early this morning when I left my house, nor when I came up to the courtroom here, nor at any point in my argument in anything I was about to say. And yet in many places, in other arguments, it has checked me right in the middle of speaking; but today it has not opposed me in any way, in none of my deeds, in none of my words. What do I take to be the reason? I will tell you. Very likely what has fallen to me is good, and those among us who think that death is an evil are wrong. There has been convincing indication of this. For the accustomed sign would surely have opposed me, if I were not in some way acting for good.

Let us also consider a further reason for high hope that death is good. Death is one of two things. Either to be dead is not to exist, to have no awareness at all, or it is, as the stories tell, a kind of alteration, a change of abode for the soul from this place to another. And if it is to have no awareness, like a sleep when the sleeper sees no dream, death would be a wonderful gain; for I suppose if someone had to pick out that night in which he slept and saw no dream, and put the other days and nights of his life beside it, and had to say after inspecting them how many days and nights he had lived in his life which were better and sweeter, I think that not only any ordinary person but even the Great King himself would find them easily numbered in relation to other days, and other nights. If death is that, I say it is gain; for the whole of time then turns out to last no longer than a single night. But if on the contrary death is like taking a journey, passing from here to another place, and the stories told are true, and all who have died are there—what greater good might there be, my Judges? For if a man once goes to the place of the dead, and takes leave of those who claim to be judges here, he will find the true judges who are said to sit in judgment there—Minos, Rhadamanthus, Aeacus, Triptolemus, and the other demigods and heroes who lived just lives. Would that journey be worthless? And again, to meet Orpheus and Musaeus, Hesiod and Homer—how much would any of you give? I at least would be willing to die many times over, if these things are true. I would find a wonderful pursuit there, when I met Palamedes, and Ajax, son of Telemon, and any others among the ancients done to death by unjust verdicts, and compared my experiences with theirs. It would not, I think, be unamusing. But the greatest thing, surely, would be to test and question there as I did here— who among them is wise? Who thinks he is and is not? How much might one give, my Judges, to examine the man who led the great army against Troy, or Odysseus, or Sisyphus, or a thousand other men and women one might mention—to converse with them, to associate with them, to examine them— why, it would be inconceivable happiness. Especially since they surely do not kill you for it there. For they are happier there than men are here in other ways, and they are already immortal for the rest of time, if the stories told are true.

But you too, my Judges, must be of good hope concerning death. You must recognize that this one thing is true: that there is no evil for a good man either in living or in dying, and that the gods do not neglect his affairs. What has now come to me did not come of its own initiative. It is clear to me that to die now and be released from my affairs is better for me. That is why the sign did not turn me back, and I bear no anger whatever toward those who voted to condemn me, or toward my accusers. And yet, it was not with this in mind that they accused and convicted me. They thought to do harm, and for that they deserve blame. But this much would I ask of them: when my sons are grown, Gentlemen, exact a penalty of them: give pain to them exactly as I gave pain to you, if it seems to you that they care more for wealth or anything else than they care for virtue.

And if they seem to be something and are nothing, rebuke them as I rebuked you, because they do not care for what they ought, because they think themselves something and are worth nothing. And should you do that, both I and my sons will have been justly dealt with at your hands.

But it is already the hour of parting—I to die and you to live. Which of us goes to the better is unclear to all but the God. ∽

INTERPRETIVE QUESTIONS
FOR DISCUSSION

Is Socrates' primary aim in the *Apology* to defend himself or to continue to examine the citizens of Athens?

1. Is the tone of Socrates' defense humble or proud?

2. Why does Socrates say he will make his defense "in the same words I customarily use at the tables in the Agora"? (52)

3. Why doesn't Socrates answer Meletus' charge by stating his religious beliefs directly? Why does Socrates display his method of inquiry to the court by questioning Meletus? (59–64)

4. Why does Socrates mention as part of his defense his belief that he will be convicted?

5. Why does Socrates tell the judges, even before they have found him guilty, that he is not afraid of the death penalty? (65–66)

6. Why does Socrates tell the judges that if they try to prohibit him from continuing his inquiry, "I shall obey the God rather than you"? (66)

7. Why does Socrates compare the city to a large, well-bred horse that has grown sluggish and sleepy and needs a gadfly to awaken it? (67)

8. Why does Socrates say that a man who intends to fight for what is just must avoid public life in order to survive? (68)

9. Why does Socrates propose as a penalty "some good thing" after the judges have found him guilty? Why doesn't he worry that this will offend them? (73)

Suggested textual analyses
Pages 64–65: beginning, "Gentlemen of Athens, I do not think further defense is needed," and ending, "be he god or man, is shameful evil."

Pages 67–68: beginning, "Please do not make a disturbance," and ending, "rather than a public life."

Why does Socrates preach that "the unexamined life is not for man worth living"?

1. Why does Socrates begin to investigate the meaning of the oracle "with great reluctance"? Why does he persevere in this course, despite "perceiving with grief and fear" that he was becoming hated? (56)

2. Why does Socrates believe that in testing the oracle he is helping and obeying the god?

3. Why does Socrates interpret the oracle to mean that the wisest person is one who "realizes that he is truly worth nothing in respect to wisdom"? (58) According to Socrates, does wisdom consist solely in recognizing how little we know? (55–58, 65)

4. Why does Socrates think that his examination of Athens' citizens is the greatest good the city has ever gained? Why does he think he is "a gift from the God to the City"? (66–67)

5. Why does the voice that guides Socrates only turn him away from what he is about to do, and never toward it? (68–69)

6. Why does Socrates think that it is so important to discover who is wise that, if it is possible, he will continue to question people in the afterlife? (77–78)

Suggested textual analyses
Pages 55–57: beginning, "Please, Gentlemen of Athens," and ending, "that it was better to be as I am."

Pages 73–74: beginning, "The man demands death for me," and ending, "you will believe what I say still less."

Does the condemnation of Socrates stand as proof that he failed in his mission to improve and educate the people of Athens?

1. Why is Socrates found guilty and sentenced to death by the gentlemen of Athens?

2. Why does Socrates find that those men with the greatest reputation for wisdom "fell little short of being most deficient"? Why does Socrates find it difficult to find even one citizen of Athens who is wise—or at least wise to some small extent? (56–58)

3. Does Socrates believe that no one is qualified to educate young people? (54, 59–61)

4. Why does Socrates fear "the grudging slander of the multitude" more than the accusations of his public accusers? (64) Does Socrates oppose the principle of majority rule? (68–69)

5. Why does Socrates tell the judges, "I have never been teacher to anyone"? (69) Why does he say, "I rouse you. I persuade you. I upbraid you," but then deny he is a teacher? (67)

6. Why does Socrates tell the judges that he is making his defense for their sake rather than for his own? (67)

7. Why does Socrates claim that he makes the citizens of Athens "happy in truth"? (73)

Suggested textual analyses
Pages 65–66: beginning, "So as against evils," and ending, "to die for it many times over."

Pages 68–70: beginning, "I shall offer you a convincing indication," and ending, "he is not telling the truth."

For Further Reflection

1. Do you agree with Socrates that "he who intends to fight for what is just . . . must of necessity live a private rather than a public life"?

2. Does society need gadflies like Socrates to improve it? Do we have someone like him now?

3. How does knowing that you don't know anything promote virtue?

4. Do you agree with Socrates that it is irrational to fear death, and that it is easier to live a life of virtue if one does not fear death? Do you agree with Socrates that "there is no evil for a good man either in living or in dying"?

5. What is wisdom? Is it more or less nonexistent, as Socrates suggests, or much more common?

6. Is Socrates a good role model for young people?

7. Would you have condemned Socrates?

A Real Life

Alice Munro

ALICE MUNRO (1931–   ), one of
Canada's most respected authors,
was born in southwestern Ontario,
the setting of most of her fiction.
Although Munro does not explicitly
identify herself as a feminist, most of
her stories focus on the lives of women—
their perceptions, their social roles,
and their relationships with men.
Munro has received the Governor
General's Award for Fiction three times,
and her work is widely translated.
"A Real Life" is from her collection
of short stories *Open Secrets*.

A MAN CAME ALONG and fell in love with Dorrie Beck. At least, he wanted to marry her. It was true.

"If her brother was alive, she would never have needed to get married," Millicent said. What did she mean? Not something shameful. And she didn't mean money either. She meant that love had existed, kindness had created comfort, and in the poor, somewhat feckless life Dorrie and Albert lived together, loneliness had not been a threat. Millicent, who was shrewd and practical in some ways, was stubbornly sentimental in others. She believed always in the sweetness of affection that had eliminated sex.

She thought it was the way that Dorrie used her knife and fork that had captivated the man. Indeed, it was the same way as he used his. Dorrie kept her fork in her left hand and used the right only for cutting. She did not shift her fork continually to the right hand to pick up her food. That was because she had been to Whitby Ladies College when she was young. A last spurt of the Becks' money. Another thing she had learned there was a beautiful handwriting, and that might have been a factor as well, because after the first meeting the entire courtship appeared to have been conducted by letter. Millicent loved the sound of Whitby Ladies *College,* and it was her plan—not shared with anybody—that her own daughter would go there someday.

Millicent was not an uneducated person herself. She had taught school. She had rejected two serious boyfriends—one because she couldn't stand his mother, one because he tried putting his tongue in her mouth—before she agreed to marry Porter, who was nineteen years older than she was. He owned three farms, and he promised her a bathroom within a year, plus a dining-room suite and a chesterfield and chairs. On their wedding night he said, "Now you've got to take what's coming to you," but she knew it was not unkindly meant.

This was in 1933.

She had three children, fairly quickly, and after the third baby she developed some problems. Porter was decent—mostly, after that, he left her alone.

The Beck house was on Porter's land, but he wasn't the one who had bought the Becks out. He bought Albert and Dorrie's place from the man who had bought it from them. So, technically, they were renting their old house back from Porter. But money did not enter the picture. When Albert was alive, he would show up and work for a day when important jobs were undertaken—when they were pouring the cement floor in the barn or putting the hay in the mow. Dorrie had come along on those occasions, and also when Millicent had a new baby, or was housecleaning. She had remarkable strength for lugging furniture about and could do a man's job, like putting up the storm windows. At the start of a hard job—such as ripping the wallpaper off a whole room—she would settle back her shoulders and draw a deep, happy breath. She glowed with resolution. She was a big, firm woman with heavy legs, chestnut-brown hair, a broad bashful face, and dark freckles like dots of velvet. A man in the area had named a horse after her.

In spite of Dorrie's enjoyment of housecleaning, she did not do a lot of it at home. The house that she and Albert had lived in—that she lived in alone, after his death—was large and handsomely laid out but practically without furniture. Furniture would come up in Dorrie's conversation—the oak sideboard, Mother's wardrobe, the spool bed—but tacked onto this mention was always the phrase "that went at the Auction." The Auction sounded like a natural disaster, something like a flood and windstorm together, about which it would be pointless to complain. No carpets remained, either, and no pictures. There was just the calendar from Nunn's Grocery, which Albert used to work for. Absences of such customary things—and the presence of others, such as Dorrie's traps and guns and the boards for stretching rabbit and muskrat skins—had made the rooms lose their designations, made the notion of cleaning them seem frivolous. Once, in the summer, Millicent saw a pile of dog dirt at the head of the stairs. She didn't see it while it was fresh, but it was fresh enough to seem an offense. Through the summer it changed, from brown to gray. It became stony, dignified, stable—and strangely, Millicent herself found less and less need to see it as anything but something that had a right to be there.

Delilah was the dog responsible. She was black, part Labrador. She chased cars, and eventually this was how she was going to get herself killed. After Albert's death, both she and Dorrie may have come a little unhinged. But this was not something anybody could spot right away. At first, it was just that there was no man coming home and so no set time to get supper. There were no men's clothes to wash—cutting out the ideas of regular washing. Nobody to talk to, so Dorrie talked more to Millicent or to both Millicent and Porter. She talked about Albert and his job, which had been driving Nunn's Grocery Wagon, later their truck, all over the countryside. He had gone to college, he was no dunce, but when he came home from the Great War he was not very well, and he thought it best to be out-of-doors, so he got the job driving for Nunn's and kept it until he died. He was a man of inexhaustible sociability and did more than simply deliver groceries. He gave people a lift to town. He brought patients home from the hospital. He had a crazy woman on his route, and once when he was getting her groceries out of the truck, he had a compulsion to turn around. There she stood with a hatchet, about to brain him. In fact her swing had already begun, and when he slipped out of range she had to continue, chopping neatly into the box of groceries and cleaving a pound of butter. He continued to deliver to her, not having the heart to turn her over to the authorities, who would take her to the asylum. She never took up the hatchet again but gave him cupcakes sprinkled with evil-looking seeds, which he threw into the grass at the end of the lane. Other women—more than one—had appeared to him naked. One of them arose out of a tub of bathwater in the middle of the kitchen floor, and Albert bowed low and set the groceries at her feet. "Aren't some people amazing?" said Dorrie. And she told further about a bachelor whose house was overrun by rats, so that he had to keep his food slung in a sack from the kitchen beams. But the rats ran out along the beams and leaped upon the sack and clawed it apart, and eventually the fellow was obliged to take all his food into bed with him.

"Albert always said people living alone are to be pitied," said Dorrie—as if she did not understand that she was now one of them. Albert's heart had given out—he had only had time to pull to the side of the road and stop the truck. He died in a lovely spot, where black oaks grew in a bottomland, and a sweet clear creek ran beside the road.

Dorrie mentioned other things Albert had told her concerning the Becks in the early days. How they came up the river in a raft, two brothers, and started a mill at the Big Bend, where there was nothing but the wildwoods. And nothing now, either, but the ruins of their mill and dam. The farm was never a livelihood but a hobby, when they built the big house and brought out the furniture from Edinburgh. The bedsteads, the chairs, the carved chests that went in the Auction. They brought it round the Horn, Dorrie said, and up Lake Huron and so up the river. Oh, Dorrie, said Millicent, that is not possible, and she brought a school geography book she had kept, to point out the error. It must have been a canal, then, said Dorrie. I recall a canal. The Panama Canal? More likely it was the Erie Canal, said Millicent.

"Yes," said Dorrie. "Round the Horn and into the Erie Canal."

"Dorrie is a true lady, no matter what anybody says," said Millicent to Porter, who did not argue. He was used to her absolute, personal judgments. "She is a hundred times more a lady than Muriel Snow," said Millicent, naming the person who might be called her best friend. "I say that, and I love Muriel Snow dearly."

Porter was used to hearing that too.

"I love Muriel Snow dearly and I would stick up for her no matter what," Millicent would say. "I love Muriel Snow, but that does not mean I approve of everything she *does*."

The smoking. And saying hot damn, Chrissakes, *poop. I nearly pooped my pants.*

Muriel Snow had not been Millicent's first choice for best friend. In the early days of her marriage she had set her sights high. Mrs. Lawyer Nesbitt. Mrs. Dr. Finnegan. Mrs. Doud. They let her take on a donkey's load of work in the Women's Auxiliary at the church, but they never asked her to their tea parties. She was never inside their houses, unless it was to a meeting. Porter was a farmer. No matter how many farms he owned, a farmer. She should have known.

She met Muriel when she decided that her daughter Betty Jean would take piano lessons. Muriel was the music teacher. She taught in the schools as well as privately. Times being what they were, she charged only twenty cents a lesson. She played the organ at the church, and directed various choirs, but some of that was for nothing. She and Millicent got on so well that soon she was in Millicent's house as often as Dorrie was, though on a rather different footing.

Muriel was over thirty and had never been married. Getting married was something she talked about openly, jokingly, and plaintively, particularly when Porter was around. "Don't you know any men, Porter?" she would say. "Can't you dig up just one decent man for me?" Porter would say maybe he could, but maybe she wouldn't think they were so decent. In the summers Muriel went to visit a sister in Montreal, and once she went to stay with some cousins she had never met, only written to, in Philadelphia. The first thing she reported on, when she got back, was the man situation.

"Terrible. They all get married young, they're Catholics, and the wives never die—they're too busy having babies.

"Oh, they had somebody lined up for me but I saw right away he would never pan out. He was one of those ones with the mothers.

"I did meet one, but he had an awful failing. He didn't cut his toenails. Big yellow toenails. Well? Aren't you going to ask me how I found out?"

Muriel was always dressed in some shade of blue. A woman should pick a color that really suits her and wear it all the time, she said. Like your perfume. It should be your signature. Blue was widely thought to be a color for blondes, but that was incorrect. Blue often made a blonde look more washed-out than she was to start with. It suited best a warm-looking skin, like Muriel's—skin that took a good tan and never entirely lost it. It suited brown hair and brown eyes, which were hers as well. She never skimped on clothes—it was a mistake to. Her fingernails were always painted—a rich and distracting color, apricot or blood-ruby or even gold. She was small and round, she did exercises to keep her tidy waistline. She had a dark mole on the front of her neck, like a jewel on an invisible chain, and another like a tear at the corner of one eye.

"The word for you is not pretty," Millicent said one day, surprising herself. "It's *bewitching*." Then she flushed at her own tribute, knowing she sounded childish and excessive.

Muriel flushed a little too, but with pleasure. She drank in admiration, frankly courted it. Once, she dropped in on her way to a concert in Walley, which she hoped would yield rewards. She had an ice-blue dress on that shimmered.

"And that isn't all," she said. "Everything I have on is new, and everything is silk."

It wasn't true that she never found a man. She found one fairly often but hardly ever one that she could bring to supper. She found them in other towns, where she took her choirs to massed concerts, in Toronto at piano recitals to which she might take a promising student. Sometimes she found them in the students' own homes. They were the uncles, the fathers, the grandfathers, and the reason that they would not come into Millicent's house, but only wave—sometimes curtly, sometimes with bravado—from a waiting car, was that they were married. A bedridden wife, a drinking wife, a vicious shrew of a wife? Perhaps. Sometimes no mention at all—a ghost of a wife. They escorted Muriel to musical events, an interest in music being the ready excuse. Sometimes there was even a performing child, to act as chaperon. They took her to dinners in restaurants in distant towns. They were referred to as friends. Millicent defended her. How could there be any harm when it was all so out in the open? But it wasn't, quite, and it would all end in misunderstandings, harsh words, unkindness. A warning from the school board. Miss Snow will have to mend her ways. A bad example. A wife on the phone. Miss Snow, I am sorry we are canceling— Or simply silence. A date not kept, a note not answered, a name never to be mentioned again.

"I don't expect so much," Muriel said. "I expect a friend to be a friend. Then they hightail it off at the first whiff of trouble after saying they'd always stand up for me. Why is that?"

"Well, you know, Muriel," Millicent said once, "a wife is a wife. It's all well and good to have friends, but a marriage is a marriage."

Muriel blew up at that, she said that Millicent thought the worst of her like everybody else, and was she never to be permitted to have a good time, an innocent good time? She banged the door and ran her car over the calla lilies, surely on purpose. For a day Millicent's face was blotchy from weeping. But enmity did not last and Muriel was back, tearful as well, and taking blame on herself.

"I was a fool from the start," she said, and went into the front room to play the piano. Millicent got to know the pattern. When Muriel was happy and had a new friend, she played mournful tender songs, like "Flowers of the Forest." Or:

She dressed herself in male attire,
And gaily she was dressed—

Then when she was disappointed, she came down hard and fast on the keys, she sang scornfully.

Hey Johnny Cope are ye waukin' yet?

Sometimes Millicent asked people to supper (though not the Finnegans or the Nesbitts or the Douds), and then she liked to ask Dorrie and Muriel as well. Dorrie was a help to wash up the pots and pans afterward, and Muriel could entertain on the piano.

She asked the Anglican minister to come on Sunday, after evensong, and bring the friend she had heard was staying with him. The Anglican minister was a bachelor, but Muriel had given up on him early. Neither fish nor fowl, she said. Too bad. Millicent liked him, chiefly for his voice. She had been brought up an Anglican, and though she'd switched to United, which was what Porter said he was (so was everybody else, so were all the important and substantial people in the town), she still favored Anglican customs. Evensong, the church bell, the choir coming up the aisle in as stately a way as they could manage, singing—instead of just all clumping in together and sitting down. Best of all the words. *But thou O God have mercy upon us miserable offenders. Spare thou them, O Lord, which confess their faults. Restore thou them that are penitent, according to the Promise. . . .*

Porter went with her once and hated it.

Preparations for this evening supper were considerable. The damask was brought out, the silver serving-spoon, the black dessert plates painted with pansies by hand. The cloth had to be pressed and all the silverware polished, and then there was the apprehension that a tiny smear of polish might remain, a gray gum on the tines of a fork or among the grapes round the rim of the wedding teapot. All day Sunday, Millicent was torn between pleasure and agony, hope and suspense. The things that could go wrong multiplied. The Bavarian cream might not set (they had no refrigerator yet and had to chill things in summer by setting them on the cellar floor). The angel food cake might not rise to its full glory. If it did rise, it might be dry. The biscuits might taste of tainted flour or a beetle might crawl out of the salad. By five o'clock she was in such a state of tension and misgiving that nobody could stay in the kitchen with her. Muriel had arrived early to help out, but she had not chopped the potatoes finely enough, and had managed to scrape her knuckles while grating carrots, so she was told off for being useless, and sent to play the piano.

Muriel was dressed up in turquoise crêpe and smelled of her Spanish perfume. She might have written off the minister but she had not seen his visitor yet. A bachelor, perhaps, or a widower, since he was traveling alone. Rich, or he would not be traveling at all, not so far. He came from England, people said. Someone had said no, Australia.

She was trying to get up the "Polovtsian Dances."

Dorrie was late. It threw a crimp in things. The jellied salad had to be taken down cellar again, lest it should soften. The biscuits put to warm in the oven had to be taken out, for fear of getting too hard. The three men sat on the veranda—the meal was to be eaten there, buffet style—and drank fizzy lemonade. Millicent had seen what drink did in her own family—her father had died of it when she was ten—and she had required a promise from Porter, before they married, that he would never touch it again. Of course he did—he kept a bottle in the granary—but when he drank he kept his distance and she truly believed the promise had been kept. This was a fairly common pattern at that time, at least among farmers—drinking in the barn, abstinence in the house. Most men would have felt there was something the matter with a woman who didn't lay down such a law.

But Muriel, when she came out on the veranda in her high heels and slinky crêpe, cried out at once, "Oh, my favorite drink! Gin and lemon!" She took a sip and pouted at Porter. "You did it again. You forgot the gin again!" Then she teased the minister, asking if he didn't have a flask in his pocket. The minister was gallant, or perhaps made reckless by boredom. He said he wished he had.

The visitor who rose to be introduced was tall and thin and sallow, with a face that seemed to hang in pleats, precise and melancholy. Muriel did not give way to disappointment. She sat down beside him and tried in a spirited way to get him into conversation. She told him about her music teaching and was scathing about the local choirs and musicians. She did not spare the Anglicans. She twitted the minister and Porter, and told about the live chicken that walked onto the stage during a country school concert.

Porter had done the chores early, washed, and changed into his suit, but he kept looking uneasily toward the barnyard, as if he recalled something that was left undone. One of the cows was bawling loudly in the field, and at last he excused himself to go and see what was wrong with her. He found that her calf had got caught in the wire fence and managed to strangle itself. He did not speak of this loss when he came back with newly washed hands. "Calf caught up in the fence" was all he said. But he connected the mishap somehow with this entertainment, with dressing up and having to eat off your knees. He thought that was not natural.

"Those cows are as bad as children," Millicent said. "Always wanting your attention at the wrong time!" Her own children, fed earlier, peered from between the bannisters to watch the food being carried to the veranda. "I think we will have to commence without Dorrie. You men must be starving. This is just a simple little buffet. We sometimes enjoy eating outside on a Sunday evening."

"Commence, commence!" cried Muriel, who had helped to carry out the various dishes—the potato salad, carrot salad, jellied salad, cabbage salad, the deviled eggs and cold roast chicken, the salmon loaf and warm biscuits, and relishes. Just when they had everything set out, Dorrie came around the side of the house, looking warm from her walk across the field, or from excitement. She was wearing her good summer dress, a navy-blue organdie with white dots and white collar, suitable for a little girl or an old lady. Threads showed where she had pulled the torn lace off the collar instead of mending it, and in spite of the hot day a rim of undershirt was hanging out of one sleeve. Her shoes had been so recently and sloppily cleaned that they left traces of whitener on the grass.

"I would have been on time," Dorrie said, "but I had to shoot a feral cat. She was prowling around my house and carrying on so. I was convinced she was rabid."

She had wet her hair and crimped it into place with bobby pins. With that, and her pink shiny face, she looked like a doll with a china head and limbs attached to a cloth body, firmly stuffed with straw.

"I thought at first she might have been in heat, but she didn't really behave that way. She didn't do any of the rubbing along on her stomach such as I'm used to seeing. And I noticed some spitting. So I thought the only thing to do was to shoot her. Then I put her in a sack and called up Fred Nunn to see if he would run her over to Walley, to the vet. I want to know if she really was rabid, and Fred always likes the excuse to get out in his car. I told him to leave the sack on the step if the vet wasn't home on a Sunday night."

"I wonder what he'll think it is?" said Muriel. "A present?"

"No. I pinned on a note, in case. There was definite spitting and dribbling." She touched her own face to show where the dribbling had been. "Are you enjoying your visit here?" she said to the minister, who had been in town for three years and had been the one to bury her brother.

"It is Mr. Speirs who is the visitor, Dorrie," said Millicent. Dorrie acknowledged the introduction and seemed unembarrassed by her mistake. She said that the reason she took it for a feral cat was that its coat was all matted and hideous, and she thought that a feral cat would never come near the house unless it was rabid.

"But I will put an explanation in the paper, just in case. I will be sorry if it is anybody's pet. I lost my own pet three months ago—my dog Delilah. She was struck down by a car."

It was strange to hear that dog called a pet, that big black Delilah who used to lollop along with Dorrie all over the countryside, who tore across the fields in such savage glee to attack cars. Dorrie had not been distraught at the death; indeed she had said she had expected it someday. But now, to hear her say "pet," Millicent thought, there might have been grief she didn't show.

"Come and fill up your plate or we'll all have to starve," Muriel said to Mr. Speirs. "You're the guest, you have to go first. If the egg yolks look dark it's just what the hens have been eating—they won't poison you. I grated the carrots for that salad myself, so if you notice some blood it's just where I got a little too enthusiastic and grated in some skin off my knuckles. I had better shut up now or Millicent will kill me."

And Millicent was laughing angrily, saying, "Oh, they are not! Oh, you did *not*!"

Mr. Speirs had paid close attention to everything Dorrie said. Maybe that was what had made Muriel so saucy. Millicent thought that perhaps he saw Dorrie as a novelty, a Canadian wild woman who went around shooting things. He might be studying her so that he could go home and describe her to his friends in England.

Dorrie kept quiet while eating and she ate quite a lot. Mr. Speirs ate a lot too—Millicent was happy to see that—and he appeared to be a silent person at all times. The minister kept the conversation going describing a book he was reading. It was called *The Oregon Trail*.

"Terrible the hardships," he said.

Millicent said she had heard of it. "I have some cousins living out in Oregon but I cannot remember the name of the town," she said. "I wonder if they went on that trail."

The minister said that if they went out a hundred years ago it was most probable.

"Oh, I wouldn't think it was that long," she said. "Their name was Rafferty."

"Man the name of Rafferty used to race pigeons," said Porter, with sudden energy. "This was way back, when there was more of that kind of thing. There was money going on it, too. Well, he sees he's got a problem with the pigeons' house, they don't go in right away, and that means they don't trip the wire and don't get counted in. So he took an egg one of his pigeons was on, and he blew it clear, and he put a beetle inside. And the beetle inside made such a racket the pigeon naturally thought she had an egg getting ready to hatch. And she flew a beeline home and tripped the wire and all the ones that bet on her made a lot of money. Him, too, of course. In fact this was over in Ireland, and this man that told the story, that was how he got the money to come out to Canada."

Millicent didn't believe that the man's name had been Rafferty at all. That had just been an excuse.

"So you keep a gun in the house?" said the minister to Dorrie. "Does that mean you are worried about tramps and suchlike?"

Dorrie put down her knife and fork, chewed something up carefully, and swallowed. "I keep it for shooting," she said.

After a pause she said that she shot groundhogs and rabbits. She took the groundhogs over to the other side of town and sold them to the mink farm. She skinned the rabbits and stretched the skins, then sold them to a place in Walley which did a big trade with the tourists. She enjoyed fried or boiled rabbit meat but could not possibly eat it all herself, so she often took a rabbit carcass, cleaned and skinned, around to some family that was on Relief. Many times her offering was refused. People thought it was as bad as eating a dog or a cat. Though even that, she believed, was not considered out of the way in China.

"That is true," said Mr. Speirs. "I have eaten them both."

"Well, then, you know," said Dorrie. "People are prejudiced."

He asked about the skins, saying they must have to be removed very carefully, and Dorrie said that was true and you needed a knife you could trust. She described with pleasure the first clean slit down the belly. "Even more difficult with the muskrats, because you have to be more careful with the fur, it is more valuable," she said. "It is a denser fur. Waterproof."

"You do not shoot the muskrats?" said Mr. Speirs.

No, no, said Dorrie. She trapped them. Trapped them, yes, said Mr. Speirs, and Dorrie described her favorite trap, on which she had made little improvements of her own. She had thought of taking out a patent but had never gotten around to it. She spoke about the spring watercourses, the system of creeks she followed, tramping for miles day after day, after the snow was mostly melted but before the leaves came out, when the muskrats' fur was prime. Millicent knew that Dorrie did these things but she had thought she did them to get a little money. To hear her talk now, it would seem that she was truly fond of that life. The blackflies out already, the cold water over her boot tops, the drowned rats. And Mr. Speirs listened like an old dog, perhaps a hunting dog, that has been sitting with his eyes half shut, just prevented, by his own good opinion of himself, from falling into an unmannerly stupor. Now he has got a whiff of something nobody else can understand—his eyes open all the way and his nose quivers and his muscles answer, ripples pass over his hide as he remembers some day of recklessness and dedication. How far, he asked, and how high is the water, how much do they weigh and how many could you count on in a day and for muskrats is it still the same sort of knife?

Muriel asked the minister for a cigarette and got one, smoked for a few moments, and stubbed it out in the middle of the Bavarian cream.

"So I won't eat it and get fat," she said. She got up and started to help clear the dishes, but soon ended up at the piano, back at the "Polovtsian Dances."

Millicent was pleased that there was conversation with the guest, though its attraction mystified her. Also, she thought that the food had been good and there had not been any humiliation, no queer taste or sticky cup handle.

"I had thought the trappers were all up north," said Mr. Speirs. "I thought that they were beyond the Arctic Circle or at least on the Precambrian shield."

"I used to have an idea of going there," Dorrie said. Her voice thickened for the first time, with embarrassment—or excitement. "I thought I could live in a cabin and trap all winter. But I had my brother, I couldn't leave my brother. And I know it here."

Late in the winter Dorrie arrived at Millicent's house with a large piece of white satin. She said that she intended to make a wedding dress. That was the first anybody had heard of a wedding—she said it would be in May—or learned the first name of Mr. Speirs. It was Wilkinson. Wilkie.

When and where had Dorrie seen him, since that supper on the veranda?

Nowhere. He had gone off to Australia, where he had property. Letters had gone back and forth between them.

Sheets were laid down on the dining-room floor, with the dining table pushed against the wall. The satin was spread out over them. Its broad bright extent, its shining vulnerability, cast a hush over the whole house. The children came to stare at it, and Millicent shouted to them to clear off. She was afraid to cut into it. And Dorrie, who could so easily slit the skin of an animal, laid the scissors down. She confessed to shaking hands.

A call was put in to Muriel to drop by after school. She clapped her hand to her heart when she heard the news, and called Dorrie a slyboots, a Cleopatra, who had fascinated a millionaire.

"I bet he's a millionaire," she said. "Property in Australia— what does that mean? I bet it's not a pig farm! All I can hope is maybe he'll have a brother. Oh, Dorrie, am I so mean I didn't even say congratulations!"

She gave Dorrie lavish loud kisses—Dorrie standing still for them as if she were five years old.

What Dorrie had said was that she and Mr. Speirs planned to go through "a form of marriage." What do you mean, said Millicent, do you mean a marriage ceremony is that what you mean, and Dorrie said yes.

Muriel made the first cut into the satin, saying that somebody had to do it, though maybe if she was doing it again it wouldn't be in quite that place.

Soon they got used to mistakes. Mistakes and rectifications. Late every afternoon, when Muriel got there, they tackled a new stage—the cutting, the pinning, the basting, the sewing— with clenched teeth and grim rallying cries. They had to alter the pattern as they went along, to allow for problems unforeseen, such as the tight set of a sleeve, the bunching of the heavy satin at the waist, the eccentricities of Dorrie's figure. Dorrie was a menace at the job, so they set her to sweeping up scraps and filling the bobbin. Whenever she sat at the sewing machine, she clamped her tongue between her teeth. Sometimes she had nothing to do, and she walked from room to room in Millicent's house, stopping to stare out the windows at the snow and sleet, the long-drawn-out end of winter. Or she stood like a docile beast in her woolen underwear, which smelled quite frankly of her flesh, while they pulled and tugged the material around her.

Muriel had taken charge of clothes. She knew what there had to be. There had to be more than a wedding dress. There had to be a going-away outfit, and a wedding nightgown and a matching dressing gown, and of course an entire new supply of underwear. Silk stockings, and a brassiere—the first that Dorrie had ever worn.

Dorrie had not known about any of that. "I considered the wedding dress as the major hurdle," she said. "I could not think beyond it."

The snow melted, the creeks filled up, the muskrats would be swimming in the cold water, sleek and sporty with their treasure on their backs. If Dorrie thought of her traps, she did not say so. The only walk she took these days was across the field from her house to Millicent's.

Made bold by experience, Muriel cut out a dressmaker suit of fine russet wool, and a lining. She was letting her choir rehearsals go all to pot.

Millicent had to think about the wedding luncheon. It was to be held in the Brunswick Hotel. But who was there to invite, except the minister? Lots of people knew Dorrie, but they knew her as the lady who left skinned rabbits on doorsteps, who went through the fields and the woods with her dog and gun and waded along the flooded creeks in her high rubber boots. Few people knew anything about the old Becks, though all remembered Albert and had liked him. Dorrie was not quite a joke—something protected her from that, either Albert's popularity or her own gruffness and dignity—but the news of her marriage had roused up a lot of interest, not exactly of a sympathetic nature. It was being spoken of as a freakish event, mildly scandalous, possibly a hoax. Porter said that bets were being laid on whether the man would show up.

Finally, Millicent recalled some cousins who had come to Albert's funeral. Ordinary respectable people. Dorrie had their addresses, invitations were sent. Then the Nunn brothers from the grocery, whom Albert had worked for, and their wives. A couple of Albert's lawn-bowling friends and their wives. The people who owned the mink farm where Dorrie sold her groundhogs? The woman from the bakeshop who was going to ice the cake?

The cake was being made at home, then taken to the shop to be iced by the woman who had got a diploma in cake decorating from a place in Chicago. It would be covered with white roses, lacy scallops, hearts and garlands and silver leaves and those tiny silver candies you can break your tooth on. Meanwhile it had to be mixed and baked, and this was where Dorrie's strong arms could come into play, stirring and stirring a mixture so stiff it appeared to be all candied fruit and raisins and currants, with a little gingery batter holding it together like glue. When Dorrie got the big bowl against her stomach and took up the beating spoon, Millicent heard the first satisfied sigh to come out of her in a long while.

Muriel decided that there had to be a maid of honor. Or a matron of honor. It could not be her, because she would be playing the organ. "O Perfect Love." And the Mendelssohn.

It would have to be Millicent. Muriel would not take no for an answer. She brought over an evening dress of her own, a long sky-blue dress, which she ripped open at the waist—how confident and cavalier she was by now about dressmaking!—and proposed a lace midriff, of darker blue, with a matching lace bolero. It will look like new and suit you to a T, she said.

Millicent laughed when she first tried it on and said, "There's a sight to scare the pigeons!" But she was pleased. She and Porter had not had much of a wedding—they had just gone to the rectory, deciding to put the money saved into furniture. "I suppose I'll need some kind of thingamajig," she said. "Something on my head."

"Her veil!" cried Muriel. "What about Dorrie's veil? We've been concentrating so much on wedding dresses, we've forgotten all about a veil!"

Dorrie spoke up unexpectedly and said that she would never wear a veil. She could not stand to have that draped over her, it would feel like cobwebs. Her use of the word "cobwebs" gave Muriel and Millicent a start, because there were jokes being made about cobwebs in other places.

"She's right," said Muriel. "A veil would be too much." She considered what else. A wreath of flowers? No, too much again. A picture hat? Yes, get an old summer hat and cover it with white satin. Then get another and cover it with the dark blue lace.

"Here is the menu," said Millicent dubiously. "Creamed chicken in pastry shells, little round biscuits, molded jellies, that salad with the apples and the walnuts, pink and white ice cream with the cake—"

Thinking of the cake, Muriel said, "Does he by any chance have a sword, Dorrie?"

Dorrie said, "Who?"

"Wilkie. Your Wilkie. Does he have a sword?"

"What would he have a sword for?" Millicent said.

"I just thought he might," said Muriel.

"I cannot enlighten you," said Dorrie.

Then there was a moment in which they all fell silent, because they had to think of the bridegroom. They had to admit him to the room and set him down in the midst of all this. Picture hats. Creamed chicken. Silver leaves. They were stricken with doubts. At least Millicent was, and Muriel. They hardly dared to look at each other.

"I just thought since he was English, or whatever he is," said Muriel.

Millicent said, "He is a fine man anyway."

ꙮ

The wedding was set for the second Saturday in May. Mr. Speirs was to arrive on the Wednesday and stay with the minister. The Sunday before this, Dorrie was supposed to come over to have supper with Millicent and Porter. Muriel was there, too. Dorrie didn't arrive, and they went ahead and started without her.

Millicent stood up in the middle of the meal. "I'm going over there," she said. "She better be sharper than this getting to her wedding."

"I can keep you company," said Muriel.

Millicent said no thanks. Two might make it worse.

Make what worse?

She did not know.

She went across the field by herself. It was a warm day, and the back door of Dorrie's house was standing open. Between the house and where the barn used to be there was a grove of walnut trees whose branches were still bare, since walnut trees are among the very latest to get their leaves. The hot sunlight pouring through bare branches seemed unnatural. Her feet did not make any sound on the grass.

And there on the back platform was Albert's old armchair, never taken in all winter.

What was in her mind was that Dorrie might have had an accident. Something to do with a gun. Maybe while cleaning her gun. That happened to people. Or she might be lying out in a field somewhere, lying in the woods among the old dead leaves and the new leeks and bloodroot. Tripped while getting over a fence. Had to go out one last time. And then, after all the safe times, the gun had gone off. Millicent had never had any such fears for Dorrie before, and she knew that in some ways Dorrie was very careful and competent. It must be that what had happened this year made anything seem possible. The proposed marriage, such wild luck, could make you believe in calamity also.

But it was not an accident that was on her mind. Not really. Under this busy fearful imagining of accidents, she hid what she really feared.

She called Dorrie's name at the open door. And so prepared was she for an answering silence, the evil silence and indifference of a house lately vacated by somebody who had met with disaster (or not vacated yet by the body of the person who had

met with, who had *brought about,* that disaster)—so prepared
was she for the worst that she was shocked, she went watery in
the knees, at the sight of Dorrie herself, in her old field pants
and shirt.

"We were waiting for you," she said. "We were waiting for
you to come to supper."

Dorrie said, "I must've lost track of the time."

"Oh, have all your clocks stopped?" said Millicent, recover-
ing her nerve as she was led through the back hall with its familiar mysterious debris. She could smell cooking.

The kitchen was dark because of the big, unruly lilac pressing against the window. Dorrie used the house's original wood
cookstove, and she had one of those old kitchen tables with a
drawer for the knives and forks. It was a relief to see that the
calendar on the wall was for this year.

Dorrie was cooking some supper. She was in the middle of
chopping up a purple onion to add to the bits of bacon and
sliced potatoes she had frying up in the pan. So much for losing
track of the time.

"You go ahead," said Millicent. "Go ahead and make your
meal. I did get something to eat before I took it into my head to
go and look for you."

"I made tea," said Dorrie. It was keeping warm on the back
of the stove and, when she poured it out, was like ink.

"I can't leave," she said, prying up some of the bacon that
was sputtering in the pan. "I can't leave here."

Millicent decided to treat this as she would a child's
announcement that she could not go to school.

"Well, that'll be a nice piece of news for Mr. Speirs," she said.
"When he has come all this way."

Dorrie leaned back as the grease became fractious.

"Better move that off the heat a bit," Millicent said.

"I can't leave."

"I heard that before."

Dorrie finished her cooking and scooped the results onto a
plate. She added ketchup and a couple of thick slices of bread

soaked in the grease that was left in the pan. She sat down to eat, and did not speak.

Millicent was sitting too, waiting her out. Finally she said, "Give a reason."

Dorrie shrugged and chewed.

"Maybe you know something I don't," Millicent said. "What have you found out? Is he poor?"

Dorrie shook her head. "Rich," she said.

So Muriel was right.

"A lot of women would give their eyeteeth."

"I don't care about that," Dorrie said. She chewed and swallowed and repeated, "I don't care."

Millicent had to take a chance, though it embarrassed her.

"If you are thinking about what I think you may be thinking about, then it could be that you are worried over nothing. A lot of time when they get older, they don't even want to bother."

"Oh, it isn't that! I know all about that."

Oh, do you, thought Millicent, and if so, how? Dorrie might imagine she knew, from animals. Millicent had sometimes thought that if she really knew, no woman would get married.

Nevertheless she said, "Marriage takes you out of yourself and gives you a real life."

"I have a life," Dorrie said.

"All right then," said Millicent, as if she had given up arguing. She sat and drank her poisonous tea. She was getting an inspiration. She let time pass and then she said, "It's up to you, it certainly is. But there is a problem about where you will live. You can't live here. When Porter and I found out you were getting married, we put this place on the market, and we sold it."

Dorrie said instantly, "You are lying."

"We didn't want it standing empty to make a haven for tramps. We went ahead and sold it."

"You would never do such a trick on me."

"What kind of a trick would it be when you were getting married?"

Millicent was already believing what she said. Soon it could come true. They could offer the place at a low enough price, and somebody would buy it. It could still be fixed up. Or it could be torn down, for the bricks and the woodwork. Porter would be glad to be rid of it.

Dorrie said, "You would not put me out of my house."

Millicent kept quiet.

"You are lying, aren't you?" said Dorrie.

"Give me your Bible," Millicent said. "I will swear on it."

Dorrie actually looked around. She said, "I don't know where it is."

"Dorrie, listen. All of this is for your own good. It may seem like I am pushing you out, Dorrie, but all it is is making you do what you are not quite up to doing on your own."

"Oh," said Dorrie. "Why?"

Because the wedding cake is made, thought Millicent, and the satin dress is made, and the luncheon has been ordered, and the invitations have been sent. All this trouble that has been gone to. People might say that was a silly reason, but those who said that would not be the people who had gone to the trouble. It was not fair to have your best efforts squandered.

But it was more than that, for she believed what she had said, telling Dorrie that this was how she could have a life. And what did Dorrie mean by "here"? If she meant that she would be homesick, let her be! Homesickness was never anything you couldn't get over. Millicent was not going to pay any attention to that "here." Nobody had any business living a life out "here" if they had been offered what Dorrie had. It was a kind of sin to refuse such an offer. Out of mulishness, out of fearfulness, and idiocy.

She had begun to get the feeling that Dorrie was cornered. Dorrie might be giving up, or letting the idea of giving up seep through her. Perhaps. She sat as still as a stump, but there was a chance such a stump might be pulpy within.

But it was Millicent who began suddenly to weep. "Oh, Dorrie," she said. "Don't be stupid!" They both got up, and grabbed hold of each other, and then Dorrie had to do the comforting, patting and soothing in a magisterial way, while Millicent wept and repeated some words that did not hang together. *Happy. Help. Ridiculous.*

"I will look after Albert," she said, when she had calmed down somewhat. "I'll put flowers. And I won't mention this to Muriel Snow. Or to Porter. Nobody needs to know."

Dorrie said nothing. She seemed a little lost, absent-minded, as if she was busy turning something over and over, resigning herself to the weight and strangeness of it.

"That tea is awful," said Millicent. "Can't we make some that's fit to drink?" She went to throw the contents of her cup into the slop pail.

There stood Dorrie in the dim window light—mulish, obedient, childish, female—a most mysterious and maddening person whom Millicent seemed now to have conquered, to be sending away. At greater cost to herself, Millicent was thinking—greater cost than she had understood. She tried to engage Dorrie in a somber but encouraging look, canceling her fit of tears. She said, "The die is cast."

Dorrie walked to her wedding.

Nobody had known that she intended to do that. When Porter and Millicent stopped the car in front of her house to pick her up, Millicent was still anxious.

"Honk the horn," she said. "She better be ready now."

Porter said, "Isn't that her down ahead?"

It was. She was wearing a light gray coat of Albert's over her satin dress, and was carrying her picture hat in one hand, a bunch of lilacs in the other. They stopped the car and she said, "No, I want the exercise. It will clear out my head."

They had no choice but to drive on and wait at the church and see her approaching down the street, people coming out of shops to look, a few cars honking sportively, people waving and calling out, "Here comes the bride!" As she got closer to the church, she stopped and removed Albert's coat, and then she was gleaming, miraculous, like the Pillar of Salt in the Bible.

Muriel was inside the church playing the organ, so she did not have to realize, at this last moment, that they had forgotten all about gloves and that Dorrie clutched the woody stems of the lilac in her bare hands. Mr. Speirs had been in the church, too, but he had come out, breaking all rules, leaving the minister to stand there on his own. He was as lean and yellow and wolfish as Millicent remembered, but when he saw Dorrie fling the old coat into the back of Porter's car, and settle the hat on her head—Millicent had to run up and fix it right—he appeared nobly satisfied. Millicent had a picture of him and Dorrie mounted high, mounted on elephants, panoplied, borne cumbrously forward, adventuring. A vision. She was filled with optimism and relief and she whispered to Dorrie, "He'll take you everywhere! He'll make you a Queen!"

"I have grown as fat as the Queen of Tonga," wrote Dorrie from Australia, some years on. A photograph showed that she was not exaggerating. Her hair was white, her skin brown, as if all her freckles had got loose and run together. She wore a vast garment, colored like tropical flowers. The war had come and put an end to any idea of traveling, and then when it was over, Wilkie was dying. Dorrie stayed on, in Queensland, on a great property where she grew sugarcane and pineapples, cotton, peanuts, tobacco. She rode horses, in spite of her size, and had learned to fly an airplane. She took up some travels of her own in that part of the world. She had shot crocodiles. She died in the fifties, in New Zealand, climbing up to look at a volcano.

Millicent told everybody what she had said she would not mention. She took credit, naturally. She recalled her inspiration, her stratagem, with no apologies. "Somebody had to take the bull by the horns," she said. She felt that she was the creator of a life—more effectively, in Dorrie's case, than in the case of her own children. She had created happiness, or something close. She forgot the way she had wept, not knowing why.

The wedding had its effect on Muriel. She handed in her resignation, she went off to Alberta. "I'll give it a year," she said. And within a year she had found a husband—not the sort of man she had ever had anything to do with in the past. A widower with two small children. A Christian minister. Millicent wondered at Muriel's describing him that way. Weren't all ministers Christian? When they came back for a visit—by this time there were two more children, their own—she saw the point of the description. Smoking and drinking and swearing were out, and so was wearing makeup, and the kind of music that Muriel used to play. She played hymns now, of the sort she had once made fun of. She wore any color at all and had a bad permanent—her hair, going gray, stood up from her forehead in frizzy bunches. "A lot of my former life turns my stomach just to think about it," she said, and Millicent got the impression that she and Porter were seen mostly as belonging to those stomach-turning times.

The house was not sold or rented. It was not torn down, either, and its construction was so sound that it did not readily give way. It was capable of standing for years and years and presenting a plausible appearance. A tree of cracks can branch out among the bricks, but the wall does not fall down. Window sashes settle at an angle, but the window does not fall out. The doors were locked, but it was probable that children got in, to write things on the walls and break up the crockery that Dorrie had left behind. Millicent never went in to see.

There was a thing that Dorrie and Albert used to do, and then Dorrie did alone. It must have started when they were children. Every year, in the fall, they—and then, she—collected up all the walnuts that had fallen off the trees. They kept going, collecting fewer and fewer walnuts, until they were reasonably sure that they had got the last, or the next-to-last, one. Then they counted them, and they wrote the final total on the cellar wall. The date, the year, the total. The walnuts were not used for anything once they were collected. They were just dumped along the edge of the field and allowed to rot.

Millicent did not continue this useless chore. She had plenty of other chores to do, and plenty for her children to do. But at the time of year when the walnuts would be lying in the long grass, she would think of that custom, and how Dorrie must have expected to keep it up until she died. A life of customs, of seasons. The walnuts drop, the muskrats swim in the creek. Dorrie must have believed that she was meant to live so, in her reasonable eccentricity, her manageable loneliness. Probably she would have got another dog.

But I would not allow that, thinks Millicent. She would not allow it, and surely she was right. She has lived to be an old lady, she is living yet, though Porter has been dead for decades. She doesn't often notice the house. It is just there. But once in a while she does see its cracked face and the blank, slanted windows. The walnut trees behind, losing again, again, their delicate canopy of leaves.

I ought to knock that down and sell the bricks, she says, and seems puzzled that she has not already done so. ∽

INTERPRETIVE QUESTIONS
FOR DISCUSSION

Why is Millicent so intent on convincing Dorrie that marriage to Mr. Speirs will give Dorrie "a real life"?

1. Why does Millicent have a premonition that Dorrie does not want to go through with the marriage? (106–107)

2. What does Millicent mean when she tells Dorrie that marriage gives a woman "a real life"? (108) Why does Millicent think that "nobody had any business living a life out 'here' if they had been offered what Dorrie had"? (109)

3. Does Millicent suddenly begin to weep—and to repeat the words "happy," "help," "ridiculous"—because she fears Dorrie will refuse Mr. Speirs' offer of marriage, or because she fears Dorrie will accept it? (110)

4. When comforting Millicent, what is Dorrie turning over and over in her mind, "resigning herself to the weight and strangeness of it"? Why is Dorrie described as comforting Millicent in a "magisterial" way? (110)

5. Why does Millicent think that it is at "greater cost to herself, . . . greater cost than she had understood" that she has persuaded Dorrie to go away? (110)

6. Why do people in the community react so unkindly to the news of Dorrie's marriage, regarding it as a "freakish event, mildly scandalous, possibly a hoax"? (103)

7. Why does Millicent insist that her friend Dorrie is "a true lady, no matter what anybody says"? (91) Why does Millicent think that it was Dorrie's feminine graces—the way she used her knife and fork, her beautiful handwriting—that captivated Mr. Speirs? (87–88)

8. At the wedding, why does Millicent have a vision of Dorrie and Mr. Speirs mounted high "on elephants, panoplied, borne cumbrously forward, adventuring"? Why does Millicent idealize the couple, telling Dorrie that her new husband will make her "a Queen"? (111)

9. Why does Millicent look upon herself as the creator of Dorrie's life, more than in the case of her own children? (111–112)

10. Why does Millicent remember every fall Albert and Dorrie's tradition of collecting and tallying the walnuts that fell from the trees in their walnut grove? (112–113)

11. Why doesn't Millicent, who rarely notices the old Beck house, knock it down and sell it for bricks? (113)

12. Why does Millicent think that if Albert hadn't died, Dorrie would never have needed to get married? (87)

Suggested textual analysis
Pages 106–110: beginning, "What was in her mind was that Dorrie might have had an accident," and ending, "The die is cast."

Are we meant to think that Dorrie is better off for having married Mr. Speirs?

1. Why doesn't Dorrie think of herself as one of those people to be pitied because they live alone? (90)

2. Why does the notion of cleaning Dorrie's house, whose rooms had lost their customary designations, seem frivolous to

Millicent? Why does Millicent come to see the dog dirt at the head of the stairs as "something that had a right to be there"? (89)

3. Why does the wealthy Mr. Speirs choose the eccentric Dorrie to be his wife? Why is he fascinated by Dorrie's description of her hunting activities? (100–101)

4. Why does the author stress Dorrie's lack of feminine charm, comparing her to "a doll with a china head and limbs attached to a cloth body, firmly stuffed with straw"? Why are we told that Dorrie's one good summer dress is "suitable for a little girl or an old lady"? (97)

5. Why do we learn that it had been Dorrie's dream to go beyond the Arctic Circle, where she could live in a cabin and trap all winter? (101)

6. Why does Dorrie stop tramping through the countryside and tending her traps after she begins preparations for her wedding? (103) Why are we told that the first satisfied sigh to come out of Dorrie in a long while occurs when she uses her strong arms to beat the stiff batter for the wedding cake? (104)

7. Why are Millicent and Muriel "stricken with doubts" when they have to admit the reality of the groom to their preparations for the wedding? (105) Why is Dorrie described as standing "like a docile beast" while Millicent and Muriel adjust the fit of the wedding dress? (102–103)

8. Why does Dorrie say, "I can't leave here," and want to back out of the marriage? (107)

9. Why does the author describe Dorrie in her satin wedding dress as "gleaming, miraculous, like the Pillar of Salt in the Bible"? (111)

10. Is Dorrie's insistence on walking to her wedding meant to suggest that she maintains her independence even as a married woman? (110)

11. Why are we told that Dorrie grows "as fat as the Queen of Tonga" after her marriage to Mr. Speirs? (111)

12. Are we meant to think that Millicent was right not to let Dorrie live out her life of customs and seasons and "manageable loneliness"? (113)

Suggested textual analysis
Pages 102–105: beginning, "Muriel made the first cut into the satin," and ending, "He is a fine man anyway."

After Dorrie's wedding, why does Muriel settle for marriage with the sort of man she would never have had anything to do with in the past?

1. Why do Millicent and Muriel get on so well, even though Millicent doesn't approve of her friend's smoking and vulgar language? (91)

2. Is the all-new silk underwear that Muriel boasts about to Millicent evidence of Muriel's sensuality, or simply another means for her to attract a man? (93)

3. Why does Muriel, who is seeking a husband, generally date married men? Why does the conventional Millicent defend Muriel, asserting that there isn't any harm in Muriel's going out with married men? (93)

4. Why does Millicent tell Muriel, "It's all well and good to have friends, but a marriage is a marriage," when Muriel complains about her male friends deserting her? (93)

5. Why does Muriel, knowing that Millicent forbids liquor, tease Porter by pretending that he has forgotten to add gin to the lemonade? Why does Muriel try to impress Mr. Speirs by criticizing the local choirs and musicians? (96)

6. Why are we told that Millicent and Dorrie, afraid to cut into the "broad bright extent" and "shining vulnerability" of the white satin for Dorrie's wedding dress, have to call in Muriel to make the first cut? (101–102)

7. Why isn't Muriel able to separate her friendship with Millicent and Porter from the parts of her former life that she rejects? (112)

8. Why does Muriel become a different person after her marriage to the Christian minister—playing only hymns, wearing any color at all, and forswearing smoking, drinking, and wearing makeup? (112)

Suggested textual analyses
Pages 91–94: beginning, "Dorrie is a true lady," and ending, *"Hey Johnny Cope are ye waukin' yet?"*

Page 112: beginning, "The wedding had its effect on Muriel," and ending, "those stomach-turning times."

FOR FURTHER REFLECTION

1. Is marriage a threat to women's sense of personal identity?

2. Does each of us have at least one mysterious moment when the course of our life changes, for better or worse?

3. Is it more difficult for women than for men to reconcile their private sense of who they are with their public identity?

4. Is being an "outsider" preferable to being an "insider"? Why does society need its outsiders?

5. Do women's friendships run deeper than men's?

A ROOM OF ONE'S OWN

(selection)

Virginia Woolf

Virginia Woolf (1882–1941),
English novelist, essayist, and critic, was
an innovator in the form of the novel,
experimenting with the presentation of
consciousness, characterization, and
temporality through the technique of stream
of consciousness. She was educated at home
by governesses and her father, Sir Leslie
Stephen, a prominent literary critic and
biographer. With her husband, Leonard
Woolf, she founded the Hogarth Press in
1917. Among other works, Hogarth Press
published the poetry of T. S. Eliot and
English translations of Freud. Woolf's
literary masterpieces are generally acknowledged to be the novels *Mrs. Dalloway* and
To the Lighthouse. She also is known for
her extended feminist essays, *A Room of
One's Own* and *Three Guineas*. Woolf's
literary criticism appeared in two volumes,
The Common Reader and *The Second
Common Reader*.

T HE SCENE, if I may ask you to follow me, was now changed.[1] The leaves were still falling, but in London now, not Oxbridge; and I must ask you to imagine a room, like many thousands, with a window looking across people's hats and vans and motorcars to other windows, and on the table inside the room a blank sheet of paper on which was written in large letters WOMEN AND FICTION, but no more. The inevitable sequel to lunching and dining at Oxbridge seemed, unfortunately, to be a visit to the British Museum. One must strain off what was

---

1. [In 1928, Virginia Woolf was invited to lecture on "Women and Fiction" at two women's colleges, Newnham and Girton, at Cambridge University. A year later she published the revised and expanded lectures as *A Room of One's Own*, in which she creates a persona for herself—Mary Beton—and describes her visit to "Oxbridge," an imaginary university based on Oxford and Cambridge. After lunching richly with the men and sharing a poor dinner at the women's college, she begins to wonder why women are poor and what effect poverty has on the creation of works of art. In our selection, Woolf pursues these and other questions.]

personal and accidental in all these impressions and so reach the pure fluid, the essential oil of truth. For that visit to Oxbridge and the luncheon and the dinner had started a swarm of questions. Why did men drink wine and women water? Why was one sex so prosperous and the other so poor? What effect has poverty on fiction? What conditions are necessary for the creation of works of art?—a thousand questions at once suggested themselves. But one needed answers, not questions; and an answer was only to be had by consulting the learned and the unprejudiced, who have removed themselves above the strife of tongue and the confusion of body and issued the result of their reasoning and research in books which are to be found in the British Museum. If truth is not to be found on the shelves of the British Museum, where, I asked myself, picking up a notebook and a pencil, is truth?

Thus provided, thus confident and enquiring, I set out in the pursuit of truth. The day, though not actually wet, was dismal, and the streets in the neighborhood of the Museum were full of open coal holes, down which sacks were showering; four-wheeled cabs were drawing up and depositing on the pavement corded boxes containing, presumably, the entire wardrobe of some Swiss or Italian family seeking fortune or refuge or some other desirable commodity which is to be found in the boarding-houses of Bloomsbury in the winter. The usual hoarse-voiced men paraded the streets with plants on barrows. Some shouted; others sang. London was like a workshop. London was like a machine. We were all being shot backwards and forwards on this plain foundation to make some pattern. The British Museum was another department of the factory. The swing doors swung open; and there one stood under the vast dome, as if one were a thought in the huge bald forehead which is so splendidly encircled by a band of famous names. One went to the counter; one took a slip of paper; one opened a volume of the catalogue, and . . . . . the five dots here indicate five separate minutes of stupefaction, wonder, and bewilderment. Have you any notion how many books are written about women in the course of one year? Have you any notion how many are written by men? Are you aware that you are, perhaps, the most discussed animal in the universe? Here had I come with a notebook and a pencil proposing to spend a morning reading, supposing that at the end of the morning I should have transferred the truth to my notebook. But I should need to be a herd of elephants, I thought, and a wilderness of spiders, desperately referring to the animals that are reputed longest lived and most multitudinously eyed, to cope with all this. I should need claws of steel and beak of brass even to penetrate the husk. How shall I ever find the grains of truth embedded in all this mass of paper, I asked myself, and in despair began running my eye up and down the long list of titles. Even the names of the books gave me food for thought. Sex and its nature might well attract doctors and biologists; but what was surprising and difficult of explanation was the fact that sex—woman, that is to say—also attracts agreeable essayists, light-fingered novelists, young men who have taken the M.A. degree; men who have taken no degree; men who have no apparent qualification save that they are not women. Some of these books were, on the face of it, frivolous and facetious; but many, on the other hand, were serious and prophetic, moral and hortatory. Merely to read the titles suggested innumerable schoolmasters, innumerable clergymen mounting their platforms and pulpits and holding forth with a loquacity which far exceeded the hour usually allotted to such discourse on this one subject. It was a most strange phenomenon; and apparently—here I consulted the letter M— one confined to male sex. Women do not write books about men—a fact that I could not help welcoming with relief, for if I had first to read all that men have written about women, then all that women have written about men, the aloe that flowers once in a hundred years would flower twice before I could set pen to paper. So, making a perfectly arbitrary choice of a dozen volumes or so, I sent my slips of paper to lie in the wire tray, and waited in my stall, among the other seekers for the essential oil of truth.

What could be the reason, then, of this curious disparity, I wondered, drawing cartwheels on the slips of paper provided by the British taxpayer for other purposes. Why are women, judging from this catalogue, so much more interesting to men than men are to women? A very curious fact it seemed, and my mind wandered to picture the lives of men who spend their time in writing books about women; whether they were old or young, married or unmarried, red-nosed or humpbacked—anyhow, it was flattering, vaguely, to feel oneself the object of such attention, provided that it was not entirely bestowed by the crippled and the infirm—so I pondered until all such frivolous thoughts were ended by an avalanche of books sliding down onto the desk in front of me. Now the trouble began. The student who has been trained in research at Oxbridge has no doubt some method of shepherding his question past all distractions till it runs into its answer as a sheep runs into its pen. The student by my side, for instance, who was copying assiduously from a scientific manual was, I felt sure, extracting pure nuggets of the essential ore every ten minutes or so. His little grunts of satisfaction indicated so much. But if, unfortunately, one has had no training in a university, the question far from being shepherded to its pen flies like a frightened flock hither and thither, helter-skelter, pursued by a whole pack of hounds. Professors, schoolmasters, sociologists, clergymen, novelists, essayists, journalists, men who had no qualification save that they were not women, chased my simple and single question—Why are women poor?—until it became fifty questions; until the fifty questions leapt frantically into mid-stream and were carried away. Every page in my notebook was scribbled over with notes. To show the state of mind I was in, I will read you a few of them, explaining that the page was headed quite simply, WOMEN AND POVERTY, in block letters; but what followed was something like this:

Condition in Middle Ages of,
Habits in the Fiji Islands of,
Worshipped as goddesses by,

Weaker in moral sense than,
Idealism of,
Greater conscientiousness of,
South Sea Islanders, age of puberty among,
Attractiveness of,
Offered as sacrifice to,
Small size of brain of,
Profounder subconsciousness of,
Less hair on the body of,
Mental, moral, and physical inferiority of,
Love of children of,
Greater length of life of,
Weaker muscles of,
Strength of affections of,
Vanity of,
Higher education of,
Shakespeare's opinion of,
Lord Birkenhead's opinion of,
Dean Inge's opinion of,
La Bruyère's opinion of,
Dr. Johnson's opinion of,
Mr. Oscar Browning's opinion of, . . .

Here I drew breath and added, indeed, in the margin, Why does Samuel Butler say, "Wise men never say what they think of women"? Wise men never say anything else apparently. But, I continued, leaning back in my chair and looking at the vast dome in which I was a single but by now somewhat harassed thought, what is so unfortunate is that wise men never think the same thing about women. Here is Pope:

Most women have no character at all.

And here is La Bruyère:

Les femmes sont extrêmes; elles sont meilleures ou pires que
les hommes—[2]

a direct contradiction by keen observers who were contemporary. Are they capable of education or incapable? Napoleon
thought them incapable. Dr. Johnson thought the opposite.[3]
Have they souls or have they not souls? Some savages say they
have none. Others, on the contrary, maintain that women are
half divine and worship them on that account.[4] Some sages hold
that they are shallower in the brain; others that they are deeper
in the consciousness. Goethe honoured them; Mussolini despises
them. Wherever one looked men thought about women and
thought differently. It was impossible to make head or tail of it
all, I decided, glancing with envy at the reader next door who
was making the neatest abstracts, headed often with an A or
a B or a C, while my own notebook rioted with the wildest
scribble of contradictory jottings. It was distressing, it was
bewildering, it was humiliating. Truth had run through my fingers. Every drop had escaped.

I could not possibly go home, I reflected, and add as a serious contribution to the study of women and fiction that women
have less hair on their bodies than men, or that the age of
puberty among the South Sea Islanders is nine—or is it ninety?—
even the handwriting had become in its distraction indecipher-
able. It was disgraceful to have nothing more weighty or
respectable to show after a whole morning's work. And if I
could not grasp the truth about W. (as for brevity's sake I had

---

2. [Women are the extremes; they are better or worse than men.]

3. "'Men know that women are an overmatch for them, and therefore they choose the weak-
est or the most ignorant. If they did not think so, they never could be afraid of women
knowing as much as themselves.'... In justice to the sex, I think it but candid to acknowledge that, in a subsequent conversation, he told me that he was serious in what he said." —
BOSWELL, *The Journal of a Tour to the Hebrides.*

4. "The ancient Germans believed that there was something holy in women, and accordingly
consulted them as oracles." —FRAZER, *Golden Bough.*

come to call her) in the past, why bother about W. in the future? It seemed pure waste of time to consult all those gentlemen who specialise in woman and her effect on whatever it may be— politics, children, wages, morality—numerous and learned as they are. One might as well leave their books unopened.

But while I pondered I had unconsciously, in my listlessness, in my desperation, been drawing a picture where I should, like my neighbour, have been writing a conclusion. I had been draw-ing a face, a figure. It was the face and the figure of Professor von X. engaged in writing his monumental work entitled *The Mental, Moral, and Physical Inferiority of the Female Sex*. He was not in my picture a man attractive to women. He was heav-ily built; he had a great jowl; to balance that he had very small eyes; he was very red in the face. His expression suggested that he was labouring under some emotion that made him jab his pen on the paper as if he were killing some noxious insect as he wrote, but even when he had killed it that did not satisfy him; he must go on killing it; and even so, some cause for anger and irritation remained. Could it be his wife, I asked, looking at my picture. Was she in love with a cavalry officer? Was the cavalry officer slim and elegant and dressed in astrachan? Had he been laughed at, to adopt the Freudian theory, in his cradle by a pretty girl? For even in his cradle the professor, I thought, could not have been an attractive child. Whatever the reason, the pro-fessor was made to look very angry and very ugly in my sketch, as he wrote his great book upon the mental, moral, and physi-cal inferiority of women. Drawing pictures was an idle way of finishing an unprofitable morning's work. Yet it is in our idle-ness, in our dreams, that the submerged truth sometimes comes to the top. A very elementary exercise in psychology, not to be dignified by the name of psychoanalysis, showed me, on look-ing at my notebook, that the sketch of the angry professor had been made in anger. Anger had snatched my pencil while I dreamt. But what was anger doing there? Interest, confusion, amusement, boredom—all these emotions I could trace and name as they succeeded each other throughout the morning.

Had anger, the black snake, been lurking among them? Yes, said the sketch, anger had. It referred me unmistakably to the one book, to the one phrase, which had roused the demon; it was the professor's statement about the mental, moral, and physical inferiority of women. My heart had leapt. My cheeks had burnt. I had flushed with anger. There was nothing specially remarkable, however foolish, in that. One does not like to be told that one is naturally the inferior of a little man—I looked at the student next me—who breathes hard, wears a ready-made tie, and has not shaved this fortnight. One has certain foolish vanities. It is only human nature, I reflected, and began drawing cartwheels and circles over the angry professor's face till he looked like a burning bush or a flaming comet—anyhow, an apparition without human semblance or significance. The professor was nothing now but a faggot burning on the top of Hampstead Heath. Soon my own anger was explained and done with; but curiosity remained. How explain the anger of the professors? Why were they angry? For when it came to analysing the impression left by these books there was always an element of heat. This heat took many forms; it showed itself in satire, in sentiment, in curiosity, in reprobation. But there was another element which was often present and could not immediately be identified. Anger, I called it. But it was anger that had gone underground and mixed itself with all kinds of other emotions. To judge from its odd effects, it was anger disguised and complex, not anger simple and open.

Whatever the reason, all these books, I thought, surveying the pile on the desk, are worthless for my purposes. They were worthless scientifically, that is to say, though humanly they were full of instruction, interest, boredom, and very queer facts about the habits of the Fiji Islanders. They had been written in the red light of emotion and not in the white light of truth. Therefore they must be returned to the central desk and restored each to his own cell in the enormous honeycomb. All that I had retrieved from that morning's work had been the one fact of anger. The professors—I lumped them together thus—were angry. But why, I asked myself, having returned the books, why, I repeated, standing under the colonnade among the pigeons and the prehistoric canoes, why are they angry? And, asking myself this question, I strolled off to find a place for luncheon. What is the real nature of what I call for the moment their anger? I asked. Here was a puzzle that would last all the time that it takes to be served with food in a small restaurant somewhere near the British Museum. Some previous luncher had left the lunch edition of the evening paper on a chair, and, waiting to be served, I began idly reading the headlines. A ribbon of very large letters ran across the page. Somebody had made a big score in South Africa. Lesser ribbons announced that Sir Austen Chamberlain was at Geneva. A meat axe with human hair on it had been found in a cellar. Mr. Justice ——— commented in the Divorce Courts upon the Shamelessness of Women. Sprinkled about the paper were other pieces of news. A film actress had been lowered from a peak in California and hung suspended in midair. The weather was going to be foggy. The most transient visitor to this planet, I thought, who picked up this paper could not fail to be aware, even from this scattered testimony, that England is under the rule of a patriarchy. Nobody in their senses could fail to detect the dominance of the professor. His was the power and the money and the influence. He was the proprietor of the paper and its editor and subeditor. He was the Foreign Secretary and the Judge. He was the cricketer; he owned the racehorses and the yachts. He was the director of the company that pays two hundred per cent to its shareholders. He left millions to charities and colleges that were ruled by himself. He suspended the film actress in midair. He will decide if the hair on the meat axe is human; he it is who will acquit or convict the murderer, and hang him, or let him go free. With the exception of the fog he seemed to control everything. Yet he was angry. I knew that he was angry by this token. When I read what he wrote about women I thought, not of what he was saying, but of himself. When an arguer argues dispassionately he thinks only of the argument; and the reader cannot help thinking of the argument too. If he had written dispassionately about women, had used indisputable proofs to establish his argument and had shown no trace of wishing that the result should be one thing rather than another, one would not have been angry either. One would have accepted the fact, as one accepts the fact that a pea is green or a canary yellow. So be it, I should have said. But I had been angry because he was angry. Yet it seemed absurd, I thought, turning over the evening paper, that a man with all this power should be angry. Or is anger, I wondered, somehow, the familiar, the attendant sprite on power? Rich people, for example, are often angry because they suspect that the poor want to seize their wealth. The professors, or patriarchs, as it might be more accurate to call them, might be angry for that reason partly, but partly for one that lies a little less obviously on the surface. Possibly they were not "angry" at all; often, indeed, they were admiring, devoted, exemplary in the relations of private life. Possibly when the professor insisted a little too emphatically upon the inferiority of women, he was concerned not with their inferiority, but with his own superiority. That was what he was protecting rather hotheadedly and with too much emphasis, because it was a jewel to him of the rarest price. Life for both sexes—and I looked at them, shouldering their way along the pavement—is arduous, difficult, a perpetual struggle. It calls for gigantic courage and strength. More than anything, perhaps, creatures of illusion as we are, it calls for confidence in oneself. Without self-confidence we are as babes in the cradle. And how can we generate this imponderable quality, which is yet so invaluable, most quickly? By thinking that other people are inferior to oneself. By feeling that one has some innate superiority—it may be wealth, or rank, a straight nose, or the portrait of a grandfather by Romney—for there is no end to the pathetic devices of the human imagination—over other people. Hence the enormous importance to a patriarch who has to conquer, who has to rule, of feeling that great numbers of people, half the human race indeed, are by nature inferior to himself. It must indeed be one of the chief sources of his power. But let me turn the light of this observation onto real life, I thought. Does it help to explain some of those psychological puzzles that one notes in the margin of daily life? Does it explain my astonishment the other day when Z, most humane, most modest of men, taking up some book by Rebecca West and reading a passage in it, exclaimed, "The arrant feminist! She says that men are snobs!" The exclamation, to me so surprising—for why was Miss West an arrant feminist for making a possibly true if uncomplimentary statement about the other sex?—was not merely the cry of wounded vanity; it was a protest against some infringement of his power to believe in himself. Women have served all these centuries as looking glasses possessing the magic and delicious power of reflecting the figure of man at twice its natural size. Without that power probably the earth would still be swamp and jungle. The glories of all our wars would be unknown. We should still be scratching the outlines of deer on the remains of mutton bones and bartering flints for sheepskins or whatever simple ornament took our unsophisticated taste. Supermen and Fingers of Destiny would never have existed. The Czar and the Kaiser would never have worn their crowns or lost them. Whatever may be their use in civilised societies, mirrors are essential to all violent and heroic action. That is why Napoleon and Mussolini both insist so emphatically upon the inferiority of women, for if they were not inferior, they would cease to enlarge. That serves to explain in part the necessity that women so often are to men. And it serves to explain how restless they are under her criticism; how impossible it is for her to say to them this book is bad, this picture is feeble, or whatever it may be, without giving far more pain and rousing far more anger than a man would do who gave the same criticism. For if she begins to tell the truth, the figure in the looking glass shrinks; his fitness for life is diminished. How is he to go on giving judgement, civilising natives, making laws, writing books, dressing up and speechifying at banquets, unless he can see himself at breakfast and at dinner at least twice the size he really is? So I reflected, crumbling my bread and stirring my coffee and now and again looking at the people in the street. The looking-glass vision is of supreme importance because it charges the vitality; it stimulates the nervous system. Take it away and man may die, like the drug fiend deprived of his cocaine. Under the spell of that illusion, I thought, looking out of the window, half the people on the pavement are striding to work. They put on their hats and coats in the morning under its agreeable rays. They start the day confident, braced, believing themselves desired at Miss Smith's tea party; they say to themselves as they go into the room, I am the superior of half the people here, and it is thus that they speak with that self-confidence, that self-assurance, which have had such profound consequences in public life and lead to such curious notes in the margin of the private mind.

But these contributions to the dangerous and fascinating subject of the psychology of the other sex—it is one, I hope, that you will investigate when you have five hundred a year of your own—were interrupted by the necessity of paying the bill. It came to five shillings and ninepence. I gave the waiter a ten-shilling note and he went to bring me change. There was another ten-shilling note in my purse; I noticed it, because it is a fact that still takes my breath away—the power of my purse to breed ten-shilling notes automatically. I open it and there they are. Society gives me chicken and coffee, bed and lodging, in return for a certain number of pieces of paper which were left me by an aunt, for no other reason than that I share her name.

My aunt, Mary Beton, I must tell you, died by a fall from her horse when she was riding out to take the air in Bombay. The news of my legacy reached me one night about the same time that the act was passed that gave votes to women. A solicitor's letter fell into the postbox and when I opened it I found that she had left me five hundred pounds a year forever. Of the two—the vote and the money—the money, I own, seemed infinitely the more important. Before that I had made my living by cadging odd jobs from newspapers, by reporting a donkey show here or a wedding there; I had earned a few pounds by addressing envelopes, reading to old ladies, making artificial flowers, teaching the alphabet to small children in a kindergarten. Such were the chief occupations that were open to women before 1918. I need not, I am afraid, describe in any detail the hardness of the work, for you know perhaps women who have done it; nor the difficulty of living on the money when it was earned, for you may have tried. But what still remains with me as a worse infliction than either was the poison of fear and bitterness which those days bred in me. To begin with, always to be doing work that one did not wish to do, and to do it like a slave, flattering and fawning, not always necessarily perhaps, but it seemed necessary and the stakes were too great to run risks; and then the thought of that one gift which it was death to hide—a small one but dear to the possessor—perishing and with it myself, my soul—all this became like a rust eating away the bloom of the spring, destroying the tree at its heart. However, as I say, my aunt died; and whenever I change a ten-shilling note a little of that rust and corrosion is rubbed off; fear and bitterness go. Indeed, I thought, slipping the silver into my purse, it is remarkable, remembering the bitterness of those days, what a change of temper a fixed income will bring about. No force in the world can take from me my five hundred pounds. Food, house, and clothing are mine forever. Therefore not merely do effort and labour cease, but also hatred and bitterness. I need not hate any man; he cannot hurt me. I need not flatter any man; he has nothing to give me. So imperceptibly I found myself adopting a new attitude towards the other half of the human race. It was absurd to blame any class or any sex, as a whole. Great bodies of people are never responsible for what they do. They are driven by instincts which are not within their control. They too, the patriarchs, the professors, had endless difficulties, terrible drawbacks to contend with. Their education had been in some ways as faulty as my own. It had bred in them defects as great. True, they had money and power, but only at the cost of harbouring in their breasts an eagle, a vulture, forever tearing the liver out and plucking at the lungs—the instinct for possession, the rage for acquisition which drives them to desire other people's fields and goods perpetually; to make frontiers and flags; battleships and poison gas; to offer up their own lives and their children's lives. Walk through the Admiralty Arch (I had reached that monument), or any other avenue given up to trophies and cannon, and reflect upon the kind of glory celebrated there. Or watch in the spring sunshine the stockbroker and the great barrister going indoors to make money and more money and more money when it is a fact that five hundred pounds a year will keep one alive in the sunshine. These are unpleasant instincts to harbour, I reflected. They are bred of the conditions of life; of the lack of civilisation, I thought, looking at the statue of the Duke of Cambridge, and in particular at the feathers in his cocked hat, with a fixity that they have scarcely ever received before. And, as I realised these drawbacks, by degrees fear and bitterness modified themselves into pity and toleration; and then in a year or two, pity and toleration went, and the greatest release of all came, which is freedom to think of things in themselves. That building, for example, do I like it or not? Is that picture beautiful or not? Is that in my opinion a good book or a bad? Indeed my aunt's legacy unveiled the sky to me, and substituted for the large and imposing figure of a gentleman, which Milton recommended for my perpetual adoration, a view of the open sky.

So thinking, so speculating, I found my way back to my house by the river. Lamps were being lit and an indescribable change had come over London since the morning hour. It was as if the great machine after labouring all day had made with our help a few yards of something very exciting and beautiful— a fiery fabric flashing with red eyes, a tawny monster roaring with hot breath. Even the wind seemed flung like a flag as it lashed the houses and rattled the hoardings.

In my little street, however, domesticity prevailed. The house painter was descending his ladder; the nursemaid was wheeling the perambulator carefully in and out back to nursery tea; the coal heaver was folding his empty sacks on top of each other;

the woman who keeps the greengrocer's shop was adding up the day's takings with her hands in red mittens. But so engrossed was I with the problem you have laid upon my shoulders that I could not see even these usual sights without referring them to one centre. I thought how much harder it is now than it must have been even a century ago to say which of these employments is the higher, the more necessary. Is it better to be a coal heaver or a nursemaid; is the charwoman who has brought up eight children of less value to the world than the barrister who has made a hundred thousand pounds? It is useless to ask such questions; for nobody can answer them. Not only do the comparative values of charwomen and lawyers rise and fall from decade to decade, but we have no rods with which to measure them even as they are at the moment. I had been foolish to ask my professor to furnish me with "indisputable proofs" of this or that in his argument about women. Even if one could state the value of any one gift at the moment, those values will change; in a century's time very possibly they will have changed completely. Moreover, in a hundred years, I thought, reaching my own doorstep, women will have ceased to be the protected sex. Logically they will take part in all the activities and exertions that were once denied them. The nursemaid will heave coal. The shopwoman will drive an engine. All assumptions founded on the facts observed when women were the protected sex will have disappeared—as, for example (here a squad of soldiers marched down the street), that women and clergymen and gardeners live longer than other people. Remove that protection, expose them to the same exertions and activities, make them soldiers and sailors and engine-drivers and dock labourers, and will not women die off so much younger, so much quicker, than men that one will say, "I saw a woman today," as one used to say, "I saw an aeroplane." Anything may happen when womanhood has ceased to be a protected occupation, I thought, opening the door. But what bearing has all this upon the subject of my paper, Women and Fiction? I asked, going indoors.

It was disappointing not to have brought back in the evening some important statement, some authentic fact. Women are poorer than men because—this or that. Perhaps now it would be better to give up seeking for the truth, and receiving on one's head an avalanche of opinion hot as lava, discoloured as dishwater. It would be better to draw the curtains; to shut out distractions; to light the lamp; to narrow the enquiry and to ask the historian, who records not opinions but facts, to describe under what conditions women lived, not throughout the ages, but in England, say in the time of Elizabeth.

For it is a perennial puzzle why no woman wrote a word of that extraordinary literature when every other man, it seemed, was capable of song or sonnet. What were the conditions in which women lived, I asked myself; for fiction, imaginative work that is, is not dropped like a pebble upon the ground, as science may be; fiction is like a spider's web, attached ever so lightly perhaps, but still attached to life at all four corners. Often the attachment is scarcely perceptible; Shakespeare's plays, for instance, seem to hang there complete by themselves. But when the web is pulled askew, hooked up at the edge, torn in the middle, one remembers that these webs are not spun in midair by incorporeal creatures, but are the work of suffering human beings, and are attached to grossly material things, like health and money and the houses we live in.

I went, therefore, to the shelf where the histories stand and took down one of the latest, Professor Trevelyan's *History of England*. Once more I looked up "Women," found "position of," and turned to the pages indicated. "Wifebeating," I read, "was a recognised right of man, and was practised without shame by high as well as low. . . . Similarly," the historian goes on, "the daughter who refused to marry the gentleman of her parents' choice was liable to be locked up, beaten, and flung about the room, without any shock being inflicted on public opinion. Marriage was not an affair of personal affection, but of family avarice, particularly in the 'chivalrous' upper classes. . . . Betrothal often took place while one or both of the parties was in the cradle, and marriage when they were scarcely out of the nurses' charge." That was about 1470, soon after Chaucer's time. The next reference to the position of women is some two hundred years later, in the time of the Stuarts. "It was still the exception for women of the upper and middle class to choose their own husbands, and when the husband had been assigned, he was lord and master, so far at least as law and custom could make him. Yet even so," Professor Trevelyan concludes, "neither Shakespeare's women nor those of authentic seventeenth-century memoirs, like the Verneys and the Hutchinsons, seem wanting in personality and character." Certainly, if we consider it, Cleopatra must have had a way with her; Lady Macbeth, one would suppose, had a will of her own; Rosalind, one might conclude, was an attractive girl. Professor Trevelyan is speaking no more than the truth when he remarks that Shakespeare's women do not seem wanting in personality and character. Not being a historian, one might go even further and say that women have burnt like beacons in all the works of all the poets from the beginning of time—Clytemnestra, Antigone, Cleopatra, Lady Macbeth, Phèdre, Cressida, Rosalind, Desdemona, the Duchess of Malfi, among the dramatists; then among the prose writers: Millamant, Clarissa, Becky Sharp, Anna Karenina, Emma Bovary, Madame de Guermantes—the names flock to mind, nor do they recall women "lacking in personality and character." Indeed, if woman had no existence save in the fiction written by men, one would imagine her a person of the utmost importance; very various; heroic and mean; splendid and sordid; infinitely beautiful and hideous in the extreme; as great as a man, some think even greater.[5] But this is woman in fiction. In fact, as

---

5. "It remains a strange and almost inexplicable fact that in Athena's city, where women were kept in almost Oriental suppression as odalisques or drudges, the stage should yet have produced figures like Clytemnestra and Cassandra, Atossa and Antigone, Phèdre and Medea, and all the other heroines who dominate play after play of the 'misogynist'

Professor Trevelyan points out, she was locked up, beaten, and flung about the room.

A very queer, composite being thus emerges. Imaginatively she is of the highest importance; practically she is completely insignificant. She pervades poetry from cover to cover; she is all but absent from history. She dominates the lives of kings and conquerors in fiction; in fact she was the slave of any boy whose parents forced a ring upon her finger. Some of the most inspired words, some of the most profound thoughts in literature fall from her lips; in real life she could hardly read, could scarcely spell, and was the property of her husband.

It was certainly an odd monster that one made up by reading the historians first and the poets afterwards—a worm winged like an eagle; the spirit of life and beauty in a kitchen chopping up suet. But these monsters, however amusing to the imagination, have no existence in fact. What one must do to bring her to life was to think poetically and prosaically at one and the same moment, thus keeping in touch with fact—that she is Mrs. Martin, aged thirty-six, dressed in blue, wearing a black hat and brown shoes; but not losing sight of fiction either—that she is a vessel in which all sorts of spirits and forces are coursing and flashing perpetually. The moment, however, that one tries this method with the Elizabethan woman, one branch of illumination fails; one is held up by the scarcity of facts. One knows nothing detailed, nothing perfectly true and substantial about

---

Euripides. But the paradox of this world where in real life a respectable woman could hardly show her face alone in the street, and yet on the stage woman equals or surpasses man, has never been satisfactorily explained. In modern tragedy the same predominance exists. At all events, a very cursory survey of Shakespeare's work (similarly with Webster, though not with Marlowe or Jonson) suffices to reveal how this dominance, this initiative of women, persists from Rosalind to Lady Macbeth. So too in Racine; six of his tragedies bear their heroines' names; and what male characters of his shall we set against Hermione and Andromaque, Bérénice and Roxane, Phèdre and Athalie? So again with Ibsen; what men shall we match with Solveig and Nora, Hedda and Hilda Wangel and Rebecca West?"
—F. L. LUCAS, *Tragedy*, pp. 114–115.

her. History scarcely mentions her. And I turned to Professor
Trevelyan again to see what history meant to him. I found by
looking at his chapter headings that it meant: "The Manor
Court and the Methods of Open-field Agriculture . . . The
Cistercians and Sheep Farming . . . The Crusades . . . The
University . . . The House of Commons . . . The Hundred Years'
War . . . The Wars of the Roses . . . The Renaissance Scholars
. . . The Dissolution of the Monasteries . . . Agrarian and
Religious Strife . . . The Origin of English Sea Power . . . The
Armada . . ." and so on. Occasionally an individual woman is
mentioned, an Elizabeth, or a Mary; a queen or a great lady. But
by no possible means could middle-class women with nothing
but brains and character at their command have taken part in
any one of the great movements which, brought together, con-
stitute the historian's view of the past. Nor shall we find her in
any collection of anecdotes. Aubrey hardly mentions her. She
never writes her own life and scarcely keeps a diary; there are
only a handful of her letters in existence. She left no plays or
poems by which we can judge her. What one wants, I thought—
and why does not some brilliant student at Newnham or Girton
supply it?—is a mass of information; at what age did she marry;
how many children had she as a rule; what was her house like;
had she a room to herself; did she do the cooking; would she be
likely to have a servant? All these facts lie somewhere, presumably, in parish registers and account books; the life of the average Elizabethan woman must be scattered about somewhere,
could one collect it and make a book of it. It would be ambi-
tious beyond my daring, I thought, looking about the shelves for
books that were not there, to suggest to the students of those
famous colleges that they should rewrite history, though I own
that it often seems a little queer as it is, unreal, lopsided; but
why should they not add a supplement to history? calling it, of
course, by some inconspicuous name so that women might figure there without impropriety? For one often catches a glimpse
of them in the lives of the great, whisking away into the back-
ground, concealing, I sometimes think, a wink, a laugh, perhaps

a tear. And, after all, we have lives enough of Jane Austen; it scarcely seems necessary to consider again the influence of the tragedies of Joanna Baillie upon the poetry of Edgar Allan Poe; as for myself, I should not mind if the homes and haunts of Mary Russell Mitford were closed to the public for a century at least. But what I find deplorable, I continued, looking about the bookshelves again, is that nothing is known about women before the eighteenth century. I have no model in my mind to turn about this way and that. Here am I asking why women did not write poetry in the Elizabethan age, and I am not sure how they were educated; whether they were taught to write; whether they had sitting rooms to themselves; how many women had children before they were twenty-one; what, in short, they did from eight in the morning till eight at night. They had no money evidently; according to Professor Trevelyan they were married whether they liked it or not before they were out of the nursery, at fifteen or sixteen very likely. It would have been extremely odd, even upon this showing, had one of them suddenly written the plays of Shakespeare, I concluded, and I thought of that old gentleman, who is dead now, but was a bishop, I think, who declared that it was impossible for any woman, past, present, or to come, to have the genius of Shakespeare. He wrote to the papers about it. He also told a lady who applied to him for information that cats do not as a matter of fact go to heaven, though they have, he added, souls of a sort. How much thinking those old gentlemen used to save one! How the borders of ignorance shrank back at their approach! Cats do not go to heaven. Women cannot write the plays of Shakespeare.

Be that as it may, I could not help thinking, as I looked at the works of Shakespeare on the shelf, that the bishop was right at least in this; it would have been impossible, completely and entirely, for any woman to have written the plays of Shakespeare in the age of Shakespeare. Let me imagine, since facts are so hard to come by, what would have happened had Shakespeare had a wonderfully gifted sister, called Judith, let us say. Shakespeare himself went, very probably—his mother was an heiress—to the grammar school, where he may have learnt Latin—Ovid, Virgil, and Horace—and the elements of grammar and logic. He was, it is well known, a wild boy who poached rabbits, perhaps shot a deer, and had, rather sooner than he should have done, to marry a woman in the neighbourhood, who bore him a child rather quicker than was right. That escapade sent him to seek his fortune in London. He had, it seemed, a taste for the theatre; he began by holding horses at the stage door. Very soon he got work in the theatre, became a successful actor, and lived at the hub of the universe, meeting everybody, knowing everybody, practising his art on the boards, exercising his wits in the streets, and even getting access to the palace of the queen. Meanwhile his extraordinarily gifted sister, let us suppose, remained at home. She was as adventurous, as imaginative, as agog to see the world as he was. But she was not sent to school. She had no chance of learning grammar and logic, let alone of reading Horace and Virgil. She picked up a book now and then, one of her brother's perhaps, and read a few pages. But then her parents came in and told her to mend the stockings or mind the stew and not moon about with books and papers. They would have spoken sharply but kindly, for they were substantial people who knew the conditions of life for a woman and loved their daughter—indeed, more likely than not she was the apple of her father's eye. Perhaps she scribbled some pages up in an apple loft on the sly, but was careful to hide them or set fire to them. Soon, however, before she was out of her teens, she was to be betrothed to the son of a neighbouring wool-stapler. She cried out that marriage was hateful to her, and for that she was severely beaten by her father. Then he ceased to scold her. He begged her instead not to hurt him, not to shame him in this matter of her marriage. He would give her a chain of beads or a fine petticoat, he said; and there were tears in his eyes. How could she disobey him? How could she break his heart? The force of her own gift alone drove her to it. She made up a small parcel of her belongings, let herself down by a rope one summer's night and took the road to London. She was not seventeen.

The birds that sang in the hedge were not more musical than she was. She had the quickest fancy, a gift like her brother's, for the tune of words. Like him, she had a taste for the theatre. She stood at the stage door; she wanted to act, she said. Men laughed in her face. The manager—a fat, loose-lipped man—guffawed. He bellowed something about poodles dancing and women acting—no woman, he said, could possibly be an actress. He hinted—you can imagine what. She could get no training in her craft. Could she even seek her dinner in a tavern or roam the streets at midnight? Yet her genius was for fiction and lusted to feed abundantly upon the lives of men and women and the study of their ways. At last—for she was very young, oddly like Shakespeare the poet in her face, with the same grey eyes and rounded brows—at last Nick Greene the actor-manager took pity on her; she found herself with child by that gentleman and so—who shall measure the heat and violence of the poet's heart when caught and tangled in a woman's body?—killed herself one winter's night and lies buried at some crossroads where the omnibuses now stop outside the Elephant and Castle.

That, more or less, is how the story would run, I think, if a woman in Shakespeare's day had had Shakespeare's genius. But for my part, I agree with the deceased bishop, if such he was—it is unthinkable that any woman in Shakespeare's day should have had Shakespeare's genius. For genius like Shakespeare's is not born among labouring, uneducated, servile people. It was not born in England among the Saxons and the Britons. It is not born today among the working classes. How, then, could it have been born among women whose work began, according to Professor Trevelyan, almost before they were out of the nursery, who were forced to it by their parents and held to it by all the power of law and custom? Yet genius of a sort must have existed among women as it must have existed among the working classes. Now and again an Emily Brontë or a Robert Burns blazes out and proves its presence. But certainly it never got itself on to paper. When, however, one reads of a witch being ducked, of a woman possessed by devils, of a wise woman selling herbs, or even of a very remarkable man who had a mother, then I think we are on the track of a lost novelist, a suppressed poet, of some mute and inglorious Jane Austen, some Emily Brontë who dashed her brains out on the moor or mopped and mowed about the highways crazed with the torture that her gift had put her to. Indeed, I would venture to guess that Anon., who wrote so many poems without signing them, was often a woman. It was a woman Edward Fitzgerald, I think, suggested who made the ballads and the folk-songs, crooning them to her children, beguiling her spinning with them, or the length of the winter's night.

This may be true or it may be false—who can say?—but what is true in it, so it seemed to me, reviewing the story of Shakespeare's sister as I had made it, is that any woman born with a great gift in the sixteenth century would certainly have gone crazed, shot herself, or ended her days in some lonely cottage outside the village, half witch, half wizard, feared and mocked at. For it needs little skill in psychology to be sure that a highly gifted girl who had tried to use her gift for poetry would have been so thwarted and hindered by other people, so tortured and pulled asunder by her own contrary instincts, that she must have lost her health and sanity to a certainty. No girl could have walked to London and stood at a stage door and forced her way into the presence of actor-managers without doing herself a violence and suffering an anguish which may have been irrational—for chastity may be a fetish invented by certain societies for unknown reasons—but were none the less inevitable. Chastity had then, it has even now, a religious importance in a woman's life, and has so wrapped itself round with nerves and instincts that to cut it free and bring it to the light of day demands courage of the rarest. To have lived a free life in London in the sixteenth century would have meant for a woman who was poet and playwright a nervous stress and dilemma which might well have killed her. Had she survived, whatever she had written would have been twisted and deformed, issuing from a strained and morbid imagination. And undoubtedly, I thought, looking at the shelf where there are no plays by women, her work would have gone unsigned. That refuge she would have sought certainly. It was the relic of the sense of chastity that dictated anonymity to women even so late as the nineteenth century. Currer Bell, George Eliot, George Sand, all the victims of inner strife as their writings prove, sought ineffectively to veil themselves by using the name of a man. Thus they did homage to the convention, which if not implanted by the other sex was liberally encouraged by them (the chief glory of a woman is not to be talked of, said Pericles, himself a much-talked-of man), that publicity in women is detestable. Anonymity runs in their blood. The desire to be veiled still possesses them. They are not even now as concerned about the health of their fame as men are, and, speaking generally, will pass a tombstone or a signpost without feeling an irresistible desire to cut their names on it, as Alf, Bert, or Chas. must do in obedience to their instinct, which murmurs if it sees a fine woman go by, or even a dog, *Ce chien est à moi.* And, of course, it may not be a dog, I thought, remembering Parliament Square, the Sieges Allee and other avenues; it may be a piece of land or a man with curly black hair. It is one of the great advantages of being a woman that one can pass even a very fine negress without wishing to make an Englishwoman of her.

That woman, then, who was born with a gift of poetry in the sixteenth century, was an unhappy woman, a woman at strife against herself. All the conditions of her life, all her own instincts, were hostile to the state of mind which is needed to set free whatever is in the brain. But what is the state of mind that is most propitious to the act of creation, I asked. Can one come by any notion of the state that furthers and makes possible that strange activity? Here I opened the volume containing the tragedies of Shakespeare. What was Shakespeare's state of mind, for instance, when he wrote *Lear* and *Antony and Cleopatra*? It was certainly the state of mind most favourable to poetry that there has ever existed. But Shakespeare himself said nothing about it. We only know casually and by chance that he "never blotted a line." Nothing indeed was ever said by the artist himself about his state of mind until the eighteenth century perhaps. Rousseau perhaps began it. At any rate, by the nineteenth century self-consciousness had developed so far that it was the habit for men of letters to describe their minds in confessions and autobiographies. Their lives also were written, and their letters were printed after their deaths. Thus, though we do not know what Shakespeare went through when he wrote *Lear,* we do know what Carlyle went through when he wrote the *French Revolution;* what Flaubert went through when he wrote *Madame Bovary;* what Keats was going through when he tried to write poetry against the coming of death and the indifference of the world.

And one gathers from this enormous modern literature of confession and self-analysis that to write a work of genius is almost always a feat of prodigious difficulty. Everything is against the likelihood that it will come from the writer's mind whole and entire. Generally material circumstances are against it. Dogs will bark; people will interrupt; money must be made; health will break down. Further, accentuating all these difficulties and making them harder to bear is the world's notorious indifference. It does not ask people to write poems and novels and histories; it does not need them. It does not care whether Flaubert finds the right word or whether Carlyle scrupulously verifies this or that fact. Naturally, it will not pay for what it does not want. And so the writer, Keats, Flaubert, Carlyle, suffers, especially in the creative years of youth, every form of distraction and discouragement. A curse, a cry of agony, rises from those books of analysis and confession. "Mighty poets in their misery dead"—that is the burden of their song. If anything comes through in spite of all this, it is a miracle, and probably no book is born entire and uncrippled as it was conceived.

But for women, I thought, looking at the empty shelves, these difficulties were infinitely more formidable. In the first place, to have a room of her own, let alone a quiet room or a soundproof room, was out of the question, unless her parents were exceptionally rich or very noble, even up to the beginning of the nineteenth century. Since her pin money, which depended on the good will of her father, was only enough to keep her clothed, she was debarred from such alleviations as came even to Keats or Tennyson or Carlyle, all poor men, from a walking tour, a little journey to France, from the separate lodging which, even if it were miserable enough, sheltered them from the claims and tyrannies of their families. Such material difficulties were formidable; but much worse were the immaterial. The indifference of the world which Keats and Flaubert and other men of genius have found so hard to bear was in her case not indifference but hostility. The world did not say to her as it said to them, Write if you choose; it makes no difference to me. The world said with a guffaw, Write? What's the good of your writing? Here the psychologists of Newnham and Girton might come to our help, I thought, looking again at the blank spaces on the shelves. For surely it is time that the effect of discouragement upon the mind of the artist should be measured, as I have seen a dairy company measure the effect of ordinary milk and Grade A milk upon the body of the rat. They set two rats in cages side by side, and of the two one was furtive, timid, and small, and the other was glossy, bold, and big. Now what food do we feed women as artists upon? I asked, remembering, I suppose, that dinner of prunes and custard.[6] To answer that question I had only to open the evening paper and to read that Lord Birkenhead is of opinion—but really I am not going to trouble to copy out Lord Birkenhead's opinion upon the writing of women. What Dean Inge says I will leave in peace. The Harley Street specialist may be allowed to rouse the echoes of Harley Street with his vociferations without raising a hair on my head. I will quote, however, Mr. Oscar Browning, because Mr. Oscar Browning was a great figure in Cambridge at one time, and used to examine the students at Girton and Newnham. Mr. Oscar Browning was wont to declare "that the impression left on his mind, after

---

6. [Woolf is alluding to her very simple dinner at the women's college.]

looking over any set of examination papers, was that, irrespective of the marks he might give, the best woman was intellectually the inferior of the worst man." After saying that Mr. Browning went back to his rooms—and it is this sequel that endears him and makes him a human figure of some bulk and majesty—he went back to his rooms and found a stableboy lying on the sofa—"a mere skeleton, his cheeks were cavernous and sallow, his teeth were black, and he did not appear to have the full use of his limbs. . . . 'That's Arthur' [said Mr. Browning]. 'He's a dear boy really and most high-minded.' " The two pictures always seem to me to complete each other. And happily in this age of biography the two pictures often do complete each other, so that we are able to interpret the opinions of great men not only by what they say, but by what they do.

But though this is possible now, such opinions coming from the lips of important people must have been formidable enough even fifty years ago. Let us suppose that a father from the highest motives did not wish his daughter to leave home and become writer, painter, or scholar. "See what Mr. Oscar Browning says," he would say; and there was not only Mr. Oscar Browning; there was the *Saturday Review;* there was Mr. Greg—the "essentials of a woman's being," said Mr. Greg emphatically, "are that *they are supported by, and they minister to, men*"— there was an enormous body of masculine opinion to the effect that nothing could be expected of women intellectually. Even if her father did not read out loud these opinions, any girl could read them for herself; and the reading, even in the nineteenth century, must have lowered her vitality, and told profoundly upon her work. There would always have been that assertion— you cannot do this, you are incapable of doing that—to protest against, to overcome. Probably for a novelist this germ is no longer of much effect; for there have been women novelists of merit. But for painters it must still have some sting in it; and for musicians, I imagine, is even now active and poisonous in the extreme. The woman composer stands where the actress stood in the time of Shakespeare. Nick Greene, I thought, remembering the story I had made about Shakespeare's sister, said that a woman acting put him in mind of a dog dancing. Johnson repeated the phrase two hundred years later of women preaching. And here, I said, opening a book about music, we have the very words used again in this year of grace, 1928, of women who try to write music. "Of Mlle. Germaine Tailleferre one can only repeat Dr. Johnson's dictum concerning a woman preacher, transposed into terms of music. 'Sir, a woman's composing is like a dog's walking on his hind legs. It is not done well, but you are surprised to find it done at all.' " So accurately does history repeat itself.

Thus, I concluded, shutting Mr. Oscar Browning's life and pushing away the rest, it is fairly evident that even in the nineteenth century a woman was not encouraged to be an artist. On the contrary, she was snubbed, slapped, lectured, and exhorted. Her mind must have been strained and her vitality lowered by the need of opposing this, of disproving that. For here again we come within range of that very interesting and obscure masculine complex which has had so much influence upon the woman's movement; that deep-seated desire, not so much that *she* shall be inferior as that *he* shall be superior, which plants him wherever one looks, not only in front of the arts, but barring the way to politics too, even when the risk to himself seems infinitesimal and the suppliant humble and devoted. Even Lady Bessborough, I remembered, with all her passion for politics, must humbly bow herself and write to Lord Granville Leveson-Gower: ". . . notwithstanding all my violence in politics and talking so much on that subject, I perfectly agree with you that no woman has any business to meddle with that or any other serious business, farther than giving her opinion (if she is ask'd)." And so she goes on to spend her enthusiasm where it meets with no obstacle whatsoever upon that immensely important subject, Lord Granville's maiden speech in the House of Commons. The spectacle is certainly a strange one, I thought. The history of men's opposition to women's emancipation is more interesting perhaps than the story of that emancipation itself. An amusing book might be made of it if some young student at Girton or Newnham would collect examples and deduce a theory—but she would need thick gloves on her hands, and bars to protect her of solid gold.

But what is amusing now, I recollected, shutting Lady Bessborough, had to be taken in desperate earnest once. Opinions that one now pastes in a book labelled cock-a-doodle-dum and keeps for reading to select audiences on summer nights once drew tears, I can assure you. Among your grandmothers and great-grandmothers there were many that wept their eyes out. Florence Nightingale shrieked aloud in her agony. Moreover, it is all very well for you, who have got yourselves to college and enjoy sitting rooms—or is it only bed-sitting-rooms?—of your own to say that genius should disregard such opinions; that genius should be above caring what is said of it. Unfortunately, it is precisely the men or women of genius who mind most what is said of them. Remember Keats. Remember the words he had cut on his tombstone.[7] Think of Tennyson; think—but I need hardly multiply instances of the undeniable, if very unfortunate, fact that it is the nature of the artist to mind excessively what is said about him. Literature is strewn with the wreckage of men who have minded beyond reason the opinions of others.

And this susceptibility of theirs is doubly unfortunate, I thought, returning again to my original enquiry into what state of mind is most propitious for creative work, because the mind of an artist, in order to achieve the prodigious effort of freeing whole and entire the work that is in him, must be incandescent, like Shakespeare's mind, I conjectured, looking at the book which lay open at *Antony and Cleopatra*. There must be no obstacle in it, no foreign matter unconsumed.

For though we say that we know nothing about Shakespeare's state of mind, even as we say that, we are saying something about Shakespeare's state of mind. The reason perhaps why we

---

7. [Here lies One Whose Name was writ in Water.]

know so little of Shakespeare—compared with Donne or Ben Jonson or Milton—is that his grudges and spites and antipathies are hidden from us. We are not held up by some "revelation" which reminds us of the writer. All desire to protest, to preach, to proclaim an injury, to pay off a score, to make the world the witness of some hardship or grievance was fired out of him and consumed. Therefore his poetry flows from him free and unimpeded. If ever a human being got his work expressed completely, it was Shakespeare. If ever a mind was incandescent, unimpeded, I thought, turning again to the bookcase, it was Shakespeare's mind.

Next day the light of the October morning was falling in dusty shafts through the uncurtained windows, and the hum of traffic rose from the street. London then was winding itself up again; the factory was astir; the machines were beginning. It was tempting, after all this reading, to look out of the window and see what London was doing on the morning of the twenty-sixth of October 1928. And what was London doing? Nobody, it seemed, was reading *Antony and Cleopatra*. London was wholly indifferent, it appeared, to Shakespeare's plays. Nobody cared a straw—and I do not blame them—for the future of fiction, the death of poetry, or the development by the average woman of a prose style completely expressive of her mind. If opinions upon any of these matters had been chalked on the pavement, nobody would have stooped to read them. The nonchalance of the hurrying feet would have rubbed them out in half an hour. Here came an errand boy; here a woman with a dog on a lead. The fascination of the London street is that no two people are ever alike; each seems bound on some private affair of his own. There were the businesslike, with their little bags; there were the drifters rattling sticks upon area railings; there were affable characters to whom the streets serve for clubroom, hailing men in carts and giving information without being asked for it. Also there were funerals to which men, thus suddenly reminded of the passing of their own bodies, lifted their hats. And then a very distinguished gentleman came slowly down a doorstep and paused to avoid collision with a bustling lady who had, by some means or other, acquired a splendid fur coat and a bunch of Parma violets. They all seemed separate, self-absorbed, on business of their own.

At this moment, as so often happens in London, there was a complete lull and suspension of traffic. Nothing came down the street; nobody passed. A single leaf detached itself from the plane tree at the end of the street, and in that pause and suspension fell. Somehow it was like a signal falling, a signal pointing to a force in things which one had overlooked. It seemed to point to a river, which flowed past, invisibly, round the corner, down the street, and took people and eddied them along, as the stream at Oxbridge had taken the undergraduate in his boat and the dead leaves. Now it was bringing from one side of the street to the other diagonally a girl in patent leather boots, and then a young man in a maroon overcoat; it was also bringing a taxicab; and it brought all three together at a point directly beneath my window; where the taxi stopped; and the girl and the young man stopped; and they got into the taxi; and then the cab glided off as if it were swept on by the current elsewhere.

The sight was ordinary enough; what was strange was the rhythmical order with which my imagination had invested it; and the fact that the ordinary sight of two people getting into a cab had the power to communicate something of their own seeming satisfaction. The sight of two people coming down the street and meeting at the corner seems to ease the mind of some strain, I thought, watching the taxi turn and make off. Perhaps to think, as I had been thinking these two days, of one sex as distinct from the other is an effort. It interferes with the unity of the mind. Now that effort had ceased and that unity had been restored by seeing two people come together and get into a taxicab. The mind is certainly a very mysterious organ, I reflected, drawing my head in from the window, about which nothing whatever is known, though we depend upon it so completely. Why do I feel that there are severances and oppositions in the mind, as there are strains from obvious causes on the body? What does one mean by "the unity of the mind," I pondered, for clearly the mind has so great a power of concentrating at any point at any moment that it seems to have no single state of being. It can separate itself from the people in the street, for example, and think of itself as apart from them, at an upper window looking down on them. Or it can think with other people spontaneously, as, for instance, in a crowd waiting to hear some piece of news read out. It can think back through its fathers or through its mothers, as I have said that a woman writing thinks back through her mothers. Again if one is a woman one is often surprised by a sudden splitting off of consciousness, say in walking down Whitehall, when from being the natural inheritor of that civilisation, she becomes, on the contrary, outside of it, alien and critical. Clearly the mind is always altering its focus, and bringing the world into different perspectives. But some of these states of mind seem, even if adopted spontaneously, to be less comfortable than others. In order to keep oneself continuing in them one is unconsciously holding something back, and gradually the repression becomes an effort. But there may be some state of mind in which one could continue without effort because nothing is required to be held back. And this perhaps, I thought, coming in from the window, is one of them. For certainly when I saw the couple get into the taxicab the mind felt as if, after being divided, it had come together again in a natural fusion. The obvious reason would be that it is natural for the sexes to cooperate. One has a profound, if irrational, instinct in favour of the theory that the union of man and woman makes for the greatest satisfaction, the most complete happiness. But the sight of the two people getting into the taxi and the satisfaction it gave me made me also ask whether there are two sexes in the mind corresponding to the two sexes in the body, and whether they also require to be united in order to get complete satisfaction and happiness. And

I went on amateurishly to sketch a plan of the soul so that in each of us two powers preside, one male, one female; and in the man's brain, the man predominates over the woman, and in the woman's brain, the woman predominates over the man. The normal and comfortable state of being is that when the two live in harmony together, spiritually cooperating. If one is a man, still the woman part of the brain must have effect; and a woman also must have intercourse with the man in her. Coleridge perhaps meant this when he said that a great mind is androgynous. It is when this fusion takes place that the mind is fully fertilised and uses all its faculties. Perhaps a mind that is purely masculine cannot create, any more than a mind that is purely feminine, I thought. But it would be well to test what one meant by man-womanly, and conversely by woman-manly, by pausing and looking at a book or two.

Coleridge certainly did not mean, when he said that a great mind is androgynous, that it is a mind that has any special sympathy with women; a mind that takes up their cause or devotes itself to their interpretation. Perhaps the androgynous mind is less apt to make these distinctions than the single-sexed mind. He meant, perhaps, that the androgynous mind is resonant and porous; that it transmits emotion without impediment; that it is naturally creative, incandescent, and undivided. In fact one goes back to Shakespeare's mind as the type of the androgynous, of the man-womanly mind, though it would be impossible to say what Shakespeare thought of women. And if it be true that it is one of the tokens of the fully developed mind that it does not think specially or separately of sex, how much harder it is to attain that condition now than ever before. Here I came to the books by living writers, and there paused and wondered if this fact were not at the root of something that had long puzzled me. No age can ever have been as stridently sex-conscious as our own; those innumerable books by men about women in the British Museum are a proof of it. The Suffrage campaign was no doubt to blame. It must have roused in men an extraordinary desire for self-assertion; it must have made them lay an emphasis upon their own sex and its characteristics which they would not have troubled to think about had they not been challenged. And when one is challenged, even by a few women in black bonnets, one retaliates, if one has never been challenged before, rather excessively. That perhaps accounts for some of the characteristics that I remember to have found here, I thought, taking down a new novel by Mr. A, who is in the prime of life and very well thought of, apparently, by the reviewers. I opened it. Indeed, it was delightful to read a man's writing again. It was so direct, so straightforward after the writing of women. It indicated such freedom of mind, such liberty of person, such confidence in himself. One had a sense of physical well-being in the presence of this well-nourished, well-educated, free mind, which had never been thwarted or opposed, but had had full liberty from birth to stretch itself in whatever way it liked. All this was admirable. But after reading a chapter or two a shadow seemed to lie across the page. It was a straight dark bar, a shadow shaped something like the letter "I." One began dodging this way and that to catch a glimpse of the landscape behind it. Whether that was indeed a tree or a woman walking I was not quite sure. Back one was always hailed to the letter "I." One began to be tired of "I." Not but what this "I" was a most respectable "I"; honest and logical; as hard as a nut, and polished for centuries by good teaching and good feeding. I respect and admire that "I" from the bottom of my heart. But—here I turned a page or two, looking for something or other—the worst of it is that in the shadow of the letter "I" all is shapeless as mist. Is that a tree? No, it is a woman. But . . . she has not a bone in her body, I thought, watching Phoebe, for that was her name, coming across the beach. Then Alan got up and the shadow of Alan at once obliterated Phoebe. For Alan had views and Phoebe was quenched in the flood of his views. And then Alan, I thought, has passions; and here I turned page after page very fast, feeling that the crisis was approaching, and so it was. It took place on the beach under the sun. It was done very openly. It was done very vigorously.

Nothing could have been more indecent. But . . . I had said
"but" too often. One cannot go on saying "but." One must finish the sentence somehow, I rebuked myself. Shall I finish it,
"But—I am bored!" But why was I bored? Partly because of the
dominance of the letter "I" and the aridity, which, like the giant
beech tree, it casts within its shade. Nothing will grow there.
And partly for some more obscure reason. There seemed to be
some obstacle, some impediment of Mr. A's mind which
blocked the fountain of creative energy and shored it within
narrow lots. And remembering the lunch party at Oxbridge,
[. . .] it seemed possible that the impediment lay there. As he no
longer hums under his breath, "There has fallen a splendid tear
from the passionflower at the gate," when Phoebe crosses the
beach, and she no longer replies, "My heart is like a singing
bird whose nest is in a water'd shoot," when Alan approaches,
what can he do? Being honest as the day and logical as the sun,
there is only one thing he can do. And that he does, to do him
justice, over and over (I said, turning the pages) and over again.
And that, I added, aware of the awful nature of the confession,
seems somehow dull. Shakespeare's indecency uproots a thousand other things in one's mind, and is far from being dull. But
Shakespeare does it for pleasure; Mr. A, as the nurses say, does
it on purpose. He does it in protest. He is protesting against
the equality of the other sex by asserting his own superiority.
He is therefore impeded and inhibited and self-conscious as
Shakespeare might have been if he too had known Miss Clough
and Miss Davies.[8] Doubtless Elizabethan literature would have
been very different from what it is if the woman's movement
had begun in the sixteenth century and not in the nineteenth.

What, then, it amounts to, if this theory of the two sides
of the mind holds good, is that virility has now become self-

8. [Anne Clough, first principal of Newnham College, Cambridge; Emily Davies, pioneer in
   the movement to secure university education for women and chief founder of Girton
   College, Cambridge.]

conscious—men, that is to say, are now writing only with the male side of their brains. It is a mistake for a woman to read them, for she will inevitably look for something that she will not find. It is the power of suggestion that one most misses, I thought, taking Mr. B the critic in my hand and reading, very carefully and very dutifully, his remarks upon the art of poetry. Very able they were, acute and full of learning; but the trouble was that his feelings no longer communicated; his mind seemed separated into different chambers, not a sound carried from one to the other. Thus, when one takes a sentence of Mr. B into the mind it falls plump to the ground—dead; but when one takes a sentence of Coleridge into the mind, it explodes and gives birth to all kinds of other ideas, and that is the only sort of writing of which one can say that it has the secret of perpetual life.

But whatever the reason may be, it is a fact that one must deplore. For it means—here I had come to rows of books by Mr. Galsworthy and Mr. Kipling—that some of the finest works of our greatest living writers fall upon deaf ears. Do what she will a woman cannot find in them that fountain of perpetual life which the critics assure her is there. It is not only that they celebrate male virtues, enforce male values, and describe the world of men; it is that the emotion with which these books are permeated is to a woman incomprehensible. It is coming, it is gathering, it is about to burst on one's head, one begins saying long before the end. That picture will fall on old Jolyon's head; he will die of the shock; the old clerk will speak over him two or three obituary words; and all the swans on the Thames will simultaneously burst out singing. But one will rush away before that happens and hide in the gooseberry bushes, for the emotion which is so deep, so subtle, so symbolical to a man moves a woman to wonder. So with Mr. Kipling's officers who turn their backs; and his Sowers who sow the Seed; and his Men who are alone with their Work; and the Flag—one blushes at all these capital letters as if one had been caught eavesdropping at some purely masculine orgy. The fact is that neither Mr. Galsworthy nor Mr. Kipling has a spark of the woman in him. Thus all their qualities seem to a woman, if one may generalise, crude and immature. They lack suggestive power. And when a book lacks suggestive power, however hard it hits the surface of the mind it cannot penetrate within.

And in that restless mood in which one takes books out and puts them back again without looking at them I began to envisage an age to come of pure, of self-assertive virility, such as the letters of professors (take Sir Walter Raleigh's letters, for instance) seem to forebode, and the rulers of Italy have already brought into being. For one can hardly fail to be impressed in Rome by the sense of unmitigated masculinity; and whatever the value of unmitigated masculinity upon the state, one may question the effect of it upon the art of poetry. At any rate, according to the newspapers, there is a certain anxiety about fiction in Italy. There has been a meeting of academicians whose object it is "to develop the Italian novel." "Men famous by birth, or in finance, industry, or the Fascist corporations" came together the other day and discussed the matter, and a telegram was sent to the Duce expressing the hope "that the Fascist era would soon give birth to a poet worthy of it." We may all join in that pious hope, but it is doubtful whether poetry can come out of an incubator. Poetry ought to have a mother as well as a father. The Fascist poem, one may fear, will be a horrid little abortion such as one sees in a glass jar in the museum of some county town. Such monsters never live long, it is said; one has never seen a prodigy of that sort cropping grass in a field. Two heads on one body do not make for length of life.

However, the blame for all this, if one is anxious to lay blame, rests no more upon one sex than upon the other. All seducers and reformers are responsible, Lady Bessborough when she lied to Lord Granville; Miss Davies when she told the truth to Mr. Greg. All who have brought about a state of sex-consciousness are to blame, and it is they who drive me, when I want to stretch my faculties on a book, to seek it in that happy age, before Miss Davies and Miss Clough were born, when the writer used both sides of his mind equally. One must turn back to Shakespeare then, for Shakespeare was androgynous; and so was Keats and Sterne and Cowper and Lamb and Coleridge. Shelley perhaps was sexless. Milton and Ben Jonson had a dash too much of the male in them. So had Wordsworth and Tolstoy. In our time Proust was wholly androgynous, if not perhaps a little too much of a woman. But that failing is too rare for one to complain of it, since without some mixture of the kind the intellect seems to predominate and the other faculties of the mind harden and become barren. However, I consoled myself with the reflection that this is perhaps a passing phase; much of what I have said in obedience to my promise to give you the course of my thoughts will seem out of date; much of what flames in my eyes will seem dubious to you who have not yet come of age.

Even so, the very first sentence that I would write here, I said, crossing over to the writing table and taking up the page headed WOMEN AND FICTION, is that it is fatal for anyone who writes to think of their sex. It is fatal to be a man or woman pure and simple; one must be woman-manly or man-womanly. It is fatal for a woman to lay the least stress on any grievance; to plead even with justice any cause; in any way to speak consciously as a woman. And fatal is no figure of speech; for anything written with that conscious bias is doomed to death. It ceases to be fertilised. Brilliant and effective, powerful and masterly, as it may appear for a day or two, it must wither at nightfall; it cannot grow in the minds of others. Some collaboration has to take place in the mind between the woman and the man before the act of creation can be accomplished. Some marriage of opposites has to be consummated. The whole of the mind must lie wide open if we are to get the sense that the writer is communicating his experience with perfect fullness. There must be freedom and there must be peace. Not a wheel must grate, not a light glimmer. The curtains must be close drawn. The writer, I thought, once his experience is over, must lie back and let his mind celebrate its nuptials in darkness. He must not look or question what is being done. Rather, he must pluck the petals from a rose or watch the swans float calmly down the river. And

I saw again the current which took the boat and the undergraduate and the dead leaves; and the taxi took the man and the woman, I thought, seeing them come together across the street, and the current swept them away, I thought, hearing far off the roar of London's traffic, into that tremendous stream.

Here, then, Mary Beton ceases to speak. She has told you how she reached the conclusion—the prosaic conclusion—that it is necessary to have five hundred a year and a room with a lock on the door if you are to write fiction or poetry. She has tried to lay bare the thoughts and impressions that led her to think this. She has asked you to follow her flying into the arms of a Beadle,[9] lunching here, dining there, drawing pictures in the British Museum, taking books from the shelf, looking out of the window. While she has been doing all these things, you no doubt have been observing her failings and foibles and deciding what effect they have had on her opinions. You have been contradicting her and making whatever additions and deductions seem good to you. That is all as it should be, for in a question like this truth is only to be had by laying together many varieties of error. And I will end now in my own person by anticipating two criticisms, so obvious that you can hardly fail to make them.

No opinion has been expressed, you may say, upon the comparative merits of the sexes even as writers. That was done purposely, because, even if the time had come for such a valuation—and it is far more important at the moment to know how much money women had and how many rooms than to theorise about their capacities—even if the time had come I do not believe that gifts, whether of mind or character, can be weighed like sugar and butter, not even in Cambridge, where they are so adept at putting people into classes and fixing caps on their heads and letters after their names. I do not believe that even the Table of Precedency which you will find in Whitaker's

9. [A Beadle chased Mary Beton from the grass of the men's college.]

Almanac represents a final order of values, or that there is any sound reason to suppose that a Commander of the Bath will ultimately walk in to dinner behind a Master in Lunacy. All this pitting of sex against sex, of quality against quality; all this claiming of superiority and imputing of inferiority, belong to the private-school stage of human existence where there are "sides," and it is necessary for one side to beat another side, and of the utmost importance to walk up to a platform and receive from the hands of the Headmaster himself a highly ornamental pot. As people mature they cease to believe in sides or in Headmasters or in highly ornamental pots. At any rate, where books are concerned, it is notoriously difficult to fix labels of merit in such a way that they do not come off. Are not reviews of current literature a perpetual illustration of the difficulty of judgment? "This great book," "this worthless book," the same book is called by both names. Praise and blame alike mean nothing. No, delightful as the pastime of measuring may be, it is the most futile of all occupations, and to submit to the decrees of the measurers the most servile of attitudes. So long as you write what you wish to write, that is all that matters; and whether it matters for ages or only for hours, nobody can say. But to sacrifice a hair of the head of your vision, a shade of its colour, in deference to some Headmaster with a silver pot in his hand or to some professor with a measuring rod up his sleeve, is the most abject treachery, and the sacrifice of wealth and chastity which used to be said to be the greatest of human disasters, a mere fleabite in comparison.

Next I think that you may object that in all this I have made too much of the importance of material things. Even allowing a generous margin for symbolism, that five hundred a year stands for the power to contemplate, that a lock on the door means the power to think for oneself, still you may say that the mind should rise above such things; and that great poets have often been poor men. Let me then quote to you the words of your own Professor of Literature, who knows better than I do what goes to the making of a poet. Sir Arthur Quiller-Couch writes:

"What are the great poetical names of the last hundred years or so? Coleridge, Wordsworth, Byron, Shelly, Landor, Keats, Tennyson, Browning, Arnold, Morris, Rossetti, Swinburne—we may stop there. Of these, all but Keats, Browning, Rossetti were University men; and of these three, Keats, who died young, cut off in his prime, was the only one not fairly well-to-do. It may seem a brutal thing to say, and it is a sad thing to say: but, as a matter of hard fact, the theory that poetical genius bloweth where it listeth, and equally in poor and rich, holds little truth. As a matter of hard fact, nine out of those twelve were University men: which means that somehow or other they procured the means to get the best education England can give. As a matter of hard fact, of the remaining three you know that Browning was well-to-do, and I challenge you that, if he had not been well-to-do, he would no more have attained to write *Saul* or *The Ring and the Book* than Ruskin would have attained to writing *Modern Painters* if his father had not dealt prosperously in business. Rossetti had a small private income; and, moreover, he painted. There remains but Keats; whom Atropos slew young, as she slew John Clare in a madhouse, and James Thomson by the laudanum he took to drug disappointment. These are dreadful facts, but let us face them. It is—however dishonouring to us as a nation—certain that, by some fault in our commonwealth, the poor poet has not in these days, nor has had for two hundred years, a dog's chance. Believe me—and I have spent a great part of ten years in watching some three hundred and twenty elementary schools—we may prate of democracy, but actually, a poor child in England has little more hope than had the son of an Athenian slave to be emancipated into that intellectual freedom of which great writings are born."

Nobody could put the point more plainly. "The poor poet has not in these days, nor has had for two hundred years, a dog's chance. . . . a poor child in England has little more hope than had the son of an Athenian slave to be emancipated into that intellectual freedom of which great writings are born." That is it. Intellectual freedom depends upon material things.

Poetry depends upon intellectual freedom. And women have always been poor, not for two hundred years merely, but from the beginning of time. Women have had less intellectual freedom than the sons of Athenian slaves. Women, then, have not had a dog's chance of writing poetry. That is why I have laid so much stress on money and a room of one's own. However, thanks to the toils of those obscure women in the past, of whom I wish we knew more, thanks, curiously enough, to two wars, the Crimean which let Florence Nightingale out of her drawing room, and the European War which opened the doors to the average woman some sixty years later, these evils are in the way to be bettered. Otherwise you would not be here tonight, and your chance of earning five hundred pounds a year, precarious as I am afraid that it still is, would be minute in the extreme.

Still, you may object, why do you attach so much importance to this writing of books by women when, according to you, it requires so much effort, leads perhaps to the murder of one's aunts,[10] will make one almost certainly late for luncheon, and may bring one into very grave disputes with certain very good fellows? My motives, let me admit, are partly selfish. Like most uneducated Englishwomen, I like reading—I like reading books in the bulk. Lately my diet has become a trifle monotonous; history is too much about wars; biography too much about great men; poetry has shown, I think, a tendency to sterility, and fiction—but I have sufficiently exposed my disabilities as a critic of modern fiction and will say no more about it. Therefore I would ask you to write all kinds of books, hesitating at no subject however trivial or however vast. By hook or by crook, I hope that you will possess yourselves of money enough to travel and to idle, to contemplate the future or the past of the world, to dream over books and loiter at street corners and let the line of thought dip deep into the stream. For I am by no means confining you to fiction. If you would please me—and there are thousands like me—you would write books of travel and adven-

10. [Woolf is referring to Mary Beton's legacy.]

ture, and research and scholarship, and history and biography, and criticism and philosophy and science. By so doing you will certainly profit the art of fiction. For books have a way of influencing each other. Fiction will be much the better for standing cheek by jowl with poetry and philosophy. Moreover, if you consider any great figure of the past, like Sappho, like the Lady Murasaki, like Emily Brontë, you will find that she is an inheritor as well as an originator, and has come into existence because women have come to have the habit of writing naturally; so that even as a prelude to poetry such activity on your part would be invaluable.

But when I look back through these notes and criticise my own train of thought as I made them, I find that my motives were not altogether selfish. There runs through these comments and discursions the conviction—or is it the instinct?—that good books are desirable and that good writers, even if they show every variety of human depravity, are still good human beings. Thus when I ask you to write more books I am urging you to do what will be for your good and for the good of the world at large. How to justify this instinct or belief I do not know, for philosophic words, if one has not been educated at a university, are apt to play one false. What is meant by "reality"? It would seem to be something very erratic, very undependable—now to be found in a dusty road, now in a scrap of newspaper in the street, now in a daffodil in the sun. It lights up a group in a room and stamps some casual saying. It overwhelms one walking home beneath the stars and makes the silent world more real than the world of speech—and then there it is again in an omnibus in the uproar of Piccadilly. Sometimes, too, it seems to dwell in shapes too far away for us to discern what their nature is. But whatever it touches, it fixes and makes permanent. That is what remains over when the skin of the day has been cast into the hedge; that is what is left of past time and of our loves and hates. Now the writer, as I think, has the chance to live more than other people in the presence of this reality. It is his business to find it and collect it and communicate it to the rest of us. So at least I infer from reading *Lear* or *Emma* or *La recherche du temps perdu*. For the reading of these books seems to perform a curious couching operation on the senses; one sees more intensely afterwards; the world seems bared of its covering and given an intenser life. Those are the enviable people who live at enmity with unreality; and those are the pitiable who are knocked on the head by the thing done without knowing or caring. So that when I ask you to earn money and have a room of your own, I am asking you to live in the presence of reality, an invigorating life, it would appear, whether one can impart it or not.

Here I would stop, but the pressure of convention decrees that every speech must end with a peroration. And a peroration addressed to women should have something, you will agree, particularly exalting and ennobling about it. I should implore you to remember your responsibilities, to be higher, more spiritual; I should remind you how much depends upon you, and what an influence you can exert upon the future. But those exhortations can safely, I think, be left to the other sex, who will put them, and indeed have put them, with far greater eloquence than I can compass. When I rummage in my own mind I find no noble sentiments about being companions and equals and influencing the world to higher ends. I find myself saying briefly and prosaically that it is much more important to be oneself than anything else. Do not dream of influencing other people, I would say, if I knew how to make it sound exalted. Think of things in themselves.

And again I am reminded by dipping into newspapers and novels and biographies that when a woman speaks to women she should have something very unpleasant up her sleeve. Women are hard on women. Women dislike women. Women— but are you not sick to death of the word? I can assure you that I am. Let us agree, then, that a paper read by a woman to women should end with something particularly disagreeable.

But how does it go? What can I think of? The truth is, I often like women. I like their unconventionality. I like their subtlety. I like their anonymity. I like—but I must not run on in this way. That cupboard there—you say it holds clean table napkins only; but what if Sir Archibald Bodkin were concealed among them? Let me then adopt a sterner tone. Have I, in the preceding words, conveyed to you sufficiently the warnings and reprobation of mankind? I have told you the very low opinion in which you were held by Mr. Oscar Browning. I have indicated what Napoleon once thought of you and what Mussolini thinks now. Then, in case any of you aspire to fiction, I have copied out for your benefit the advice of the critic about courageously acknowledging the limitations of your sex. I have referred to Professor X and given prominence to his statement that women are intellectually, morally, and physically inferior to men. I have handed on all that has come my way without going in search of it, and here is a final warning—from Mr. John Langdon Davies. Mr. John Langdon Davies warns women "that when children cease to be altogether desirable, women cease to be altogether necessary." I hope you will make a note of it.

How can I further encourage you to go about the business of life? Young women, I would say, and please attend, for the peroration is beginning, you are, in my opinion, disgracefully ignorant. You have never made a discovery of any sort of importance. You have never shaken an empire or led an army into battle. The plays of Shakespeare are not by you, and you have never introduced a barbarous race to the blessings of civilisation. What is your excuse? It is all very well for you to say, pointing to the streets and squares and forests of the globe swarming with black and white and coffee-coloured inhabitants, all busily engaged in traffic and enterprise and lovemaking, we have had other work on our hands. Without our doing, those seas would be unsailed and those fertile lands a desert. We have borne and bred and washed and taught, perhaps to the age of six or seven years, the one thousand six hundred and twenty-three million human beings who are, according to statistics, at present in existence, and that, allowing that some had help, takes time.

There is truth in what you say—I will not deny it. But at the same time may I remind you that there have been at least two colleges for women in existence in England since the year 1866; that after the year 1880 a married woman was allowed by law to possess her own property; and that in 1919—which is a whole nine years ago—she was given a vote? May I also remind you that the most of the professions have been open to you for close on ten years now? When you reflect upon these immense privileges and the length of time during which they have been enjoyed, and the fact that there must be at this moment some two thousand women capable of earning over five hundred a year in one way or another, you will agree that the excuse of lack of opportunity, training, encouragement, leisure, and money no longer holds good. Moreover, the economists are telling us that Mrs. Seton has had too many children. You must, of course, go on bearing children, but, so they say, in twos and threes, not in tens and twelves.

Thus, with some time on your hands and with some book learning in your brains—you have had enough of the other kind, and are sent to college partly, I suspect, to be uneducated—surely you should embark upon another stage of your very long, very laborious, and highly obscure career. A thousand pens are ready to suggest what you should do and what effect you will have. My own suggestion is a little fantastic, I admit; I prefer, therefore, to put it in the form of fiction.

I told you in the course of this paper that Shakespeare had a sister; but do not look for her in Sir Sidney Lee's life of the poet. She died young—alas, she never wrote a word. She lies buried where the omnibuses now stop, opposite the Elephant and Castle. Now my belief is that this poet who never wrote a word and was buried at the crossroads still lives. She lives in you and in me, and in many other women who are not here tonight, for they are washing up the dishes and putting the children to bed. But she lives; for great poets do not die; they are continuing presences; they need only the opportunity to walk among us in the flesh. This opportunity, as I think, it is now coming within your power to give her. For my belief is that if we live another century or so—I am talking of the common life which is the real life and not of the little separate lives which we live as individuals—and have five hundred a year each of us and rooms of our own; if we have the habit of freedom and the courage to write exactly what we think; if we escape a little from the common sitting room and see human beings not always in their relation to each other but in relation to reality; and the sky, too, and the trees or whatever it may be in themselves; if we look past Milton's bogey, for no human being should shut out the view; if we face the fact, for it is a fact, that there is no arm to cling to, but that we go alone and that our relation is to the world of reality and not only to the world of men and women, then the opportunity will come and the dead poet who was Shakespeare's sister will put on the body which she has so often laid down. Drawing her life from the lives of the unknown who were her forerunners, as her brother did before her, she will be born. As for her coming without that preparation, without that effort on our part, without that determination that when she is born again she shall find it possible to live and write her poetry, that we cannot expect, for that would be impossible. But I maintain that she would come if we worked for her, and that so to work, even in poverty and obscurity, is worthwhile. ～

INTERPRETIVE QUESTIONS
FOR DISCUSSION

**According to Woolf, why are women in an inferior position
in society?**

1. Why does Woolf adopt the persona of a fictional woman she
   calls Mary Beton in order to argue her points?

2. Why is Woolf's persona, Mary Beton, able to begin making
   sense of the relationship between men and women when
   she acknowledges her anger? Why is she aware of "interest,
   confusion, amusement, boredom," but surprised by her
   anger? (129)

3. Why does Woolf include some positive, civilizing effects among
   the generally negative effects of women's serving as magnifying
   mirrors for men? Why does she acknowledge that "without that
   power probably the earth would still be swamp and jungle"?
   (133)

4. Does Woolf think the self-confidence necessary for success must
   be based on an illusion? (132–133)

5. Why doesn't Woolf blame men for women's inferior social
   position? Why does she assert that, because of instincts beyond
   our control, "Great bodies of people are never responsible for
   what they do"? (135)

6. Does Woolf think that men and women are inherently different?
   When she refers to the male "instinct for possession, the rage for
   acquisition," are we meant to think that women are naturally
   less acquisitive than men? (135–136)

7. Why does Woolf suggest that Mary Beton had to free herself from "pity and toleration" before she could think of things in themselves? Why is it desirable to be able to "think of things in themselves"? (136)

8. Why does Woolf suggest that when women are no longer the protected sex and take part in all occupations, they may become nearly extinct? (137)

9. Has Woolf, through Mary Beton's musings during her day at the British Museum, provided an answer to the question "Why are women poor"?

Suggested textual analysis
Pages 130–136: beginning, "Whatever the reason, all these books," and ending, "a view of the open sky."

In Woolf's view, why do women need to achieve intellectual independence before they can write fiction or poetry?

1. Why, according to Woolf, does intellectual independence require financial independence?

2. Why does Woolf consider the immaterial difficulties to be more formidable than the material difficulties that impede women's production of art? (147–148)

3. Why does Woolf counter Mr. Oscar Browning's low opinion of women's intellectual capacity by pointing to his lack of human feeling? (148–149)

4. Why, according to Woolf, are a lack of self-confidence and the resentment that accompanies it the greatest impediments to women's creation of art? (145)

5. What does Woolf mean when she says that writers, more than other people, are able to live in the presence of a reality which "fixes and makes permanent" whatever it touches? (165)

6. Why does Woolf think it is more important for women writers to "live in the presence of reality" and to "think of things in themselves" than to influence the world to higher ends? (166)

7. What does Woolf mean when she says that great works of literature allow one to see more intensely, so that the "world seems bared of its covering"? (166)

8. Why does Woolf emphasize the need for women writers to realize that their "relation is to the world of reality and not only to the world of men and women"? (169)

9. Why does Woolf think that Shakespeare's sister won't be born and write her poetry until she has a tradition of women writers to draw upon? Why doesn't it matter to Woolf if these predecessors are women who have worked in poverty and obscurity? (168–169)

Suggested textual analysis
Pages 165–169: from "But when I look back through these notes" to the end of the selection.

Why does Woolf insist that works of the imagination are created by "suffering human beings," and yet argue that the best art is impersonal?

1. In what sense does Woolf think that the best art reveals nothing of the writer? (151–152, 160)

2. Why does Woolf maintain that men and women are equally to blame for the present age of "sex-consciousness" and second-rate fiction? Why does she say that "all seducers and reformers" are responsible for having brought about this state of sex-consciousness? (159)

3. What does Woolf mean when she says that great minds, fully creative minds, are "androgynous"? (155, 159–160) What does she mean by an "incandescent" mind? (151–152, 155)

4. Why does Woolf insist that in order to create great art women must transcend any sense of personal grievance—that it is "fatal" for a woman "in any way to speak consciously as a woman"? (160)

5. Why does Woolf emphasize the need for inner harmony in the creating mind of the artist if a work is to be expressed completely? (151–152, 155, 160)

6. Is the transcendence of personality and sex that Woolf prescribes for the creation of great art consistent with her recommendation that women writers be themselves—that "it is much more important to be oneself than anything else"? (166)

7. Is Woolf's elevation of the virtue of impersonality in creating art in fact a prescription for female anonymity, for a retreat from public identity?

Suggested textual analysis
Pages 153–161: beginning, "The sight was ordinary enough;" and ending, "into that tremendous stream."

FOR FURTHER REFLECTION

1. Do you agree with Woolf that the greatest impediment to women's creation of great art is a lack of self-confidence and the resentment that accompanies it?

2. Is the best art impersonal?

3. Would Baldwin and Woolf agree that racism and sexism have the same psychological roots?

4. Do we now have a tradition of women writers sufficient for Shakespeare's sister to live and write her poetry?

5. Is Woolf too lenient with men when she concludes that their treatment of women is the result of faulty education and instincts which "are not in their control"?

6. Do you agree with Woolf that most men, in order to maintain the valuable quality of self-confidence, need to view women as inferior?

7. Do women still have more to overcome than men in becoming great artists?

A Dull Story

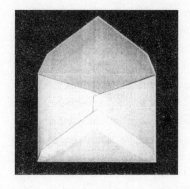

Anton Chekhov

ANTON CHEKHOV (1860–1904) was born
in Taganrog, Russia, to a grocer who had
been born a serf. At sixteen, Chekhov was
left to shift for himself when his father fled
to Moscow with the rest of the family after
going bankrupt. Chekhov finished his
schooling and moved to Moscow to study
medicine, selling short stories and comic
sketches to newspapers and magazines to
help support his family. By the time he took
his medical degree in 1884, writing had
become his main interest and occupation.
Having written most of his short stories by
his early thirties, Chekhov turned to writing
plays, several of which were produced with
great success by the Moscow Art Theater.
But Chekhov never fully left the medical
profession; known for his compassion and
humanitarianism, Chekhov helped to enact
social reforms in Russia and combated two
cholera epidemics. Just three years before
his death, Chekhov found love and married
the actress Olga Knipper, who played
leading roles in his dramas. Ravaged by
the tuberculosis he contracted in medical
school, Chekhov died at the age of
forty-four.

T
1

HERE LIVES in Russia a certain Honored Professor Nikolai Stepanovich, privy councilor and knight, who has received so many decorations, both Russian and foreign, that when he has occasion to wear them all, his students call him "the icon stand." He moves in the most aristocratic circles, and, for the last twenty-five or thirty years at least, there has not been a single eminent scholar with whom he has not been intimately acquainted. Now there is no one for him to be friends with, but if one speaks of the past, the long list of his distinguished acquaintances comes to an end with such names as Pirogov, Kalenin, and the poet Nekrasov, all of whom gave him the warmest and most sincere friendship. He is an honorary member of the faculty of every Russian university and of three universities abroad. And so forth and so on. All this, and a great deal more that might be said, constitutes what is called my "name."

This name of mine is well known. Every educated man in Russia is familiar with it, and abroad it is never mentioned in a lecture hall without adding the words "celebrated and esteemed." It is one of the few fortunate names which it is considered bad taste to take in vain, to abuse in public or in print. And that is as it should be. After all, my name is closely connected with the concept of a man who is famous, richly endowed, and unquestionably useful. I am as hard-working and persevering as a camel, and this is important; and I am gifted, which is even more important. Furthermore—and it may as well be said—I am an honest, well-bred, unassuming fellow. I have never poked my nose into literature or politics, never sought popularity by entering into polemics with ignoramuses, never made speeches at banquets or over the graves of my colleagues. . . . All things considered, my academic name is without blemish and beyond reproach. A fortunate name.

The bearer of this name, which is to say myself, appears to be a man of sixty-two, bald, with false teeth and an incurable tic. My person is as drab and ugly as my name is illustrious and beautiful. Both my head and my hands shake from weakness, my neck, as Turgenev says of one of his heroines, is like the finger board of a double bass, my chest is hollow, my shoulders narrow. When talking or lecturing, my mouth twists to one side, and when I smile my face is a mass of hoary, cadaverous wrinkles. There is nothing imposing about my miserable figure, except perhaps when I undergo a seizure of my tic, at which time a rather peculiar expression comes over my face that must suggest to anyone looking at me the grimly imposing thought: "This man, apparently, has not long to live."

I can still lecture fairly well; as in the past, I am able to hold the attention of my listeners for two consecutive hours. My fervor, humor, and command of language make the defects of my voice pass almost unnoticed, despite the fact that it is dry, cracked, and makes me sound like a canting Pharisee. But I write badly. That segment of my brain which directs the faculty of writing refuses to work. My memory is impaired, there is a lack of sequence in my thoughts, and when I set them down on paper it always seems to me that I have lost the knack of integrating them; the construction is monotonous, the sentences timid and insipid. I frequently write what I do not mean, and by the time I come to the end I have forgotten the beginning. Often I forget the simplest words and am continually forced to waste a great deal of time and energy trying to avoid superfluous phrases and unnecessary parenthetical clauses—both obvious signs of the decline of my mental processes. And it is remarkable that the simpler the letter, the greater the strain to write it. I feel far more fluent and intelligent writing a scientific article than a letter of congratulation or a report. And another thing: I find it easier to write in German or English than in Russian.

As regards my present way of life, I must note first of all insomnia, from which I have been suffering of late. If I were asked what now constitutes the chief and fundamental feature of my existence, I should answer: insomnia. As was my custom in the past, I undress and go to bed precisely at midnight. I fall asleep almost at once, but around two o'clock wake up feeling as if I had not slept. I have to get out of bed, light the lamp, and for an hour or two I pace the floor or contemplate the long-familiar photographs and pictures on my walls. When I tire of walking about, I sit down at my table. I sit motionless, thinking of nothing, desiring nothing; if a book lies before me, I automatically move it closer, and without any interest start reading it. In this way, quite mechanically and in a single night, I read an entire novel with the strange title *What the Swallow Sang*. I sometimes occupy my mind by counting to a thousand, or conjure up the face of one of my colleagues and try to recall in what year and in what circumstances he joined the faculty. I like listening to sounds. Two doors away, my daughter Liza sometimes mutters rapidly in her sleep; or my wife crosses the drawing room with a candle in her hand, invariably dropping the matchbox on the floor; or a warped cupboard creaks; or the lamp may suddenly begin to hiss, and these sounds for some reason move me.

Not to sleep at night is to be conscious of every minute that you are not normal, and for this reason I wait with impatience for morning to come, for daytime, when I have a right not to sleep. Many tedious hours pass before the cock crows in the yard. He is my first bearer of good tidings. As soon as I hear him I know that in an hour the hall porter will wake up and, coughing irascibly, come upstairs to fetch something. And gradually a pale light will appear in the windows, voices will be heard in the street. . . .

My day begins with the appearance of my wife. She comes into the room in her petticoat, before her hair has been done, but already washed and smelling of flower-scented eau de cologne; she looks as if she had come in by chance, and invariably says exactly the same thing.

"Excuse me, I've come only for a minute. . . . Have you had another bad night?"

Then she puts out the lamp, sits down at the table, and begins talking. I am no prophet, but I know in advance what she will say. Every morning the same thing. As a rule, following her anxious inquiries about my health, she abruptly brings up the subject of our son, an officer serving in Warsaw. We send him fifty rubles after the twentieth of every month—and this serves as our chief topic of conversation.

"Of course, it's hard for us," sighs my wife, "but until he is definitely on his feet, it is our duty to help him. The boy is in a strange place, his pay is low. . . . However, if you like, we can send him forty rubles next month instead of fifty. What do you think?"

Daily experience might have taught my wife that our expenses are not reduced by talking about them, but she is impervious to experience, and regularly, every morning, talks about our son, tells me that the price of bread, thank God, has gone down, while sugar has gone up two kopecks—and all with an air of conveying news.

I listen, automatically saying yes to everything, and, probably because I have not slept, I am possessed by strange and futile thoughts. I gaze at my wife in childish wonder. Bewildered, I ask myself: is it possible that this corpulent, ungainly old woman with the dull expression that comes of petty concerns and anxiety over her daily bread, with eyes dimmed by the perpetual brooding on debt and want, and who is capable of talking only of expenses, who smiles at nothing but lowered prices—is it really possible that this woman was once the slender Varya whom I so passionately loved for her fine clear mind, her pure soul, her beauty, and, as Othello loved Desdemona, "that she did pity me"? Is it possible that this is my wife Varya, who once bore me a son?

I gaze intently at the puffy face of this clumsy old woman, searching for my Varya in her, but nothing remains of the past except her anxiety over my health and her manner of calling my salary "our salary," and my cap "our cap." It is painful for me to look at her, but I try to humor her by letting her talk as much as she likes, saying nothing even when she criticizes people unjustly, or nags me for not publishing a textbook and not having a private practice.

Our conversations always end in the same way. Suddenly my wife is dismayed at remembering that I have not had my tea.

"What am I thinking of sitting here?" she exclaims, getting up. "The samovar has been on the table for ever so long, and here I sit chattering. Good heavens, how forgetful I'm becoming!"

She goes quickly to the door, then stops and says:

"You know, don't you, that we owe Yegor five months' wages? I don't know how many times I've told you that it doesn't do to let the servants' wages lapse. It's much easier to pay ten rubles every month than fifty rubles every five months!"

Once outside the door, she stops again to say:

"There's nobody I pity as I do our poor Liza. Studying at the conservatory the child is constantly in good society, and just look at the way she's dressed! It's a disgrace to appear in the street in such a fur coat. If she were anyone else's daughter it wouldn't matter, but everyone knows her father is a famous professor, a privy councilor!"

And having reproached me with my rank and reputation, she at last goes. This how my day begins. And it does not improve as it goes on.

While I am drinking my tea, my daughter Liza comes into the room in her fur coat and hat, carrying her music, and ready to go to the conservatory. She is twenty-two years old but looks younger, a handsome girl, rather like my wife in her youth. Kissing me tenderly on the forehead, then dropping a kiss on my hand, she says:

"Good morning, Papa! Are you well?"

As a child she was very fond of ice cream, and I often took her to the confectioner's. Ice cream was for her the gauge of excellence in everything. If she wanted to praise me, she would say: "Papa, you are creamy!" One little finger was called pistachio, another cream, another raspberry, and so on. When she used to come to my room to say good morning, I would take her on my knee, kiss her fingers, and say "Cream . . . pistachio . . . lemon . . ."

And I still kiss Liza's fingers in memory of those days, murmuring:

"Pistachio . . . cream . . . lemon . . ." but it isn't the same. I am cold as ice, and feel ashamed. When my daughter comes to me and touches my forehead with her lips, I start as if a bee had stung me, and with a forced smile turn my face away. Ever since I began suffering from insomnia, the thought sticks in my brain like a nail: my daughter often sees me, an elderly and celebrated man, blush painfully because of owing money to my footman; she sees how my anxiety over petty debts forces me to drop my work and spend hours pacing the floor and thinking—yet why is it she has never once come to me in secret and whispered: "Father, here is my watch, my bracelets, my earrings, my dresses—pawn them, you need money" . . . ? How is it, when she sees that her mother and I put ourselves in a false position in an effort to hide our poverty, that she does not relinquish the luxury of studying music? I would not accept her watch, her bracelets, the sacrifice of her lessons—God forbid! That is not what I want.

And this brings me to the thought of my son, an officer in Warsaw. He is an intelligent, honest, sober fellow. But that is not enough for me. I think that if I had an old father, and knew that there were moments when he was mortified by his poverty, I should give up my commission and hire myself out as a workman. Such thoughts about my children are poisoning me. And what good are they? Only a narrow-minded or embittered man harbors feelings of rancor against ordinary human beings because they are not heroes. But enough of this.

At a quarter to ten I must go and give a lecture to my dear boys. I dress and set off on a road I have known for thirty years, a road that has a history for me. There is the big gray house with the chemist's shop; here at one time stood a little house in which there was an alehouse, and it was in this alehouse that I thought out my dissertation and wrote my first love letter to Varya. I wrote it in pencil on a sheet of paper with the heading "Historia morbi." Over there is the grocer's shop, at one time kept by a little Jew who sold me cigarettes on credit, later by a stout woman who was fond of students because "every one of them has a mother," and now by a redheaded merchant, a stolid man who sits drinking tea out of a copper teapot. And here are the gloomy university gates, which have long been in need of repair, the bored yardman in his sheepskin, the broom, the heaps of snow. . . .

Such gates cannot produce a very salutary impression on a fresh young boy from the provinces who imagines that a temple of learning must really be a temple. In a history of Russian pessimism a prominent place among the predisposing causes would have to be given to the generally dilapidated state of university buildings, the gloominess of their corridors, the grimy walls, inadequate light, the dismal aspect of the staircases, cloakrooms, and benches. . . .

And there is our park. It seems to have grown neither better nor worse since my student days. I have never liked it. It would be far more sensible if, instead of emaciated lime trees, yellow acacias, and skimpy cropped lilacs, there were tall pines and great oaks. The student, whose state of mind in the majority of cases is influenced by his surroundings, should see before him only what is lofty, powerful, elegant. . . . The Lord preserve him from sickly trees, broken windowpanes, gray walls, and doors covered with torn oilcloth.

When I come to the wing where I work, the door is thrown open and I am met by my old fellow worker, contemporary, and namesake, the doorman Nikolai. As he lets me in, he clears his throat and says: "A frost, Your Excellency!" Or, if my fur coat is wet: "Rainy, Your Excellency!" Then he runs ahead of me to open all the doors on my way. In my office he carefully helps me off with my coat, and while doing so always manages to give me some item of university news. Thanks to the intimacy existing between all the university doormen and porters, he knows everything that goes on in all four faculties, the chancellor's office, the rector's study, and the library. There is nothing he does not know. When there is news such as the resignation of the rector or of one of the deans, I hear him in conversation with a young watchman naming all the candidates for the position, explaining that this one would not be approved by the minister, that one would himself refuse the post, then going into fabulous details about certain mysterious documents received in the chancellor's office, secret conversations said to have been held between the minister and one of the trustees, and so on. Apart from such details, he almost always turns out to be right. If you want to know in what year someone defended his dissertation, joined the university staff, retired, or died, you have only to draw on the vast memory of this veteran, and he will tell you the year, the month, and the day, and will further supply you with every detail of the circumstances accompanying the event. His is the memory of one who loves.

He is the guardian of university traditions. Having inherited from his predecessors a store of legends pertaining to university life, he has added to this wealth treasures of his own, amassed during years of service, and, should you wish, can relate many a tale, both long and short. He can tell of extraordinary sages who knew all there is to know, of remarkable workers who could go for weeks without sleep, of innumerable martyrs and victims of science; and good always triumphs over evil in these stories, the weak vanquish the strong, the wise man the fool, the humble the proud, the young the old. . . . There is no need to take all these legends and marvels at face value, but filter them, and the essentials remain: our splendid traditions and the names of the real heroes, recognized as such by all.

In our society all that is known of the academic world is summed up in anecdotes about the extraordinary absent-mindedness of old professors and a few witticisms variously ascribed to Gruber, myself, and Babukin. For the educated public this is not very much. If it loved science, learned men, and students as Nikolai does, our literature would long ago have been enriched by epics, biographies, and sayings, all of which, unfortunately, it now lacks.

After telling me the news, Nikolai's face takes on a solemn expression and we proceed to business. If an outsider were to hear how freely Nikolai uses our terminology, he might think him a scientist in disguise. As a matter of fact, rumors about the erudition of university watchmen are greatly exaggerated. It is true that Nikolai is familiar with more than a hundred Latin terms, knows how to put a skeleton together, occasionally prepares certain equipment, amuses the students with some lengthy scientific quotation, but such a relatively simple thing as the circulation of the blood, for instance, is as obscure to him today as it was twenty years ago.

Seated at a table in my office, bent low over a book or laboratory apparatus, is my prosecutor, Pyotr Ignatyevich, a modest, hard-working, but rather mediocre individual of thirty-five, already grown bald and paunchy. He works from morning till night, reads masses of material, and remembers absolutely everything he reads, which makes him worth his weight in gold to me; apart from this, he is a draft horse, in other words, a learned clod. The characteristic features of the draft horse, which distinguish him from the man of talent, are narrowness of vision and an extremely circumscribed specialization; outside his specialization he is as simple as a child.

I recall coming into my office one morning and saying: "Think what a misfortune! They say Skobelev is dead!" Nikolai crossed himself; but Pyotr Ignatyevich turned to me and asked: "Who's Skobelev?" Another time, somewhat earlier, I told him that Professor Perov had died. And my good Pyotr Ignatyevich asked: "What was his field?"

I believe that Patti herself might sing into his ear, a horde of Chinese invade Russia, or an earthquake occur, and he would not turn a hair, but would go on placidly squinting into his microscope. In a word, what's Hecuba to him? I'd give anything to see how this dry stick sleeps with his wife.

Another characteristic: his fanatical faith in the infallibility of science, and, above all, in anything written by a German. He is confident of himself and of his demonstrations, knows his goal in life, and is entirely immune to the doubts and disillusionments that turn a gifted man's hair gray. A slavish reverence for authority and a total lack of any need for independent thought. Hard to shake his convictions, and impossible to quarrel with him. How can you argue with a man who is firmly convinced that medicine is the very best of sciences, doctors the very best of men, and medical traditions the very best of all traditions that exist? Only one imperfect tradition has survived—the wearing of a white tie by doctors. For the scientist, for any educated man in fact, there can be only university traditions as a whole, with no differentiation between medicine, law, and so on, but you would have a hard time getting Pyotr Ignatyevich to agree with this; he would argue with you till doomsday.

His future is quite clear to me. He will do a few hundred impeccable dissections in the course of his lifetime, write numerous arid but tolerable papers, and make a dozen conscientious translations, but he will never set the world on fire—that requires imagination, originality, intuition, none of which he has. To put it briefly, he is not the master, but the servant, of science.

Pyotr Ignatyevich, Nikolai, and I speak in undertones. We are not quite at ease. Hearing the murmur of a sea of voices behind the door in the lecture hall gives rise to a peculiar feeling. In thirty years I have not grown accustomed to this sensation and experience it every morning. I nervously button my frock coat, ask Nikolai unnecessary questions, lose my temper. . . . Anyone would think I was afraid, but this is not fear, it is something else, something I can neither put a name to nor describe.

I needlessly look at my watch and say: "Well? Time to go in."

And we proceed in the following order: Nikolai goes first, carrying the apparatus or the charts, I follow him, and after me trudges the draft horse, with humbly hanging head; or, when required, a cadaver is carried in on a stretcher, followed by Nikolai, and so on. At my appearance the students rise, sit down again, and the sea of sound instantly subsides. A calm ensues.

I know what I am going to lecture on, but not how, nor where I shall begin and end. There is not a single ready-made phrase in my head. But I have only to look at my audience (ranged before me in the amphitheater) and pronounce the stereotyped phrase: "At our last lecture we stopped at . . ." and a long sequence of sentences pours from my soul—and I'm off!

I speak with irrepressible rapidity and fervor; there is no power on earth that can stem the flow of my speech. To lecture well, that is, with profit to your listeners and without boring them, requires not talent alone but experience and skill; you must have a thorough grasp of your subject and be in absolute control of your own powers and your audience. In addition to all this, you must keep your wits about you and never lose sight of the point in question for an instant.

A good conductor, conveying a composer's ideas, does twenty things at once: he follows the score, waves his baton, keeps an eye on the singers, makes a sign to the drums, the French horn, and so on. It is the same with me when lecturing. I see a hundred and fifty faces before me, each one different from the others, three hundred eyes staring into my face. My aim is to conquer this many-headed Hydra. If, at every moment I am lecturing, I have a clear conception of the degree of its attention and the measure of its comprehension, it is in my power. My other adversary resides within myself—it is the infinite variety of forms, phenomena, and laws, a great many of them conditioned by my own and others' thoughts.

At all times I must have the skill to pluck from this mass of material what is most important and essential and, keeping pace with my own speech, to present my thoughts in a form that is both accessible to the monster's mind and effective in rousing its interest; at the same time I must see to it that my ideas are presented not as they come to me, but in the order required for a proper composition of the picture I wish to paint.

Moreover, I endeavor to make my style literary, with sentences as simple and elegant as possible, and definitions brief and exact. I continually have to remind myself that I have only an hour and forty minutes at my disposal. In short, I must be scientist, teacher, orator all in one, and woe is me if the orator gets the upper hand of the teacher and scientist, or vice versa!

You lecture for a quarter of an hour, a half hour perhaps, and you begin to notice that the students are staring at the ceiling or at Pyotr Ignatyevich; one fumbles for his handkerchief, another shifts to a more comfortable position, a third smiles at his own thoughts. . . . This means that attention is flagging. Measures must be taken. At the first suitable opportunity I introduce a pun. All hundred and fifty faces smile broadly, eyes sparkle merrily, and a momentary murmur of the sea is heard. . . . I join in the laughter. Attention is revived and I can go on.

No scientific debate, no sort of game or entertainment, has ever given me so much pleasure as lecturing. Only then have I been able to abandon myself entirely to a passion, to have realized that inspiration is not an invention of the poets, but is real. And it seems to me that Hercules, after the most piquant of his exploits, never knew such voluptuous exhaustion as I have experienced after every lecture.

That is how it used to be. Now I experience nothing but torture when I lecture. Before half an hour has passed I begin to feel an overwhelming weakness in my legs and shoulders; I sit down, but am not accustomed to lecturing sitting down; a moment later I get up and go on, then sit down again. My mouth is dry, my voice grows husky, my head swims. . . . In an effort to conceal my condition from my audience I sip water, cough, blow my nose as if troubled by a cold, make irrelevant puns, and end by announcing the recess sooner than I ought to. But it is chiefly shame that I feel.

My conscience and my mind both tell me that the best thing I could do would be to deliver a farewell lecture to the boys, say my last word, give them my blessing, and yield my place to a younger, stronger man. But—God forgive me—I have not the courage to follow the dictates of my conscience.

Unfortunately, I am neither a philosopher nor a theologian. I know quite well that I have no more than six months to live; it would seem that now I ought to be concerned primarily with the mystery beyond the grave, with the visions that may visit me in my sepulchral sleep. But for some reason my soul declines to face these questions, though my mind acknowledges them as important. Now, on the threshold of death, the only thing that interests me is what interested me twenty or thirty years ago—science. Even as I breathe my last, I shall go on believing that science is the most important, most beautiful, most essential thing in the life of man, that it always has been and always will be the highest manifestation of love, that by means of it alone will man conquer nature and himself. It may be that this belief is naive and fundamentally incorrect, but I cannot help believing as I do, and for me to overcome this belief of mine would be impossible.

But this is not the point. I only ask indulgence for my weakness, and that it be understood that to sever a man from his professorship and pupils, when to him the destiny of bone marrow is of more interest than the ultimate purpose of the universe, would be tantamount to nailing him up in his coffin before he is dead.

Sleeplessness, and the consequent strain of trying to combat my increasing weakness, have caused something strange to happen to me. In the middle of the lecture tears suddenly choke me, my eyes begin to smart, and I have a passionate, hysterical desire to stretch out my arms and break into a loud lament. I feel like crying out in a loud voice that I, a famous man, have been sentenced by fate to capital punishment, that in six months or so another man will be holding sway in this lecture hall. I want to cry out that I have been poisoned; new thoughts, never before known to me, have poisoned the last days of my life and even now are stinging my brain like mosquitoes. At such moments my situation seems to me so horrifying that I want my listeners to be horrified, to leap from their seats panic-stricken, and rush to the exit with a desperate shriek.

It is not easy to get through such moments.

2

After the lecture I stay at home and work. I read journals, monographs, prepare my next lecture, and occasionally write something. I do not work uninterruptedly, as I am obliged to receive visitors.

The bell rings. A colleague has come to discuss a professional matter. He comes in, hat and stick in hand, holds them both out to me, and says:

"I've come only for a minute, only a minute! Sit down, *collega*! I just want a couple of words with you!"

We begin by trying to show each other how extraordinarily polite we are, and how absolutely delighted to see each other. I offer him a chair, he offers me a chair; we cautiously pat each other on the back, make tentative buttonholing gestures, as if trying to reach out to one another but afraid of burning our fingers. We both laugh, although nothing amusing has been said. Once seated, we lean toward each other and begin talking in subdued voices. However sincere our relations, we cannot refrain from gilding our conversation in the most Celestial Chinese manner: "as you have so justly observed," or "as I have once before had the honor to inform you," and never fail to laugh at each other's witticisms, no matter how unfortunate they may be. Our business concluded, my colleague abruptly rises, and, with a wave of his hat in the direction of my work, takes his leave. Again we start laughing and patting one another. I accompany him into the hall where I help him on with his coat, while he does his utmost to forestall this superlative honor. Then, when Yegor opens the front door for him, my friend assures me I will catch cold as I make a show of accompanying him out to the street. When at last I return to my room, my face goes on smiling—from inertia, I suppose.

A little later there is another ring. Someone is a long time removing his things and clearing his throat. Yegor announces that a student wishes to see me. I tell him to ask him to come in. A moment later a young man of pleasing appearance enters. For a year now there have been strained relations between this young man and me: he makes a deplorable showing on my examinations and I give him the lowest mark. Every year there are about seven of these young hopefuls whom, to use their language, I "kick out" or "flunk." Those of them who fail the examinations because of illness or inability, as a rule bear their cross with fortitude and do not try to bargain with me; the ones who do try, and who come to my house for this purpose, are the self-confident, easygoing types whose failure perhaps spoils their appetites or interferes with their regular attendance at the opera. I make allowances for the former, but the latter I pitch into throughout the entire year.

"Sit down," I say to my visitor. "What have you to say?"

"Excuse me for troubling you, professor . . . " he begins, stammering and not looking me in the eye. "I wouldn't have ventured to trouble you if it had not been for . . . Well, I've been up for your examinations five times now, and . . . and failed. I beg of you, please be so good as to give me a passing mark, because . . ."

The argument that all idlers produce in their own favor is the same: they have passed all their other examinations brilliantly and failed only mine, which is particularly surprising inasmuch as they have always studied my subject most assiduously and know it so very well, and if they have failed it must be owing to some unaccountable misunderstanding.

"Excuse me, my friend," I say to my visitor. "I cannot give you a passing mark. Go and read up on the lectures again, then come back, and we shall see."

A pause. I have an inclination to torment a student who prefers beer and opera to science, and remark with a sigh:

"In my opinion, the best thing for you to do now is to give up medicine altogether. If, with your abilities, you cannot manage to pass the examination, it is evident that you have neither the vocation nor the desire to become a doctor."

The face of this sanguine young man lengthens.

"Excuse me, professor," he says with a laugh, "but that would be odd, to say the least. After studying for five years, to suddenly—give up!"

"Not at all! Better to have lost five years than to spend the rest of your life in an occupation that doesn't appeal to you."

But the next moment I feel sorry for him and hasten to add: "However, you know best. Well, then, do a little studying and come back."

"When?" the young idler asks in a hollow voice.

"Whenever you like. Tomorrow if you are ready."

In his good-natured eyes I read: "I can come all right, but you'll flunk me again, and you know it, you swine!"

"Of course," I add, "it won't make you any more erudite to take my examination another fifteen times, but it will develop your character. That's something to be thankful for."

A silence follows. I get up and wait for my visitor to go, but he stands staring at the window, plucking at his beard and thinking. This becomes boring.

The voice of this sanguine young man is agreeably mellow, his eyes intelligent and mocking, but his genial face looks a little blowzy from frequent indulgence in beer and prolonged repose on the sofa; no doubt he could tell me a great many things about the opera, the company he keeps, his amorous adventures, but, unfortunately, such conversations are hardly appropriate, or I should gladly have listened.

"Professor! I give you my word of honor that if you pass me, I'll . . . "

When matters reach the word of honor stage, I wave my hands and sit down at my desk. The student ponders for a moment and says dejectedly:

"In that case, good-bye. . . . Excuse me. . . ."

"Good-bye, my friend. Good luck to you."

He irresolutely goes out to the hall, slowly puts on his coat, and leaves, probably still pondering. Having dismissed me from his thoughts with "That old devil!" he goes off to some miserable restaurant to drink beer and eat dinner, then home to sleep. Peace to thy ashes, honest toiler!

A third ring. In comes a young doctor wearing a new black suit, gold-rimmed spectacles, and, of course, a white tie. He introduces himself. I invite him to sit down and ask what I can do for him. This young priest of science begins by telling me, not without emotion, that he passed his doctor's examination this year, and now has only to write his dissertation. He would like to work with me, under my guidance, and would be infinitely obliged if I would supply him with a subject for his thesis.

"I should be happy to be of service to you, *collega*," I say, "but let us come to an understanding as to the meaning of a dissertation. The word is generally taken to mean a work that is the product of independent creative effort. Is that not so? Anything written on another man's theme and under his guidance is called something else. . . ."

The aspirant makes no reply. I become incensed and jump up from my chair.

"Why is it that you all come to me, I'd like to know?" I shout angrily. "Do you think I keep a shop? I'm not dealing in themes. For the thousandth time, I ask you all to leave me in peace! Excuse me if I seem rude, but after all, I'm fed up with this!"

The aspirant continues to remain silent, but a faint flush appears in the region of his cheekbones. His face expresses a profound respect for my great name and learning, but his eyes reveal his contempt for my voice, my pitiful figure, and my nervous gestures. In my anger I impress him as being merely odd.

"I don't keep a shop!" I repeat angrily. "And this is an amazing thing! Why don't you want to be independent? Why is freedom so odious to you?"

I go on and on, and he says not one word. Gradually I calm down and, of course, give in. He gets his theme from me, though it's not worth much, writes—under my supervision—a dissertation that will be of no use to anyone, and defends it in a dreary debate to receive a degree that will be of no use to him.

The bell goes on ringing endlessly, but I shall confine myself to describing the first four callers. When it rings for a fourth time, I hear familiar footsteps, the rustle of a dress, a voice I love. . . .

Eighteen years ago a friend of mine, an oculist, died, leaving a seven-year-old daughter, Katya, and about sixty thousand rubles. In his will he appointed me her guardian. She lived with us till she was ten, then was sent to boarding school and was at home only during the summer holidays. I had no time to look after her upbringing, took notice of her only sporadically, and consequently can say very little about her childhood.

My earliest memory concerning her, and one that I hold dear, is the extraordinary trustfulness she displayed on coming into my home, and later in allowing herself to be treated by doctors—a trustfulness that always lit up her little face. She might be sitting apart, with a bandaged cheek, but she never failed to take a lively interest in whatever was going on around her; whether she watched me writing or leafing through a book, my wife bustling about the house, the cook peeling potatoes, or the dog frolicking, her eyes invariably expressed the same thought: "Everything that happens in this world is wise and wonderful." She was extremely curious and loved talking to me. Sometimes she would sit at the table opposite me, following my movements and asking questions. She wanted to know what I was reading, what I did at the university, whether I was not afraid of dead bodies, what I did with my salary.

"Do the students fight at the university?" she would ask.

"Yes, darling, they do."

"And do you make them stand in the corner?"

"I do."

And she thought it so funny that university students fought and were made to stand in the corner that she burst out laughing. She was a gentle, patient, good child. More than once I saw something taken away from her, saw her unjustly punished, or her curiosity left unsatisfied; at such times a look of sadness mingled with the invariable expression of confidence in her face—but that was all. I did not know how to defend her, but when I saw her sadness, I felt like drawing her close to me and consoling her like an old nurse: "My dear little orphan!"

I also remember that she loved dressing nicely and sprinkling herself with perfume. In this respect she was like me. I too like fine clothes and good scent.

I regret that I had neither the time nor the inclination to follow the rise and development of what became Katya's ruling passion from the time she was fourteen or fifteen years old. I refer to her ardent love for the theater. When she came home from boarding school for the summer, there was nothing she talked of with such eagerness and pleasure as plays and actors; she wore us out with her incessant chatter about the theater. My wife and children would not listen to her. I was the only one who had not the heart to deny her my attention. When she felt a desire to share her enthusiasm with someone, she would come into my study and in a beseeching voice say to me:

"Nikolai Stepanych, do let me talk to you about the theater!"

I would point to the clock and say: "I'll give you half an hour—go ahead!"

Soon she was bringing home dozens of pictures of actors and actresses she adored, later she tried her hand at amateur the-atricals, and finally, when she had finished school, she came to me and announced that she was born to be an actress.

I never shared Katya's enthusiasm for the theater. In my opinion, if a play is good, you don't need actors to produce the desired effect: just reading it is enough. And if the play is poor, then no acting can make it good.

In my youth I often went to the theater, and now my family takes a box twice a year and carries me off for an "airing." This, of course, does not entitle me to be a judge of the theater, so I will say very little about it. In my opinion, the theater is no better today than it was thirty or forty years ago. Now as then I can never find a decent glass of water in the corridors or foyers. The cloakroom attendants, as in the past, fine me twenty kopecks for my coat, though there would seem to be nothing reprehensible in wearing warm clothes in winter. Also as in the past, and for no reason whatsoever, music is played during the intermissions, which adds something new and uncalled-for to the impression made by the play, and men still go to the buffet to drink. If there is no progress to be seen in these minor matters, it would be futile to look for it in the essentials.

When an actor, cloaked from head to foot in theatrical traditions and conventions, tries to recite a simple ordinary monologue like "To be or not to be" with the inevitable hissing and contortions of the body, or when he tries to convince me by every means that Chatsky—who spends all his time talking with fools and is in love with a fool—is an exceedingly clever man, and that *Woe from Wit* is not a dull play, then the stage smells of the same routine that bored me forty years ago, when I was regaled with classical wailing and breast-beating. And I leave the theater every time a greater conservative than I entered it.

The credulous and sentimental public may be persuaded that the theater in its present form is a school, but anyone who is acquainted with a school in its true sense will not swallow that bait. I do not know how it will be fifty or a hundred years from now, but in its present condition the theater can serve as nothing but entertainment. And this entertainment is far too costly for us to go on enjoying it. It robs the state of thousands of gifted, healthy young men and women who, if they had not dedicated themselves to the theater, might have been good doctors, farmers, schoolteachers, officers; it robs the public of its evening hours— the best time for intellectual work and conversations with friends. Not to mention the financial waste or the moral damage inflicted on the spectator by seeing murder, adultery, and slander erroneously interpreted on the stage.

Katya, however, was of quite a different opinion. She assured me that the theater, even in its present state, was superior to the lecture hall, to books, to everything in the world. It was a force uniting within itself all the arts, and actors were its missionaries. No art or science by itself was capable of exercising so positive and powerful an effect on the human spirit as the stage, and it was not without reason that even a mediocre actor was more popular than the greatest scientist or painter. No other public activity was able to afford such gratification and enjoyment as the theater.

One fine day Katya joined a theatrical troupe and went away, to Ufa, I believe, taking with her a large sum of money, a multitude of rainbow-tinted hopes, and a very aristocratic view of her work.

Her first letters, written on the road, were wonderful. I read them and was simply amazed that those small sheets of paper could contain so much youth, purity of spirit, and blessed innocence, combined with a subtle, practical judgment that would have done credit to a first-class masculine mind. The Volga, nature, the towns she visited, her companions, her failures and successes, were not so much described as celebrated; every line breathed the confidence I was accustomed to reading in her face—but with all that, there were countless grammatical errors and scarcely any punctuation whatsoever.

Before six months had passed, I received a highly poetical, rapturous letter beginning with the words: "I have fallen in love." The letter was accompanied with a photograph of a clean-shaven young man in a broad-brimmed hat and a plaid flung over one shoulder. The letters that followed were as marvelous as before, but punctuation marks began to make their appearance, mistakes in grammar disappeared, and there was a strong smack of masculinity about them.

Katya now wrote about how splendid it would be to build a big theater somewhere on the Volga, by forming a partnership, of course, and attracting the wealthy merchants and shipowners to the enterprise; there would be plenty of money, the box office receipts would be enormous, actors would work on a cooperative basis. . . . This might be all very well, I told myself; but such schemes could originate only in the mind of a man.

However that may have been, for a year and a half everything seemed to go well: Katya was in love, believed in her work, and was happy; but then I commenced to notice obvious signs of a decline. It began with her complaining to me of her companions—this was the first and most ominous symptom; if a young scientist or writer begins his career by complaining bitterly of scientific or literary men, it is a sure sign that he is enervated and not fit for his work. Katya wrote that her comrades failed to attend rehearsals and never knew their parts, that the absurdity of the plays produced and the way the actors conducted themselves on the stage showed the utmost contempt for the audience; that in the interests of box office receipts, which was all they talked of, dramatic actresses degraded themselves by singing chansonettes, tragedians sang comic songs making fun of deceived husbands and the pregnancy of unfaithful wives, and so on. In fact, it was a wonder the provincial theater had survived and could still maintain itself in this meager and corrupt vein.

In reply I sent Katya a long and, I must confess, boring letter. Among other things I wrote:

"I have not infrequently had occasion to have long talks with old actors, men of the very highest principles, who have been good enough to bestow their affection on me; from my conversations with them I could see that their occupation is governed not so much by their own reason and choice as by fashion and the disposition of the public; the best of them in their time have been obliged to play not only in tragedies, but in operettas,

French farces, and pantomimes, and in every case they have been equally certain that they were getting ahead and being of use. So, as you see, the root of the evil must be sought not in the actor, but deeper, in the art itself, and in the attitude of society to it."

This letter of mine only irritated Katya, and she replied:

"We are talking at cross-purposes. I was not writing to you about the high-principled men who bestowed their affection on you, but about a band of adventurers who have no principles whatever—a horde of savages who have gone on the stage only because they wouldn't have been accepted anywhere else, and who call themselves artists out of sheer insolence. Not one of them is talented; they are a lot of mediocrities, drunkards, schemers, and backbiters. I cannot tell you how bitter it makes me to see that the art I love so much has fallen into the hands of people I detest; how bitter, too, that the best men view this evil only from a distance, not caring to come closer, and instead of taking one's part, write heavy-handed commonplaces and utterly superfluous sermons. . . ."

And so on in the same style.

A short time elapsed, and I received the following letter:

"I have been brutally deceived. I cannot go on living. Dispose of my money as you see fit. I have loved you as my father and my only friend. Good-bye."

And it turned out that *he* too belonged to the "horde of savages." Later I gathered from certain hints that there had been an attempt at suicide. It appeared that Katya had tried to poison herself. She must have been seriously ill after this, for the next letter I received was from Yalta, where in all probability she had been sent by a doctor. Her last letter contained a request to send her a thousand rubles as quickly as possible, and ended with the words:

"Forgive me if my letter is gloomy. Yesterday I buried my child."

After living in the Crimea for nearly a year, she returned home.

She had been away for about four years, and during all that time, I must admit, I had played a strange and not very admirable role with regard to her. Earlier, when she announced her intention of going on the stage, when she wrote me of her love, had periodic fits of extravagance and demanded that I send her now a thousand, now two thousand rubles, then wrote me of her wish to die and later of the death of her child, on each occasion I had lost my head, and my concern for her fate was expressed only in thinking about her and writing long, boring letters. And yet, I had taken the place of her father, and loved her like a daughter.

Now Katya lives not half a verst from me. She has rented a five-room apartment and installed herself quite comfortably in a style all her own. If anyone were to paint a picture of her surroundings, the predominant mood of the painting would have to be indolence. Soft couches and soft ottomans for an indolent body, soft rugs for indolent feet, pale, drab, faded colors for indolent eyes, for the indolent soul a profusion of cheap fans strewn over the walls along with trivial pictures in which originality of execution prevails over content, an abundance of little tables and shelves covered with utterly useless worthless objects, and anomalous scraps of material in place of curtains. . . . All this in combination with an avoidance of bright colors, symmetry, and space, reveals not only laziness, but a perversion of natural taste. Katya lies on a couch for whole days reading—mostly novels and short stories. She goes out of the house only once a day, in the afternoon, to come and see me.

I go on working and Katya sits not far from me on the sofa, wrapped in a shawl as if she were cold. Either because I am fond of her, or because I grew accustomed to her frequent visits when she was a little girl, her presence does not prevent me from concentrating. From time to time I mechanically ask her a question and she gives me a brief reply; or, to relax for a moment, I turn and watch her dreamily looking through a medical journal or newspaper. At such moments I observe that her face has lost its former trusting look. Her expression is cold, apathetic, abstracted, like the faces of travelers who have had to wait a long time for a train. She still dresses beautifully and simply, but has grown careless; it is clear that her dress and hair owe something of their appearance to her habit of lolling in rocking chairs or lying about on couches all day. And she has lost her curiosity and never asks questions, as if, having experienced everything in life, she no longer expects to hear anything new.

About four o'clock there begin to be sounds of activity in the hall and drawing room. This means that Liza has come back from the conservatory and brought some of her girlfriends with her. We hear them playing the piano, singing a note or two, and laughing; in the dining room Yegor is setting the table with a clatter of dishes.

"Good-bye," says Katya. "I won't go in and see them today. They must excuse me. I have no time. Come and see me."

I go to the door with her and she inspects me severely from head to foot, remarking with vexation:

"You keep getting thinner and thinner! Why don't you consult a doctor? I'm going to see Sergei Fyodorovich and ask him to have a look at you."

"There's no need, Katya."

"I can't understand what your family can be thinking of! They're a fine lot, I must say!"

She pulls on her coat with a jerk, and two or three hairpins, as usual, fall from her carelessly arranged hair. She is too lazy or in too great a hurry to set it to rights and clumsily pushes the falling curls under her hat and leaves.

When I go into the dining room, my wife asks:

"Wasn't that Katya with you just now? Why didn't she come in to see us? That's really very odd. . . ."

"Mama!" Liza says to her reproachfully. "If she doesn't care to come in, let her go. We don't have to go down on our knees to her."

"Well, in any case, it's very rude. To sit there in the study for three hours and never give a thought to us! But then, she must do as she pleases, of course."

Both Varya and Liza hate Katya. This hatred is incomprehensible to me; one would probably have to be a woman to understand it. I am ready to swear that of the hundred and fifty young men I see every day in my lecture hall, and of the hundreds of elderly men I meet in the course of the week, hardly one could be found who would be able to comprehend this hatred and repugnance for Katya's past—for the fact that she bore a child out of wedlock, for the illegitimate child itself; and at the same time I cannot think of a single woman or girl of my acquaintance who, consciously or unconsciously, would not harbor the same feeling. And this is not because women are any purer or more virtuous than men: after all, purity and virtue are not very different from vice if they are tinged with malice. I simply attribute it to the backwardness of women. The melancholy feeling of compassion and the pangs of conscience experienced by the modern man at the sight of misfortune is to my mind far greater proof of culture and moral development than hatred and disgust. Modern women are just as lachrymose and callous as were women in the Middle Ages. And in my opinion those who advocate giving women the same education as men are right.

My wife also dislikes Katya for having been an actress, for her ingratitude, her pride, her eccentricity, for all those countless vices that one woman can always find in another.

Besides the family and two or three of Liza's girlfriends, her admirer and suitor, Aleksandr Adolfovich Gnekker, is dining with us. He is a fair-haired young man, not over thirty, of medium height, stout, broad-shouldered, with reddish whiskers and a little waxed mustache that gives his smooth plump face a doll-like expression. He wears an extremely short jacket, a flowered waistcoat, checked trousers that are very wide at the top, very narrow at the bottom, and tan shoes without heels. He has the bulging eyes of a crayfish, wears a tie that looks like the tail of a crayfish, and it seems to me that this young man even gives off a smell of crayfish soup. He visits us daily, but no one in the

family knows anything about his origins, where he was educated, or what he lives on. He neither plays nor sings, but has
some connection with music and singing, sells mysterious grand
pianos to mysterious customers, goes frequently to the conservatory, is acquainted with all the celebrities, and has something
to do with concerts; his judgments on music are delivered with
great authority, and I observe that everyone is eager to agree
with him.

Rich people always have their hangers-on, and it is the same
with the arts and sciences. I don't suppose that any one of the
arts or sciences anywhere in the world is free from such "foreign
bodies" as this Mr. Gnekker. I am not a musician, and perhaps
I am mistaken about Gnekker, whom, moreover, I hardly know,
but the air of authority, the dignity with which he stands at the
piano and listens when anyone plays or sings, look very suspicious to me.

You may be a gentleman a hundred times over, and a privy
councilor, but nothing can save you from that atmosphere of
middle-class vulgarity which courting, matchmaking, and wed-
dings insinuate into your home and state of mind. I can never
reconcile myself, for instance, to the expression of triumph on
my wife's face whenever Gnekker visits us, or to the bottles of
Lafitte, port, and sherry that are brought out, only on his
account, so that he may see for himself the lavish and luxurious
scale on which we live. Nor can I endure the staccato laugh that
Liza has picked up at the conservatory, or her way of screwing
up her eyes when there are men present. But above all I cannot
for the life of me understand why it is that a creature who is
utterly alien to my habits, my profession, my whole way of life,
who is totally different from the sort of people I like, should
come to my house every day, and dine with me every day.
My wife and the servants whisper mysteriously that "he is a
suitor," but I still can't make out why he should be here; his
presence arouses in me the same perplexity I should feel if they
were to set a Zulu next to me at the table. And it also seems

strange to me that my daughter, whom I am accustomed to look on as a child, should love that necktie, those eyes, those pudgy cheeks. . . .

In the old days I would either enjoy my dinner or be indifferent to it; now it induces in me nothing but boredom and irritation. Ever since I became an "Excellency" and was made a dean of faculty, my family has, for some reason, found it necessary to make a complete change in our menu and dining habits. Instead of the simple dishes I was in the habit of eating when I was a student and in practice, I am now fed soup purée with some sort of stalactites floating in it, and kidneys in Madeira sauce. My rank and fame have deprived me forever of cabbage soup and little savory pies, of goose with apple sauce, of bream with buckwheat. They also have deprived me of the housemaid Agasha, a garrulous, laughter-loving old woman in whose place the pompous, dull-witted Yegor now serves dinner with a white glove on his right hand. The intervals between courses are shorter, but seem inordinately long because of being so empty. Gone is the gaiety of the old days, the spontaneous talk, the jokes and laughter, all the mutual affection and joy that used to animate my wife and children when we came together at the table. For a busy man like me, dinner was a time of relaxation and reunion, and for my wife and children a festivity—brief, it is true, but bright and gay—when they knew that for half an hour I belonged, not to science and my students, but to them alone. Gone forever the feeling of exhilaration from one glass of wine, gone Agasha, buckwheat and bream, and the uproar that greeted every little dinner-table drama such as the cat and dog fighting under the table, or Katya's bandage falling into the soup.

To describe our dinners nowadays would be as unappetizing as to eat them. Along with her usual worried look, my wife's face wears an expression of triumph and ostentatious dignity. She glances uneasily at our plates and says: "I see you don't like the meat. Tell me: you really don't care for it, do you?" And I have to reply: "There's nothing to be concerned about, my dear, the meat is delicious." Then she says: "You're always trying to spare my feelings, Nikolai Stepanych, and you never tell me the truth. . . . And why is Aleksandr Adolfovich eating so little?" This goes on throughout the entire meal. Liza breaks into her staccato laugh and screws up her eyes. I look from one to the other, and only now, at the dinner table, does it become clear to me that long ago their inner lives slipped from my control. I feel as if there had once been a time when I lived in my own home with a real family, and that now I am dining in the home of an unreal wife, looking at an unreal Liza. A startling change has taken place in both of them; somehow I failed to observe the long process that produced this change—no wonder I am unable to understand it. Why did the change take place? I do not know. Perhaps the real trouble is that God did not endow my wife and daughter with the same strength He gave to me. Since childhood I have accustomed myself to resist external influences, have steeled myself against them; such catastrophes as fame, high rank, the transition from mere sufficiency to living beyond one's means, acquaintance with celebrities and so on, have scarcely touched me. I have remained intact and unharmed; but all this has fallen like an avalanche on my wife and daughter, weak and undisciplined as they are, and has crushed them.

Gnekker and the young ladies discuss fugues, counterpoint, singers, pianists, Bach, and Brahms, while my wife—lest she be suspected of musical ignorance—smiles sympathetically and murmurs: "Delightful . . . Really? . . . You don't say so! . . ." And Gnekker gravely eats, gravely jests, and listens condescendingly to the young ladies' remarks. Every now and then he has an urge to speak bad French, and then, for some reason, he finds it necessary to call me *"Votre Excellence."*

And I am morose. Evidently they put me under constraint and I put them under constraint. Never before have I had any personal experience of class antagonism, but now I am tormented by the thought that someone outside my own circle should be sitting here as my daughter's suitor. His presence has a bad influence on me in another respect. Generally, when I am alone or in the society of people I like, I never think of my own achievements, or if I should happen to give them a momentary thought, they appear as trifling as if I had become a qualified scientist only yesterday; but in the company of people like Gnekker they seem to tower like mountain peaks that disappear into the clouds, while down below the Gnekkers are shuffling about, barely visible to the naked eye.

After dinner I return to my study and smoke a pipe, the only one of the entire day, sole relic of my former filthy habit of smoking from morning to night. While I am smoking my wife comes in and sits down to have a talk with me. And, as in the morning, I know beforehand what the conversation will be.

"I must talk to you seriously, Nikolai Stepanych," she begins. "It's about Liza. . . . Why don't you show any interest?"

"In what?"

"You pretend not to notice anything . . . it's not right. It's simply impossible to go on being so unconcerned. . . . Gnekker has intentions with regard to Liza. . . . What do you think about it?"

"That he is no good, I cannot say, because I don't know him, but that I do not like him—I've already told you a thousand times."

"This is impossible . . . impossible. . . ."

She gets up and paces the floor in agitation.

"It's just impossible to take that attitude to such a serious matter . . ." she says. "When it's a question of your daughter's happiness, all personal considerations should be set aside. I know you don't like him. . . . Very well, then . . . suppose we refuse him now, break it off—how can you be sure that Liza will not hold it against us for the rest of her life? Suitors are not so plentiful nowadays, goodness knows, and it may very well happen that no one else will turn up. . . . He's terribly in love with Liza, and as far as I can see she likes him too. . . . Of course, he has no settled position, but that can't be helped. Please God, in time he'll get established somewhere. He comes of a good family and is rich."

"Where did you learn that?"

"He told me. His father has a big house in Kharkov and an estate in the neighborhood. So, you see, Nikolai Stepanych, you absolutely must go to Kharkov."

"What for?"

"You can make inquiries. . . . You know some of the professors there, they'll help you. I'd go myself, but I am a woman. I can't. . . ."

"I am not going to Kharkov," I say glumly.

My wife is appalled; an expression of extreme anguish comes over her face.

"For God's sake, Nikolai Stepanych!" she implores me, sobbing. For God's sake, relieve me of this burden! I am suffering!"

It pains me to look at her.

"Very well, Varya," I say kindly. "I'll go to Kharkov if you want me to, and do all that you wish."

She presses her handkerchief to her eyes and goes off to her room to cry. I am left alone.

Soon a lamp is brought in. The armchairs and lampshade cast the same old tiresome shadows on the walls and floor and the sight of them makes me feel as though night had come and now my accursed insomnia would begin. I lie down on the bed, get up and walk about the room, lie down again. . . . As a rule it is after dinner, at the approach of evening, that my nervous tension reaches its highest pitch.

I begin crying for no reason, and bury my head in the pillow. At such moments I am afraid someone may come in, afraid I may suddenly die; I am ashamed of my tears, and something altogether unendurable prevails in my soul. I feel that I can no longer bear the sight of my lamp, my books, the shadows on the floor; I cannot bear the sound of the voices coming from the drawing room. Some incomprehensible, unseen force is violently pushing me out of the house. I leap up, hastily put on my hat and coat, and go out, taking every precaution not to be observed by any member of the household. But where am I to go?

The answer to this question has long been in my mind: to Katya.

3

I generally find her lying on a Turkish couch or sitting on an ottoman reading. When she sees me, she raises her head languidly, sits up, and holds out her hand.

"Lolling about as usual . . ." I say, after pausing to recover my breath. "It's bad for you. You ought to find something to do!"

"Hm?"

"I say you ought to find something to do."

"What? There's nothing a woman can do but be a simple worker or an actress."

"Well? If you can't be a worker, then be an actress."

She says nothing.

"You ought to get married," I say, half in jest.

"There's no one to marry. And no reason to, either."

"You can't live like this."

"Without a husband? A lot that matters! I could have as many men as I like, if that were what I wanted."

"That's ugly, Katya."

"What's ugly?"

"What you just said."

Seeing that she has upset me, and wishing to smooth over the disagreeable impression she has made, Katya says:

"Come with me. Come . . . this way. . . . Here."

She leads me into a cozy little room, and, pointing to a writing table, says:

"There you are. . . . I prepared this for you. You shall work here. Come every day and bring your work. They don't let you work in peace at home. Will you work here? Would you like to?"

Not to wound her by refusing, I tell her that I will and that I like the room very much. Then we sit down in the comfortable little room and begin talking.

Warm cozy surroundings and the presence of a sympathetic person no longer arouse in me the feeling of gratification they once did, but are a powerful incentive to grumbling and complaining. I somehow feel that if I fret and indulge in a little self-pity, I will feel better.

"Things are in a bad way with me, my dear," I begin, sighing deeply. "Very bad."

"What's the matter?"

"You see, dear, it's like this. . . . The highest and most sacred prerogative of kings is the right to pardon. And I have always felt myself a king, for I have made unlimited use of this right. I have never judged, but have always been indulgent, showering my pardons right and left. Where others have protested or expressed indignation, I have merely counseled and persuaded. All my life I have endeavored to make my company tolerable to my family, students, colleagues, and servants. And this attitude of mine, I know, has been edifying to those around me. But I am no longer a king. Something worthy only of a slave is going on inside me: evil thoughts prowl through my mind day and night, and my soul is a hotbed of feelings such as I have never known before. I feel hatred, contempt, indignation, resentment, fear. I have grown excessively severe, exacting, irritable, discourteous, suspicious. Things that in the old days would have provoked no more than a pun or a good-natured laugh, now evoke dark feelings in me. Even my sense of logic has undergone a change: in the old days it was only money I despised, now I harbor feelings of bitterness not with regard to money, but the rich, as if they were to blame; in those days I detested tyranny and violence, now I detest the men who practice it, as if they alone were guilty, and not every one of us who is incapable of bringing out the best in one another. What is the meaning of this? If these thoughts and feelings have arisen from a change in my convictions, then what has caused the change? Can the world have grown worse and I better, or is it that I have been blind till now, and indifferent? If the change results from a general decline of my mental and physical powers—I am a sick man, you know, losing weight every day—then my situation is indeed pitiable: it means my new ideas are abnormal, morbid, that I ought to be ashamed of them and consider them of no importance. . . ."

"It has nothing to do with illness," Katya interrupts me. "It's simply that your eyes have been opened, that's all. You have seen what you refused to see before. In my opinion, what you ought to do first of all is to break with your family and go away."

"You're talking nonsense."

"You no longer care for them, why be a hypocrite? And is that what you call a family? Nonentities! If they died today, tomorrow no one would miss them."

Katya despises my wife and daughter as much as they hate her. In these days one can hardly speak of people having a right to despise one another, but if one looks at it from Katya's point of view, and acknowledges the existence of such a right, one can see that she has just as much right to despise my wife and Liza as they have to hate her.

"Nonentities!" she repeats. "Have you had dinner today? How is it they didn't forget to call you to the table? How is it they still remember your existence?"

"Katya!" I say sternly. "I want you to stop talking like this."

"Do you think I enjoy talking about them? I'd be happier not even knowing them. Listen to me, dear: give it all up and go away. Go abroad. The sooner the better."

"What nonsense! And what about the university?"

"Give that up too. What's the university to you? It makes no sense. You've been lecturing there for thirty years, and where are your students now? How many of them are well-known scientists? Just count them! It doesn't require a good and talented man to increase the number of doctors who exploit ignorance and pile up hundreds of thousands of rubles for themselves. You are not needed."

"My God, how bitter you are!" I exclaim, appalled. "How bitter! Stop, or I shall leave. I don't know how to reply to such harshness."

The maid comes in and summons us to tea. When we sit down before the samovar our conversation, I am glad to say, changes. Having poured out my complaints, I now feel like indulging in another weakness of old age—reminiscing. I tell Katya about my past, and, to my great astonishment, recount incidents that I had not suspected still lived in my memory. And she listens to me with sympathy, with pride, with bated breath. I am particularly fond of telling her of how I once studied at the seminary, and how I dreamed of going to the university.

"Sometimes I would walk in our seminary garden," I tell her, "and if a breeze brought me the sound of singing and the whine of an accordion from some distant tavern, or if a troika flew by the seminary wall with bells jingling, that alone was enough to make me feel a rush of joy surging, not just in my breast, but in my stomach, in my arms and legs. . . . I would listen to the accordion, to the receding sound of bells, and imagine myself a doctor—painting pictures for myself one better than another. And, as you see, my dreams came true. I have had more than I dared to dream of. For thirty years I have been an admired professor, I have had splendid comrades, have enjoyed a notable fame. I have loved, married for passionate love, had children. In short, looking back, I see my whole life as a beautiful composition, the work of a master. Now it remains for me not to spoil the finale. And this requires that I die like a man. If death is, in fact, a peril, then it must be met in a manner worthy of a teacher, a scientist, and a citizen of a Christian country: with courage and an untroubled soul. But I am spoiling the finale. Drowning, I run to you with a plea for help, and you say to me: drown, that is what you ought to do."

The doorbell rings. Katya and I both recognize the ring and say:

"That must be Mikhail Fyodorovich."

And, indeed, a minute later, in comes my friend, the philologist Mikhail Fyodorovich, a tall, well-built, clean-shaven man of fifty, with thick gray hair and black eyebrows—a good man and an excellent comrade. He comes of an old aristocratic family of rather talented, successful men, who have played important roles in the history of literature and education. He himself is talented, intelligent, and highly cultivated, but rather strange. We are all, to a certain extent strange, we all have our eccentricities, but there is something exceptional in his strangeness, something that is apt to give his friends cause for concern. I know several among them who are unable to see his good qualities just because of this strangeness.

He comes in slowly, drawing off his gloves, and says in his velvety bass:

"Good evening. Having tea? Splendid! It's infernally cold."

He sits down at the table, takes a glass of tea, and immediately begins talking. The thing that is most characteristic about his manner of speaking is a perpetually jocular tone, a blend of philosophy and drollery that reminds one of Shakespeare's gravediggers. He speaks only of serious matters, but never seriously. His judgments are always harsh and cutting, but his mild, smooth, facetious manner takes the sting out of his abuse and one soon grows accustomed to it. He comes every evening with half a dozen university anecdotes, which he generally begins relating as soon as he sits down at the table.

"Good Lord!" he sighs, with an ironical twitch of his eyebrows. "What clowns there are in this world!"

"Tell us . . ." says Katya.

"As I was coming out of my lecture this morning, I met that old idiot N. N—— on the staircase. He was coming along with that horsy chin of his stuck out, looking, as usual, for someone to listen to his complaints about his migraine, his wife, or the students who stay away from his lectures. 'Oh, he's seen me,' I thought, 'I'm done for, now I am in for it. . . .' "

And so on in the same vein. Or he will begin by saying: "Yesterday I attended a lecture for the general public given by our friend Z. Z———. I am really amazed that our alma mater—tell it not in Gath—risks making a public display of such simpletons as that Z. Z———, Europe's great dunce! You could comb the continent, I've no doubt, and not find another like him. He lectures, if you can imagine it, as if he were sucking a lollypop: smack-smack-smack. . . . He gets cold feet, loses his place in the manuscript, and his poor little thoughts crawl at the speed of a bishop on a bicycle—and the worst of it is that you have absolutely no idea what he is trying to say. The boredom is ghastly, even the flies expire. It can only be compared to our annual gathering in the auditorium for the traditional commencement address, God help us!"

Then an abrupt transition.

"Three years ago—Nikolai Stepanovich here will remember—it fell to me to deliver that address. It was hot, stifling, my uniform cut me under the arms—simply deadly! I spoke for half an hour, an hour, an hour and a half, two hours. . . . 'Thank God,' I thought, 'only ten more pages.' But since the last four pages were entirely superfluous, I counted on leaving them out. 'That,' thought I, 'leaves only six.' But then what do you think? I happened to glance up and there before me in the front row sat a general wearing some sort of decoration, and next to him a bishop. The poor devils were numb with boredom, absolutely goggle-eyed from trying to keep awake and at the same time to look attentive, and as if they understood my lecture and enjoyed it. 'Well,' I thought, 'if you like it so much, you shall have it!' And just for spite, I read the last four pages too."

When he talks, only his eyes and eyebrows seem to smile, a characteristic of ironical people. And at such times there is no trace of malice or hatred in his eyes, but a good deal of wit and that foxy sort of slyness which is seen only in the faces of very observant people. While I am speaking about his eyes, I may as well mention another peculiarity I have observed. When he accepts a glass from Katya, listens to her remarks, or watches her if she happens to leave the room for a moment, there is something gentle, something pure and beseeching in his glance. . . .

The maid removes the samovar and puts a large piece of cheese on the table with some fruit and a bottle of Crimean champagne, a rather poor wine that Katya grew fond of while living in the Crimea. Mikhail Fyodorovich takes two packs of cards from the whatnot and begins playing patience. He contends that certain varieties of patience require great concentration and sagacity, but that does not prevent him from diverting himself with conversation the whole time he is playing. Katya follows the game attentively, helping him more by her facial expressions than by anything she says. She never drinks more than two small glasses of wine in the course of the evening. I sip a quarter of a tumbler, and the rest of the bottle is left to Mikhail Fyodorovich, who can drink a great deal without ever getting drunk.

We settle a variety of questions over patience, questions for the most part of a higher order and touching on the subject nearest our hearts—science.

"Science, God knows, has become obsolete," says Mikhail Fyodorovich, speaking in measured tones. "Its song is sung. Yes. . . . Humanity has already begun to feel the need of replacing it with something else. It sprang from the soil of superstition, was nourished by superstition, and is now as much the quintessence of superstition as its defunct grandams, alchemy, metaphysics, and philosophy. And what, actually, has it given to mankind? The difference between learned Europeans and the Chinese, who get along without science, is trifling, purely external. The Chinese know nothing of science, but what have they lost?"

"Flies know nothing of science either," I say, "but what does that prove?"

"There is no need to get angry, Nikolai Stepanych. After all, I am only saying it here among ourselves. . . . I am more circumspect than you think; I have no intention of saying such things in public—God forbid! The mass of humanity cherishes the superstition that science and art are superior to agriculture, commerce, handicrafts. Our sect is maintained by this superstition, and it is not for us to destroy it. God forbid!"

As the game goes on, the younger generation is hauled over the coals too.

"Our present-day populace has degenerated," sighs Mikhail Fyodorovich. "Not to speak of ideals and all that sort of thing, but if, at least, they were capable of work and rational thought! In fact, it's a case of 'Sadly I gaze upon this generation.' "

"Yes, they have degenerated terribly," Katya agrees. "Tell me, have you had a single outstanding student in the last five or ten years?"

"I don't know about our other professors, but I can't think of any among mine."

"In my time I have seen a great many of your students and young scientists, and many actors too . . . well, I have never been so fortunate as to meet—I won't say a hero or a man of talent—even a merely interesting man. They are all colorless, mediocre, puffed up with pretentions. . . ."

These conversations about degeneration never fail to produce the same effect upon me: I feel as though I had accidentally overheard some unpleasant talk about my own daughter. Sweeping accusations based on such threadbare commonplaces, such bugaboos as degeneration, lack of ideals, and references to the glorious past, are offensive to me. Any imputation, even when made in the presence of ladies, ought to be formulated with the utmost exactness, otherwise it is not an accusation but idle vilification, and unworthy of decent people.

I am an old man, I have been teaching for thirty years, and I see neither degeneration nor an absence of ideals, and I do not find that the present is any worse than the past. My doorman Nikolai, whose experience in the matter is worth something, says that present-day students are neither better nor worse than those of the past.

If I were asked what it is I do not like in my students today, I should not be able to answer at once, nor to say very much, but I should be quite specific. I know their defects, and consequently have no need to resort to vague generalities. I do not like their smoking, drinking, and marrying late, nor the fact that they are so unconcerned, at times even so callous, as to tolerate want in their midst and to neglect paying up their arrears in the Students' Aid Society. They do not know other languages, and express themselves incorrectly in their own. Only yesterday one of my colleagues, a professor of hygienics, complained to me that he is obliged to lecture twice as long as he should because of their poor knowledge of physics and complete ignorance of meteorology. They readily succumb to the influence of the latest authors, even when they are by no means the best, but they are utterly indifferent to the classics such as Shakespeare, Marcus Aurelius, Epictetus, or Pascal, and it is this inability to distinguish the great from the inferior that more than anything else betrays their lack of practical intelligence. All complicated questions of a more or less social character (demographic problems, for instance) they solve by resorting to subscription lists rather than by means of scientific investigation and experiment, although these methods are entirely at their disposal and most appropriate to the purpose. They gladly become house physicians, assistants, laboratory technicians, externs, and are willing to stay in these positions till the age of forty, although independence, a sense of freedom, and personal initiative are no less necessary in science than, say, in art or commerce. I have plenty of pupils and listeners, but no assistants or successors, and consequently, while I am fond of them, touched by them, I am not proud of them, and so forth and so on. . . .

Such shortcomings, however numerous, give rise to pessimism or abuse only in the pusillanimous and the timid; they are all of an adventitious and transitory nature, entirely dependent on circumstances; in ten years or so they inevitably will have disappeared or have given place to other, new defects, which in their turn will alarm the faint-hearted. The students' sins frequently vex me, but this vexation is nothing compared with the joy I have experienced in the course of thirty years of talking with them, lecturing to them, observing their attitudes and comparing them to those outside their circles.

Mikhail Fyodorovich continues his obloquy, Katya listens, neither of them realizing into what depths the apparently innocent diversion of criticizing their neighbors is gradually leading them. They do not perceive how a simple conversation is degenerating by degrees into mockery and jeering, how they are both stooping to a form of slander.

"Laughable types one meets," says Mikhail Fyodorovich. "Yesterday I went to see our friend Yegor Petrovich, and there I found one of your medicos, a third-year sciolist, I believe. What a face . . . in the Dobrolyubov style . . . deep thought chiseled on the brow. We got into a conversation. 'Well, young man, quite a stir!' I said. 'I read that some German or other, I forget his name, has obtained a new alkaloid, idiotine, from the human brain.' And what do you think? He believed me, and his face was the picture of respect, as if to say: See what we fellows can do! And the other day I went to the theater. I took my seat, and there, just in front of me in the next row, sat a couple of individuals, one apparently a member of our clan, a law student, the other, a shaggy-looking fellow, a medico. The latter drunk as a lord. His attention to the stage—zero. Just sat there dozing and nodding, but the minute an actor embarked on a loud monologue, or even raised his voice, he started, nudged his companion, and said: 'What's he saying? Is it elevating?' 'Yes,' the law student replied. 'Sublime! Bra-vo-o!' the medico roared. 'Su-bli-i-me! Bravo-o!' The stupid sot, you see, goes to the theater not for art but for uplift. He craves the sublime."

Katya listens, laughing. There is something strange about her laugh: she catches her breath in quick rhythmic gasps, very much as if she were playing a concertina, and nothing in her face expresses mirth except her nostrils. I am depressed and do not know what to say. At last, beside myself, I flare up, leap from my chair, and shout:

"Stop it! Why do you sit there like a couple of toads, poisoning the air with your breath? That's enough!"

And without waiting for them to finish their malicious talk, I prepare to leave. It's time, in any case—nearly eleven.

"I'll stay a little longer," says Mikhail Fyodorovich. "May I, Yekaterina Vladimirovna?"

"Of course."

"*Bene.* Then perhaps we can have another little bottle."

They both accompany me into the hall with candles, and as I put on my overcoat Mikhail Fyodorovich says:

"You've grown terribly thin and old lately, Nikolai Stepanovich. What's the matter with you? Are you ill?"

"Yes, somewhat."

"And he won't consult a doctor," Katya puts in glumly.

"But why don't you consult someone? How can you go on like this? The Lord helps those who help themselves, my dear fellow. My regards to your family, and my apologies for not having gone to see them. In a day or two, before I go abroad, I'll drop in to say good-bye, I really will! I'm leaving next week."

I go away from Katya's feeling irritated, alarmed by the talk of my illness, and dissatisfied with myself. After all, I ask myself, why not consult one of my colleagues? And I immediately picture to myself how, after examining me, he would walk to the window in silence, think for a moment, then turn to me, and, in an effort to prevent me from reading the truth in his face, casually say:

"So far I see nothing special, *collega,* nevertheless, I would advise you to discontinue your work . . ." Thereby depriving me of my last hope.

And who is without hope? Now, when I make my own diagnosis and prescribe for myself, I can occasionally hope that I am deceived by my own ignorance, that I am mistaken about the albumin and sugar that I find, about my heart, about the edema I have twice observed in the morning; when, with the zeal of a hypochondriac, I look through the textbooks on therapy, changing my medication daily, I keep thinking I shall stumble on something comforting. It's all very petty.

Whether the heavens are covered with clouds or bright with a moon and stars, each time I look up on my way home in the evenings I think that soon death will come for me. It would seem that at such moments my thoughts would be deep as the sky, clear, momentous. . . . But no! I think about myself, my wife, Liza, Gnekker, my students, about people in general; my thoughts are mean, petty; I try to delude myself, and at these times my attitude to life might be expressed in the words of the celebrated Arakcheyev, who in one of his personal letters writes: "Everything good in this world has something bad in it, and the bad always outweighs the good." In other words, everything is vile, there is nothing to live for, and the sixty-two years that I have already lived are to be considered lost. Catching myself in such thoughts, I try to persuade myself that they are fortuitous, transitory, not deeply rooted; but the next moment I think:

"If that is so, then what draws you to those two toads every evening?"

And I make a vow never to go to Katya's again, though I know quite well that I shall go the next day.

As I ring my doorbell, and afterward going up the stairs, I feel that now I have no family and have no desire for one. Clearly the new Arakcheyev thoughts are not fortuitous and transitory, but dominate my whole being. Conscience-stricken, depressed, sluggish, barely able to move my limbs, and feeling as though a ton had been added to my weight, I get into bed and drop off to sleep.

And then—insomnia. . . .

4

With the advent of summer life changes.

One fine morning Liza comes into my room and says:

"Come, Your Excellency. Everything is ready."

My Excellency is led into the street, seated in a cab, and driven off. Having nothing better to do, I read signboards backward. The tavern sign "traktir" comes out Ritkart. A good name for a baroness—Baroness Ritkart. Driving along an open field we pass a cemetery, which makes absolutely no impression on me, though I know I shall soon be lying in it, through a wood, then more fields. Nothing of interest. After a two hours' drive, My Excellency is conducted into a summer cottage and installed in a room on the ground floor—a rather small but cheerful room with light blue wallpaper.

The night, as usual, is sleepless, but in the morning, not having to wake up and listen to my wife, I lie in bed. I do not sleep, but remain in that drowsy, half-conscious state in which you know you are not asleep, but dreaming. At noon I get up and sit at my table out of habit; now, instead of working, I amuse myself with French novels sent to me by Katya. It would, of course, be more patriotic to read Russian writers, but I must confess I have no particular liking for them. With the exception of two or three of our older writers, all contemporary writing strikes me as being not so much literature as some sort of home industry existing for no other reason than that it is being encouraged, even though its products enjoy no great success. The very best of these home products can hardly be called remarkable, and any sincere praise of them must be qualified by a "but"; and this holds true for all those literary novelties I have read in the last ten or fifteen years: not one is remarkable, not one exempt from a "but." Clever, edifying, but no talent; or talented, edifying, but not clever; or, finally, talented, clever, but not edifying.

I don't say that these French works are all edifying, talented, and clever. They don't satisfy me either. But they are less boring than Russian books, and it is not unusual to find in them the prime element of creative work—a sense of personal freedom, something that is lacking in Russian writers. I cannot recall a single one of our modern works in which the author has not taken pains from the very first page to involve himself in all sorts of conventions and covenants with his conscience. One is afraid to speak of nudity; another ties himself hand and foot with psychological analysis; a third feels he must have a "warm attitude toward humanity"; a fourth pads his book with descriptions of nature—whole pages of it—so he won't be suspected of tendentiousness. . . . One is bent on being the bourgeois at all costs, another on being the aristocrat, and so on. There is design, there is caution and a certain shrewdness, but neither the freedom nor the courage to write as one pleases, and consequently no creativeness.

All this applies to what is known as belles-lettres.

When it comes to serious articles by Russian writers on such subjects as sociology, art, and so on, I avoid reading them out of sheer timidity. In my childhood and early youth I had a fear of doormen and ushers, a fear which I retain to this day. I am still intimidated by them. It is said that we are only afraid of what we do not understand. And it is difficult, indeed, to understand why doormen and ushers are so pompous, so supercilious, so majestically rude. And when I read serious articles I feel this same undefined fear. Their extraordinary pomposity, the tone of Olympian waggery, the unceremonious treatment of foreign authors, and their dexterity and dignity in milling the wind—all this intimidates and alarms me, being so utterly unlike the modesty, the tone of gentlemanly restraint, to which I am accustomed when reading the works of naturalists or medical men.

And not only their articles, I even find it oppressive to read works translated or edited by our serious Russian writers. The vainglorious, patronizing tone of the prefaces, the superfluity of translator's notes, which prevent me from concentrating on the text, the bracketed question marks and the *sic!*s profusely scattered throughout the article or book, seem to me like so many violations of the author's personality and my independence as a reader.

I was once asked to appear as an expert in the circuit court; during a recess one of my fellow experts drew my attention to the rudeness of the prosecuting attorney to the defendants, among whom were two cultivated ladies. I believe I did not exaggerate when I told him that this rudeness was no worse than that displayed to one another by our writers of serious articles. In fact, this rudeness is so marked that I cannot speak of it without distress. Either they treat one another, or the authors they are criticizing, with a respect so exaggerated as to be undignified, or they deal with them more ruthlessly than I deal with my future son-in-law in my thoughts and in these notes. Accusations of irresponsibility, of dubious intentions, even of all sorts of crimes, are the customary adornments of these articles. All this, as young medical men are fond of saying in their articles, is the *ultima ratio*!

Such an attitude is inevitably reflected in the morals of the younger generation of writers, and consequently I am not at all surprised to find in the new works that have enriched our literature in the past ten or fifteen years, heroes who drink too much vodka and heroines who are somewhat less than chaste.

I sit reading my French novels, from time to time looking out the open window; I can see the tips of the fence palings, two or three scraggy trees, and beyond the fence a road, a meadow, and a broad strip of pine woods. Sometimes I watch a little boy and girl, both fair-haired and ragged, who clamber up the fence and laugh at my bald head. In their bright little eyes I read: "Look at baldy!" They are almost the only ones who care nothing for my rank and reputation.

People no longer come to see me every day. I will speak only of the visits of Nikolai and Pyotr Ignatyevich. Nikolai usually comes on holidays, ostensibly in connection with work, but in fact only to see me. He is always the worse for drink, which never happens in the winter.

"Well, how's everything?" I ask, going to meet him in the entry.

"Your Excellency!" he says, laying his hand on his heart and gazing at me with the ecstasy of a lover. "Your Excellency! . . . May God punish me! May lightning strike me dead on the spot! *Gaudeamus igitur Juvenestus. . . .*"

And he eagerly kisses me on the shoulder, the sleeve, the coat buttons.

"Everything all right back there?" I ask him.

"Your Excellency! As God is my witness . . ."

He tires me out with his pointless and incessant invocations, and I send him to the kitchen where they give him dinner.

Pyotr Ignatyevich also comes to see me on holidays; he comes not only to see how I am, but for the specific purpose of sharing his thoughts with me. He sits down near my table, modest, neat, circumspect, not venturing to cross his legs or lean his elbow on the table, and in an even, gentle voice and fluent bookish language recounts what to his mind are extremely interesting, piquant items of news, all gleaned from journals and books, and all resembling one another, belonging as they do to a single type: a certain Frenchman makes a discovery; some German denounces him by proving that his discovery had been made in 1870 by an American; a third person—also a German—outwits them both by proving that they both had made fools of themselves in mistaking air bubbles for dark pigment under the microscope.

Even when he wants to amuse me, Pyotr Ignatyevich speaks at great length and in the most minute detail, as if he were defending his dissertation; he enumerates all the literary sources from which his material is drawn, tries to be accurate in citing dates, issues of a journal, and names, giving every name in full—never simply Petit, but Jean Jacques Petit. Sometimes he stays to dinner with us, at which time he recounts the same piquant stories throughout the entire meal, reducing everyone at the table to a state of despair. If Gnekker and Liza turn the conversation to fugues and counterpoint, or Bach and Brahms, he lowers his eyes in modest confusion, embarrassed that such trivial subjects should be discussed in the presence of serious persons like myself and him.

In my present state of mind five minutes with him is enough to make me feel as if I had been looking at him and listening to him for an eternity. I detest the poor fellow. I simply wither under the steady sound of his soft voice and bookish language, and his anecdotes stupefy me. . . . He has nothing but the kindest feelings for me, talks for the sole purpose of giving me pleasure, and I repay him by staring at him as if I wanted to hypnotize him, all the while thinking: "Go, go, go. . . ." But he is not susceptible to mental suggestion and continues to stay, stay, stay. . . .

And as he sits before me I cannot rid myself of the thought: "When I die, it is quite possible that he will be appointed in my place"; then my poor lecture hall appears before my eyes as an oasis in which the spring is dry, and I am as ungracious, silent, and morose as if he, not I, were guilty of these thoughts. When he begins, as usual, to laud German scientists, instead of laughing at him good-naturedly, as I used to, I glumly mutter:

"A pack of asses, your Germans. . . ."

I know I am being like the late Professor Nikita Krylov, who, when bathing at Revel with Pirogov, was furious with the water for being cold, and burst out with: "These blasted Germans!" I behave badly with Pyotr Ignatyevich, and only when he has gone and I catch a glimpse of his gray hat on the other side of the garden fence do I have an impulse to call out to him and say: "Forgive me, my dear fellow!"

Our dinners are even more boring than in winter. Gnekker, whom I now loathe and despise, dines with us almost every day. Formerly I bore his presence in silence, now I direct caustic remarks at him, making my wife and Liza blush. Carried away by feelings of anger, I often say things that are simply stupid, without even knowing why I say them. Thus it happened on one occasion that I fixed my scornful gaze on him, and for no reason whatsoever blurted out:

> The eagle lower than the chick may fly,
> But never will the chick soar upward to the sky. . . .

And what I find most vexatious of all is that the chick-Gnekker shows himself to be much cleverer than the eagle-professor. Knowing that my wife and daughter are on his side, he holds to such tactics as responding to my gibes with a condescending silence (the old man's balmy—no use arguing with him) or making amiable fun of me. It is astounding to see how petty a man can become. I am capable of dreaming throughout an entire meal of how Gnekker will turn out to be an adventurer, how my wife and daughter will come to see their mistake, and how I will taunt them—this and other such absurd dreams when I have one foot in the grave!

There are now misunderstandings besides, which in the old days were known to me only by hearsay. Much as I am ashamed, I will describe one that occurred the other day after dinner.

I was sitting in my room smoking my pipe. My wife came in, as usual, sat down, and began talking about how nice it would be, now that the weather is warm and I am free, if I would go to Kharkov and find out what sort of man our Gnekker is.

"Very well, I'll go," I agreed.

Pleased with me, my wife got up and went to the door, but immediately turned back and said:

"Oh, and another thing . . . I know you'll be cross with me, but it is my duty to warn you. . . . Forgive my saying so, Nikolai Stepanych, but all our friends and neighbors have begun talking about how often you go to see Katya. She's an intelligent, educated girl, and I don't deny that she may be pleasant company, but, you know, it looks rather odd for a man of your age and social position to find pleasure in her society. . . . Besides, she has such a reputation that—"

All the blood suddenly left my brain, my eyes flashed, I sprang up, clutching my head, stamping my feet, and shouting:

"Leave me alone! Leave me alone! Leave me!"

My face must have looked awful, and my voice no doubt was strange, for all at once my wife turned pale and in a loud, unnatural voice uttered a desperate shriek. Hearing our cries Liza and Gnekker came running in, followed by Yegor. . . .

"Leave me alone!" I shouted. "Get out! Go away!"

My legs were numb, as if they no longer belonged to me. I felt myself falling into someone's arms, and was briefly aware of the sound of weeping before I fell into a swoon which lasted for two or three hours.

Now about Katya. She comes to see me every day before nightfall, and this, of course, cannot pass unnoticed by our friends and neighbors. She stops only for a minute, then takes me off for a drive with her. She has her own horse and a new little chaise, bought this summer. Altogether she lives in grand style. She has rented an expensive villa with a large garden, has moved all her furniture into it, and keeps two maids and a coachman. . . . I often ask her:

"Katya, what will you live on when you have run through all your father's money?"

"We shall see when the time comes," she replies.

"That money deserves to be treated more seriously, my dear. A good man worked hard to accumulate it."

"You have told me that before. I know."

First we drive through the meadow, then into the pine woods that I see from my window. Nature seems to me as beautiful as ever, though an evil spirit whispers that these pines and firs, these birds and white clouds overhead, will not even notice my absence, when, in three or four months, I am dead. Katya likes taking the reins; she enjoys the fine weather, and having me at her side, and, being in good spirits, refrains from saying harsh things.

"You are a very good man, Nikolai Stepanych," she says. "You are a rare specimen, the actor doesn't exist who could play you. Even a poor actor could play me, for instance, or Mikhail Fyodorych, but not you. I envy you, envy you terribly! After all, what have I made of myself? What?" She thinks for a minute, then asks: "Nikolai Stepanych, I'm nothing but a negative quantity, isn't that so? Isn't it?"

"Yes, it is," I answer.

"Hm-m. . . . And what can I do about it?"

How am I to answer her? It is easy to say: "Work," or "Give all you have to the poor," or "Know thyself," and just because it is so easy, I have no answer for her.

My colleagues who teach therapeutics advise: "Individualize each particular case." One has only to follow this advice to be convinced that the remedies recommended in textbooks as the best standard treatment prove to be absolutely useless in individual cases. This is no less true in moral disorders.

But I must give her some sort of answer, and I say:

"You have too much free time, dear. It's imperative that you find something to do. Why don't you go on the stage again, since acting is your vocation?"

"I can't."

"Why do you assume such a martyred air? I don't like that, my dear. Remember, it was you who became incensed at the people and the system, but you did nothing to improve either one. You didn't combat the evil, you were merely exhausted by it; you were the victim not of a struggle, but of your own weakness. Of course, you were young then, and inexperienced; now everything might be different. Do go on the stage again. You will be working, serving the sacred cause of art. . . . "

"Don't be so sly, Nikolai Stepanych," Katya interrupts me. "Let us agree once and for all: we will talk about actors, actresses, and writers, but leave art in peace. You are a fine, a rare person, but you do not sufficiently understand art to be able, in all conscience, to call it sacred. You've had no time to cultivate this feeling. In any case, I don't like these conversations about art!" she goes on nervously. "Don't like them at all! It has already been so vulgarized—I've had enough!"

"Who has vulgarized it?"

"Some have vulgarized it by their drinking, the newspapers by being so free with it, and clever people by their philosophy."

"Philosophy has nothing to do with it."

"Oh, yes it has. If anyone has to philosophize, that shows he doesn't understand it."

To avoid sharp words I hasten to change the subject, and then remain silent for some time. Only when we leave the woods and are driving toward Katya's house do I return to the subject and say:

"But you haven't told me why you don't want to go back to the stage."

"Nikolai Stepanych, this is really cruel!" she cries, suddenly blushing all over. "Do you want me to come right out and tell you the truth? Very well, if that's what you want. I have no talent. No talent and . . . and a great deal of vanity! There!"

After making this confession, she turns her face away from me and tugs violently at the reins to conceal the trembling of her hands.

As we drive up to the house we see Mikhail Fyodorovich walking near the gate, impatiently waiting for us.

"That Mikhail Fyodorych again!" Katya says with vexation. "Take him away from me, please! I'm fed up with him . . . such a washout. . . . I've had enough!"

Mikhail Fyodorovich was to have gone abroad some time ago, but he keeps postponing his departure from week to week. Certain changes have come over him lately: he looks drawn, drinks wine till he shows it—something he never did before— and his black eyebrows have begun to turn gray. When our chaise stops at the gate, he cannot conceal his joy and impatience. He makes a great fuss helping Katya and me to get out, bombards us with questions, laughs, rubs his hands, and that gentle, pure, imploring look, which I used to see only in his eyes, now suffuses his entire face. He is joyful, and at the same time ashamed of his joy, ashamed of his habit of spending every evening with Katya, and feels impelled to account for his presence by some such obvious absurdity as:

"I was driving by on business and thought I'd drop in for a minute."

We all go into the house; first we have tea, then the long familiar objects begin to appear on the table—the packs of cards, the big piece of cheese, fruit, the bottle of Crimean champagne. The subjects of our conversation are the same too; we talk about the very things we discussed in the winter. The theater, literature, the university and students all come in for their share; the air grows thick and stifling with malicious talk, only now, unlike the winter, it is poisoned by the breath of three toads instead of two. Besides the velvety baritone laugh and the concertinalike giggle, the maid who waits on us now hears the jarring disagreeable laugh of a stage general: he-he-he!

5

There are nights made terrible by thunder, lightning, wind, and rain—"sparrow nights," the country people call them. I experienced just such a "sparrow night" in my personal life. . . .

I woke up after midnight and instantly leaped out of bed. It suddenly seemed to me that I was about to die. What made it seem so? I experienced no particular bodily sensation that would indicate the end was near, but my soul was as oppressed by horror as if I had just seen a huge ominous glow in the sky.

Hastily lighting the lamp, I drank some water straight from the carafe and rushed to the open window. It was a magnificent night. There was the scent of new-mown hay, and something else that smelled sweet. I saw the tips of the fence palings, the gaunt drowsy trees by the window, the road, and the dark strip of woodland; the moon shone serene and bright in the cloudless sky. It was still; not a leaf stirred. I felt that everything was looking at me, holding its breath, waiting for me to die. . . .

It was sinister. I closed the window and quickly went back to bed. I felt for my pulse, and, unable to find it in my wrist, felt my temples, then my chin, and again my wrist, and wherever I touched my body it was cold and clammy. My breathing became more and more rapid, my whole body trembled, and inside me there was turmoil; I had the sensation there were cobwebs on my face and bald spot.

What should I do? Call my family? No, it would be useless. I could not imagine what my wife and Liza would do if they were to come.

I hid my head under the pillow, closed my eyes, and waited . . . and waited. . . . My back was cold, I felt as if my spine was being drawn inward; it was as if death was definitely creeping up to me from behind. . . .

"Kee-vee! Kee-vee!" a screech suddenly pierced the silence of the night, and I could not tell whether it came from outside or from within my breast.

"Kee-vee! Kee-vee!"

My God, how frightful! I wanted to take another drink of water, but I was afraid to open my eyes, afraid to raise my head. I was in the grip of an unaccountable animal fear, unable to understand what I was afraid of; was it that I wanted to live, or that some new unknown pain was in store for me?

Upstairs, in the room overhead, someone either groaned or laughed. . . . I strained my ears. Soon afterward I heard footsteps on the stairs. Someone hurried down, then went back up. A minute later, again the sound of footsteps descending, and someone stopped outside my door and listened.

"Who's there?" I cried.

The door opened. I intrepidly opened my eyes and saw my wife. Her face was pale and her eyes red from weeping.

"Are you awake, Nikolai Stepanych?" she asked.

"What is it?"

"For God's sake, come and see Liza! Something has happened to her. . . ."

"Very well . . . I'll be glad to . . ." I mumbled, relieved at not being alone. "Very well . . . at once. . . ."

I followed my wife, listening to what she was telling me, but too agitated to understand a word. Spots of light from her candle danced on the stairs and our elongated shadows trembled; it seemed to me that someone was pursuing me, trying to seize me from behind; my feet got caught in the skirts of my dressing gown and I gasped for breath.

"I'm going to die right here on the staircase," I thought. "This very minute. . . ."

But the stairs came to an end and we approached Liza's room along a dark corridor with an Italian window. Liza was sitting on the bed with her legs hanging over the side; she had nothing on but a nightgown and was moaning.

"Oh, my God . . . Oh, my God . . ." she mumbled, squinting at the light of our candles. "I cannot, I cannot. . . ."

"Liza, my child," I said, "what is it?"

When she saw me she gave a cry and flung herself on my neck.

"Papa, my good, kind Papa . . ." she sobbed. "My darling, my dearest Papa. . . . I don't know what's the matter with me . . . I'm so miserable!"

She put her arms around me and kissed me, babbling endearing expressions I had not heard from her since she was a child.

"Calm yourself, little one. God bless you," I said. "There's no need to cry. I am miserable too."

I tried to cover her up and my wife gave her something to drink; as we clumsily jostled each other at the bedside, my shoulder brushing my wife's shoulder, I was reminded of how together we used to give our children their baths.

"Help her, help her!" my wife implored me. "Do something for her!"

What could I do? I could do nothing. The poor girl's heart was burdened with something I did not understand, something I knew nothing about, and I could only murmur:

"Never mind, never mind. . . . It will pass. . . . Go to sleep, go to sleep. . . ."

To make things worse, a dog howled outside; at first it was a subdued uncertain sound, then it grew louder as two dogs commenced howling together. I had never attached any significance to such omens as the howling of dogs or the hooting of owls, but now my heart contracted painfully and I hastened to give myself an explanation of this howling.

"It's nonsense," I thought, "the influence of one organism upon another. My violent nervous tension communicated itself to my wife, to Liza, to the dog, that's all. . . . This sort of trans-ference explains prescience and forebodings."

A little later, when I returned to my room to write a pre-scription for Liza, I no longer thought about my imminent death, but felt so heavy-hearted, so depressed, that I was sorry not to die then and there. For a long time I stood motionless in the middle of the room trying to think what to prescribe for Liza; the moaning overhead ceased and I decided not to pre-scribe anything, yet I continued to stand there. . . .

The silence was deathly, a silence which, as some writer has put it, rings in your ears. Time passed slowly, the strips of moonlight on the windowsill did not move but seemed frozen there. . . . Dawn would be long in coming.

Suddenly the gate creaked, someone stole toward the house, broke a twig from one of the scraggy trees, and cautiously tapped on the window with it.

"Nikolai Stepanych!" I heard a whisper. "Nikolai Stepanych!"

I opened the window and thought I must be dreaming: hud-dled against the wall under the window, the moonlight full upon her, stood a woman in black gazing up at me with big eyes. Her face was pale, austere, fantastic in the moonlight, as if carved in marble, but her chin was quivering.

"It is I," she said. "I—Katya!"

All women's eyes look big and black in the moonlight, and everyone looks taller and paler; probably for this reason I had failed to recognize her at first.

"What's the matter?"

"Forgive me," she said. "I suddenly felt unbearably miserable . . . . I couldn't stand it and came here. . . . There was a light in your window and . . . and I decided to knock. . . . Forgive me. . . . Oh, if you only knew how wretched I am! What are you doing up?"

"Nothing . . . I couldn't sleep."

"I had a sort of foreboding. But, of course, it's nonsense."

Her eyebrows were raised, tears glistened in her eyes, and her whole face was radiant with the expression of trustfulness that I knew so well but had not seen for a long time.

"Nikolai Stepanych!" she pleaded, holding out her arms to me. "My darling, I beg you, implore you . . . if you do not scorn my friendship and respect for you, do what I ask of you!"

"What is it?"

"Take my money!"

"Come, now, what an idea! What would I do with your money?"

"You could go away somewhere for your health. You need medical treatment. Will you take the money? Will you? Yes, my darling?"

She gazed eagerly into my face and repeated:

"Yes? Will you take it?"

"No, my dear, I will not take it," I said. "Thank you."

She turned her back to me and bowed her head. No doubt there was something in the tone of my refusal which did not admit of further talk about money.

"Go home to bed," I said. "We'll see each other tomorrow."

"So you don't consider me your friend?" she asked despondently.

"I didn't say that. But your money is of no use to me now."

"I beg your pardon . . ." she said, dropping her voice a whole octave. "I understand. . . . To be indebted to a person like me— a retired actress. . . . Well, good-bye. . . ."

And she went away so quickly that I had no time to say good-bye to her.

6

I am in Kharkov.

Since it would have been useless and, indeed, beyond my strength to struggle against my present mood, I have determined that the last days of my life should be irreproachable, at least outwardly. If I have been wrong where my family is concerned, which I am well aware is the case, then I will try to do what they wish. I am asked to go to Kharkov—I go to Kharkov. Besides, I have grown so indifferent to everything of late that it does not matter to me where I go—to Kharkov, to Paris, to Berdichev.

I arrived here at midday and came to this hotel not far from the cathedral. The rocking of the train and cold drafts have left me in such a state that I can do nothing but sit on the side of the bed holding my head and waiting for my tic to begin. I ought to have gone to see some of my acquaintances among the professors today, but I have neither the strength nor the inclination.

An old hall porter comes in and asks whether I have brought my own bed linen with me. I detain him for five minutes and question him about Gnekker, on whose account I have come here. The old man turns out to be a native of Kharkov, knows the town like the palm of his hand, but does not remember any family by the name of Gnekker. I question him about the estate—same answer.

The clock in the corridor strikes one, then two, then three. . . . These last months of waiting for death to come have seemed longer to me than all the rest of my life. And never before have I been so reconciled to the slow passage of time. Formerly, if I had to wait in the station for a train, or sit through the students' examinations, a quarter of an hour seemed an eternity, but now I can sit motionless on the side of my bed all night, thinking with complete indifference that tomorrow will be followed by another such long and dismal night, and the day after tomorrow. . . .

The clock in the corridor strikes five, six. . . . It grows dark.

In order to occupy my thoughts, I try to recover the point of view I had before I became indifferent, and ask myself: why am I, a distinguished man, a privy councilor, sitting in this little hotel room, on the side of this bed with the strange gray blanket? Why am I looking at this cheap tin washstand and listening to the jangling of that wretched clock in the corridor? Is this in keeping with my reputation and high position? My answer to these questions is an ironic smile. It amuses me to think of the naiveté with which, in my youth, I exaggerated the importance of fame and the exceptional position that celebrities are supposed to enjoy. I am famous, my name is pronounced with reverence, my picture has appeared in the *Niva* and the *Illustrated World News,* I have even read my biography in a German magazine—and what of it? Here I sit, utterly alone, in a strange city, on a strange bed, rubbing my aching cheek with the palm of my hand. . . .

Family squabbles, the implacability of creditors, the rudeness of railway employees, the inconvenience of the passport system, the expensive and unwholesome food in station buffets, the universal ignorance and coarseness in human relations—all this and a great many other things which it would take too long to enumerate, concern me no less than the ordinary citizen who is known no further than his own street. Then what is so special about my situation? Let us suppose that I am celebrated a thousand times over, that I am a hero of whom my country is proud; that bulletins on the state of my health appear in all the newspapers, letters of sympathy pour in from colleagues, students, the general public; yet all this will not prevent me from dying in a strange bed, in misery and utter loneliness. . . . No one is to blame for it, of course, but, I am sorry to say, I have no love for my renown. It appears to have betrayed me.

I fall asleep around ten o'clock, sleeping soundly in spite of my tic, and had I not been awakened should have slept a long time. Shortly after one there is a knock at the door.

"Who's there?"

"A telegram."

"You might have waited till morning," I say angrily, taking the telegram from the hall porter.

"Excuse me. Your light was on, so I thought you were awake."

I open the telegram and look first at the signature: from my wife. What can she want?

"Gnekker and Liza married secretly yesterday. Return."

After reading the telegram I am momentarily alarmed, but what alarms me is not so much what Liza and Gnekker have done as my own indifference to the news of their marriage. They say that philosophers and wise men are indifferent. This is not true. Indifference is a paralysis of the soul, a premature death.

Again I go to bed and try to think of something to occupy my mind. What am I to think about? Everything has been thought over; there seems to be nothing left to arouse my interest.

When daylight comes I sit up in bed, clasping my knees, and try, for want of something better to do, to understand myself. "Know thyself" is excellent and useful advice; it is only a pity that the ancients failed to indicate a method for following it.

In the past when I wanted to understand someone, or even myself, I took into consideration, not actions, which are always conditional, but desires. Tell me what you want and I will tell you what you are.

And now I examine myself. What do I want?

I want our wives, children, friends, and students to love in us, not the fame, the label, the connections, but the ordinary man. What else? I should like to have assistants and successors. What else? I should like to wake up a hundred years from now and have a glimpse of what is going on in science. I should like to have lived another ten years. . . . Anything more?

No, nothing more. I think and think, but can think of nothing further. And no matter how much I may think, nor how far-reaching my thoughts, it is clear to me that there is nothing vital, nothing of great importance, in my desires. In my passion for science, in my desire to live, in this sitting up in a strange bed and trying to know myself, in all the thoughts, feelings, and conceptions that I formulate, there is no common element, nothing that would unify them into a whole. Each thought and feeling exists in isolation, and in all my judgments of science, the theater, literature, and my students, in all the pictures my imagination paints, even the most skillful analyst would be unable to find what is called a general idea, or the god of a living man.

And without this there is nothing.

Given such poverty of spirit, any serious ailment, the fear of death, the influence of circumstances or of people, would be enough to upset and scatter to the winds all that I have been accustomed to regard as an outlook that embodied the joy and meaning of my life. It is consequently no wonder that the last months of my life are darkened by thoughts and feelings worthy of a slave and a barbarian, and that I now am indifferent and take no heed of the dawn. When that which is higher and stronger than all external influences is lacking in a man, a good head cold is enough to upset his equilibrium and make him see an owl in every bird and hear the howl of a dog in every sound. At such times all his pessimism or optimism, all his thoughts both great and small, are significant only as symptoms, nothing more.

I am defeated. This being so, it is useless to go on thinking, useless to talk. I will sit and wait in silence for what is to come.

In the morning the porter brings me tea and a copy of the local newspaper. I mechanically read through the advertisements on the first page, the leading article, extracts from other newspapers and magazines, the news of the day. . . . Among the news items I find the following: "The celebrated scientist, Honored Professor Nikolai Stepanovich So-and-So arrived in Kharkov yesterday by express train, and is staying at the Such-and-Such Hotel."

Great names are apparently created to live a life of their own, apart from those who bear them. At this moment my name is nonchalantly parading about Kharkov; in another three months, set out in gold letters on my tombstone, it will blaze like the sun itself—while I shall be covered with moss.

A light tap on the door. Somebody to see me.

"Who's there? Come in."

The door opens, I step back in astonishment, hastily drawing my dressing gown around me. Before me stands Katya.

"How are you?" she says, out of breath from having climbed the stairs. "You weren't expecting me, were you? I too . . . I too . . . have come. . . ."

She sits down, stammering and not looking at me.

"Why don't you say something? I just arrived . . . found out you were in this hotel . . . and came to see you."

"I am very happy to see you," I say, shrugging my shoulders, "but I am surprised. . . . It's as if you had dropped from the sky. What have you come for?"

"Oh . . . I just thought . . . I'd come. . ."

Silence. All at once she jumps up and impulsively comes to me.

"Nikolai Stepanych!" she says, turning pale and pressing her hands to her breast. "Nikolai Stepanych! I cannot go on living like this! I cannot! In God's name, tell me quickly, this very minute: what am I to do? Tell me, what am I to do?"

"What can I say?" I am perplexed. "There's nothing I can say."

"Tell me, I implore you!" she goes on breathlessly, trembling from head to foot. "I swear I cannot go on like this! It's too much for me!"

She sinks into a chair and begins sobbing. Throwing back her head, she wrings her hands and stamps her feet; her hat slips off her head and dangles by its elastic, her hair is disheveled.

"Help me! Help me!" she pleads. "I can't go on any longer!"

She takes a handkerchief out of her traveling bag and with it pulls out several letters, which fall from her lap to the floor. As I pick them up, I accidentally catch sight of the word "passiona——" on one of them, and recognize Mikhail Fyodorovich's handwriting.

"There is nothing I can tell you, Katya," I say.

"Help me!" she sobs, seizing my hand and kissing it. "After all, you are my father, my only friend! And you are wise, educated, you have lived a long time! You have been a teacher! Tell me: what am I to do?"

"Honestly, Katya, I do not know. . . ."

I am utterly at a loss, bewildered, touched by her sobs, and barely able to stand on my feet.

"Come, let's have some breakfast, Katya," I say with a forced smile. "No more crying."

And then I add in a sinking voice:

"I shall soon be gone, Katya. . . ."

"Just one word, even a word!" she weeps, stretching out her hands to me. "What shall I do?"

"What a queer girl you are, really . . ." I mutter. "I don't understand. . . . Such a sensible girl, and suddenly you . . . go off into tears!"

Silence. Katya arranges her hair, puts on her hat, crumples up the letters, and stuffs them into her bag—all very deliberately and without a word. Her face, the front of her dress, and her gloves are wet with tears, but her expression is cold and austere. . . . Looking at her I feel ashamed of being happier than she is. I have discovered in myself the absence of what my philosophic colleagues call a general idea only recently, in my decline, and in the face of death, but the soul of this poor creature has never found and never in her life will find refuge . . . never in her life!

"Come, Katya, let us have breakfast," I say.

"No, thank you," she replies coldly.

Another minute passes in silence.

"I don't like Kharkov," I say. "It's so gray here. . . . Such a gray town."

"Yes, I suppose it is. . . . It's ugly. . . . I shan't be here for long. . . . I'm only passing through. I leave today."

"Where are you going?"

"To the Crimea—to the Caucasus, I mean."

"Oh! For long?"

"I don't know."

Katya gets up, smiling coldly, and without looking at me holds out her hand.

I feel like saying: "So you won't be at my funeral?" But she does not look at me; her hand is cold, like the hand of a stranger. I accompany her to the door in silence. . . . Now she has left me, and walks down the long corridor without glancing back. She knows that I am watching her and will probably look back when she reaches the turn. . . .

No, she did not look back. Her black dress has disappeared from sight for the last time, the sound of her footsteps dies away. . . . Farewell, my precious! ∾

INTERPRETIVE QUESTIONS
FOR DISCUSSION

Why, despite his great "name," talent, and reputation for goodness, can't Nikolai Stepanovich avoid spoiling the finale of his life?

1. Why does Nikolai Stepanovich emphasize the disparity between his "drab and ugly" person and his "illustrious and beautiful" name? (180) Why does he conclude that his renown "appears to have betrayed me"? (237)

2. Why has Nikolai Stepanovich lost his ability to write, but not to lecture? Why are scientific articles easier for him to write than the simplest letter of congratulation or a report? (180–181)

3. Are we meant to blame Nikolai Stepanovich for his wife's change from "the slender Varya whom I so passionately loved for her fine clear mind, her pure soul, her beauty" into a corpulent, dull, and petty woman? (182–183)

4. Why does Nikolai Stepanovich harbor poisonous thoughts about his children, who are for the most part decent people? (184–185) Why does he come to feel that he has no family and no desire for one? (221)

5. Why has no scientific debate, game, or entertainment given Nikolai Stepanovich as much pleasure as lecturing? Why does he feel a "voluptuous exhaustion" after his lectures that is greater than even Hercules knew after his exploits? (189–190)

6. Why can't Nikolai Stepanovich face the all-important questions about the "mystery beyond the grave"? Why is the destiny of bone marrow of more interest to him than the ultimate purpose of the universe? (191)

7. Why does Nikolai Stepanovich lack the courage to follow his conscience and resign his lectureship? (191)

8. Why do horrible new thoughts come to Nikolai Stepanovich during his lectures and poison the last days of his life? Why does he want his listeners to know what he is thinking and to be horrified along with him? (191–192)

9. Why does Nikolai Stepanovich tell Katya, "I see my whole life as a beautiful composition, the work of a master. Now it remains for me not to spoil the finale. And this requires that I die like a man"? (213)

10. Why, when he dislikes Katya's and Mikhail Fyodorovich's malicious talk, does Nikolai Stepanovich eventually join them and become a third "toad"? (231)

11. Why does Nikolai Stepanovich's soul become a hotbed of feelings he has never known before—"hatred, contempt, indignation, resentment, fear"? (211) Why is his "outlook that embodied the joy and meaning" of his life destroyed by his illness? (238–239)

12. Why can't Nikolai Stepanovich unify his thoughts and feelings into a general idea about life? (238) Why is he "defeated" by his attempt to know himself? (239)

Suggested textual analyses
Pages 189–192: beginning, "I know what I am going to lecture on," and ending, "It is not easy to get through such moments."

Pages 236–237: beginning, "In order to occupy my thoughts," and ending, "It appears to have betrayed me."

Why is Nikolai Stepanovich overcome with indifference after his "sparrow night"?

1. Why have the inner lives of Nikolai Stepanovich's family—whose gaiety and love used to animate his life—slipped away from his "control"? (206–207)

2. Why does the terrible "sparrow night" bring out expressions in Liza and Katya that Nikolai Stepanovich had not seen in a long time? (233, 235)

3. Why does Nikolai Stepanovich say that he knew nothing about and could not understand the cause of Liza's suffering? (233)

4. When Liza sobs and clings to her father during the "sparrow night," why does Nikolai Stepanovich say, "There's no need to cry. I am miserable too"? Why does he tell Liza that her sorrow will pass rather than try to find out more about it? (233)

5. Why is Nikolai Stepanovich so depressed after his encounter with Liza that he actually longs for the death he had feared? (234)

6. Why does Katya offer to give Nikolai Stepanovich all her money—the sacrifice he longs to hear from his children? Why doesn't this expression of love keep Nikolai Stepanovich from becoming indifferent? (235–236)

7. Why does Nikolai Stepanovich confide in no one about the fears he suffered during his "sparrow night"?

8. Why does Nikolai Stepanovich determine that the last days of his life should be "irreproachable, at least outwardly"? Why does he think that he has been wrong as far as his family is concerned, and that doing "what they wish" will make up for it? (235–236)

9. Why does Nikolai Stepanovich feel nothing when he finds out that Liza has run off with the scheming Gnekker? Why is he alarmed at his indifference? (237–238)

10. Why does Nikolai Stepanovich try to take to heart the advice of the ancients to "know thyself" as a solution to his paralyzing indifference, his "premature death"? (238)

Suggested textual analyses
Pages 231–234: beginning, "There are nights made terrible," and ending, "yet I continued to stand there. . . ."

Pages 237–239: beginning, "I open the telegram," and ending, "for what is to come."

Why can't Nikolai Stepanovich and Katya relieve each other's unhappiness, despite their affection for each other?

1. Why do Nikolai Stepanovich and Katya turn to each other when they are miserable?

2. Why does Nikolai Stepanovich in his old age love the orphan Katya, but not his own children? Why is his earliest memory concerning Katya—and the one that he holds most dear—her "extraordinary trustfulness"? (196)

3. Why is Nikolai Stepanovich, who deeply loves lecturing before an audience, unable to understand Katya's passion for the theater? (189–190, 197–199)

4. Why did Nikolai Stepanovich play "a strange and not very admirable role" with regard to Katya during her life in the theater? Why was he never able to convey to Katya how he had lost his head over what was happening to her? (200–202)

5. Why does Nikolai Stepanovich feel that Katya's advice to leave his family and the university is useless—like telling a drowning man to go drown? (212–213) Why does he think that his giving any advice to Katya would be just as pointless? (229)

6. Why does Nikolai Stepanovich tell Katya, "You didn't combat the evil, you were merely exhausted by it; you were the victim not of a struggle, but of your own weakness"? (229)

7. Why does Katya misunderstand the reason that Nikolai Stepanovich refuses to take her money? (235) Why does Katya not respond when Nikolai Stepanovich confesses that he will soon be "gone"? (240)

8. Why does Katya follow Nikolai Stepanovich to Kharkov and implore him to tell her what to do after she receives a passionate love letter from Mikhail Fyodorovich? Why does she beg Nikolai Stepanovich for "just one word"? (240)

9. Although miserable himself and moved by Katya's anguish, why does Nikolai Stepanovich reprimand Katya for her tears? Why does he make ridiculous small talk when Katya begs for help? (240–241)

10. Why does Nikolai Stepanovich feel ashamed of being happier than Katya? Why will Katya never find "refuge" in her life? (241)

11. Why does Katya act "cold and austere" and not look back when she leaves Nikolai Stepanovich? (241)

12. Why do Katya and Nikolai Stepanovich—people who follow their dreams—end up being alone and miserable? Why does Chekhov have Katya's unhappiness come early in life and Nikolai Stepanovich's come late in life?

Suggested textual analyses
Pages 211–213: beginning, "Warm cozy surroundings," and ending, "I don't know how to reply to such harshness."

Pages 239–241: from "The door opens," to the end of the story.

FOR FURTHER REFLECTION

1. Do Nikolai Stepanovich and Katya have great and sensitive souls, or are they self-absorbed failures?

2. Is Nikolai Stepanovich being wise or insensitive when he doesn't even try to comfort Liza or Katya?

3. Is "refuge" from isolation the best we can hope for in our human relationships?

4. Would having a "name" as illustrious and beautiful as Nikolai Stepanovich's give you satisfaction at the end of your life?

5. Could any advice have helped Katya?

6. How can we avoid spoiling the finale of our lives? Is it Nikolai Stepanovich's own fault that he feels miserable and alone at the end of his life, or is his a universal condition?

POETRY

T. S. Eliot

T. S. ELIOT (1888–1965), poet, critic,
playwright, and editor, was born of a
distinguished New England family in
St. Louis, Missouri. Educated at Harvard,
the Sorbonne, and Oxford, he settled in
London in 1915. With the publication of
"The Love Song of J. Alfred Prufrock" in
1915, Eliot launched the modernist age of
English poetry. His critical essays, such as
"Tradition and the Individual Talent" and
"The Metaphysical Poets," were equally
influential. In 1922, he published *The Waste
Land* and became a director of the publishing firm of Faber & Faber Ltd., a position
he held until his death. After joining the
Church of England in 1927, his poetry
became more overtly Christian, a trend
that culminated in *Four Quartets* (1943),
a single work composed of four long
poems. A writer of profound influence on
twentieth-century literature and criticism,
Eliot was awarded the Nobel Prize for
literature in 1948.

The Love Song of J. Alfred Prufrock

S' i' credesse che mia risposta fosse
a persona che mai tornasse al mondo,
questa fiamma starìa sanza più scosse;
ma però che già mai di questo fondo
non tornò vivo alcun, s' i' odo il vero,
sanza tema d' infamia ti rispondo.[1]

Let us go then, you and I,
When the evening is spread out against the sky
Like a patient etherised upon a table;
Let us go, through certain half-deserted streets,
The muttering retreats
Of restless nights in one-night cheap hotels
And sawdust restaurants with oyster-shells:
Streets that follow like a tedious argument
Of insidious intent
To lead you to an overwhelming question . . .
Oh, do not ask, "What is it?"
Let us go and make our visit.

---

1. ["If I thought my answer were to one who would ever return to the world, this flame
   should stay without another movement; but since none ever returned alive from this depth,
   if what I hear is true, I answer thee without fear of infamy." This is from Guido da
   Montefeltro's answer to Dante when asked why he is being punished in hell. Guido is
   encountered by Dante and Virgil in the Eighth Chasm of the Eighth Circle, the realm
   of the False Counselors. There each spirit is concealed within a flame, which moves
   as the spirit speaks.]

In the room the women come and go
Talking of Michelangelo.

The yellow fog that rubs its back upon the window-panes,
The yellow smoke that rubs its muzzle on the window-panes
Licked its tongue into the corners of the evening,
Lingered upon the pools that stand in drains,
Let fall upon its back the soot that falls from chimneys,
Slipped by the terrace, made a sudden leap,
And seeing that it was a soft October night,
Curled once about the house, and fell asleep.

And indeed there will be time
For the yellow smoke that slides along the street,
Rubbing its back upon the window-panes;
There will be time, there will be time
To prepare a face to meet the faces that you meet;
There will be time to murder and create,
And time for all the works and days of hands
That lift and drop a question on your plate;
Time for you and time for me,
And time yet for a hundred indecisions,
And for a hundred visions and revisions,
Before the taking of a toast and tea.

In the room the women come and go
Talking of Michelangelo.

And indeed there will be time
To wonder, "Do I dare?" and, "Do I dare?"
Time to turn back and descend the stair,
With a bald spot in the middle of my hair—
[They will say: "How his hair is growing thin!"]
My morning coat, my collar mounting firmly to the chin,
My necktie rich and modest, but asserted by a simple pin—
[They will say: "But how his arms and legs are thin!"]

Do I dare
Disturb the universe?
In a minute there is time
For decisions and revisions which a minute will reverse.

For I have known them all already, known them all—
Have known the evenings, mornings, afternoons,
I have measured out my life with coffee spoons;
I know the voices dying with a dying fall
Beneath the music from a farther room.
   So how should I presume?

And I have known the eyes already, known them all—
The eyes that fix you in a formulated phrase,
And when I am formulated, sprawling on a pin,
When I am pinned and wriggling on the wall,
Then how should I begin
To spit out all the butt-ends of my days and ways?
   And how should I presume?

And I have known the arms already, known them all—
Arms that are braceleted and white and bare
[But in the lamplight, downed with light brown hair!]
Is it perfume from a dress
That makes me so digress?
Arms that lie along a table, or wrap about a shawl.
   And should I then presume?
   And how should I begin?

      .   .   .   .   .

Shall I say, I have gone at dusk through narrow streets
And watched the smoke that rises from the pipes
Of lonely men in shirt-sleeves, leaning out of windows? . . .

I should have been a pair of ragged claws
Scuttling across the floors of silent seas.

．　．　．　．　．

And the afternoon, the evening, sleeps so peacefully!
Smoothed by long fingers,
Asleep . . . tired . . . or it malingers,
Stretched on the floor, here beside you and me.
Should I, after tea and cakes and ices,
Have the strength to force the moment to its crisis?
But though I have wept and fasted, wept and prayed,
Though I have seen my head [grown slightly bald] brought in
　　　upon a platter,
I am no prophet—and here's no great matter;
I have seen the moment of my greatness flicker,
And I have seen the eternal Footman hold my coat, and snicker,
And in short, I was afraid.

And would it have been worth it, after all,
After the cups, the marmalade, the tea,
Among the porcelain, among some talk of you and me,
Would it have been worth while,
To have bitten off the matter with a smile,
To have squeezed the universe into a ball
To roll it toward some overwhelming question,
To say: "I am Lazarus, come from the dead,
Come back to tell you all, I shall tell you all"—
If one, settling a pillow by her head,
　　Should say: "That is not what I meant at all.
　　That is not it, at all."

And would it have been worth it, after all,
Would it have been worth while
After the sunsets and the dooryards and the sprinkled streets,
After the novels, after the teacups, after the skirts that trail
　　　along the floor—
And this, and so much more?—
It is impossible to say just what I mean!
But as if a magic lantern threw the nerves in patterns on a screen:

Would it have been worth while,
If one, settling a pillow or throwing off a shawl,
And turning toward the window, should say:
 "That is not it at all,
 That is not what I meant, at all."

.   .   .   .   .

No! I am not Prince Hamlet, nor was meant to be;
Am an attendant lord, one that will do
To swell a progress, start a scene or two,
Advise the prince; no doubt, an easy tool,
Deferential, glad to be of use,
Politic, cautious, and meticulous;
Full of high sentence, but a bit obtuse;
At times, indeed, almost ridiculous—
Almost, at times, the Fool.

I grow old . . . I grow old . . .
I shall wear the bottoms of my trousers rolled.

Shall I part my hair behind? Do I dare to eat a peach?
I shall wear white flannel trousers, and walk upon the beach.
I have heard the mermaids singing, each to each.

I do not think that they will sing to me.

I have seen them riding seaward on the waves
Combing the white hair of the waves blown back
When the wind blows the water white and black.

We have lingered in the chambers of the sea
By sea-girls wreathed with seaweed red and brown
Till human voices wake us, and we drown.

T. S. Eliot

Interpretive Questions
for Discussion

Why is Prufrock never able to articulate his "overwhelming" question?

1. To whom is Prufrock addressing his monologue?

2. Why does the author introduce his poem with a quotation from Dante's *Inferno*? How seriously are we meant to take the epigraph's suggestion that the social environment Prufrock must negotiate is a kind of hell?

3. Why does Prufrock compare the evening to a "patient etherised upon a table"? (251) Is it Prufrock's internal state, or the external world, that is deadened or diseased?

4. After issuing his invitation, why does Prufrock envision walking through half-deserted streets lined with one-night cheap hotels and sawdust restaurants?

5. Aware that he is being led to an "overwhelming question," why does Prufrock back away from it? (251) What *is* Prufrock's unarticulated question?

6. Why does Prufrock feel threatened and helpless—like an insect "pinned and wriggling on the wall"—when he imagines daring to ask his question? Why does he feel vulnerable to being fixed in a "formulated phrase" by the eyes of others? (253)

7. Why does the self-effacing Prufrock tell himself that there will be time not only for indecision, but also to "murder and create"? (252)

8. Why does Prufrock vacillate between wanting to assert himself and wanting to escape from the need to act?

Does Prufrock fail to find love because he is afraid of women?

1. If Prufrock is timid in female company, why does he say that he has "known the arms already, known them all"? (253)

2. Is Prufrock unconsciously or consciously repelled by the physical? Why does he note that the arms of the women he has known are "downed with light brown hair" when viewed in lamplight? (253)

3. Why is Prufrock, who imagines people commenting on his thinning hair, so concerned that he is aging?

4. Are we meant to imagine Prufrock as middle-aged, or as a young man who is prematurely worried about aging?

5. Why does Prufrock reassure himself by thinking that he is properly dressed? Why does he focus on the way his morning coat mounts "firmly to the chin" and on his rich and modest necktie, "asserted by a simple pin"? (252)

6. Why do Prufrock's thoughts repeatedly turn to the room with the women who "come and go" if he feels that this society is meaningless—that he must stop measuring out his life "with coffee spoons"? (252, 253)

7. Why does Prufrock imagine having "bitten off the matter" and stating his question only to have a woman respond, "That is not what I meant at all. / That is not it, at all"? (254)

8. Why does Prufrock compare his life (his "days and ways") to the disgusting contents of an ashtray? (253)

9. Why is Prufrock's monologue referred to as a "love song"?

Is Prufrock's identity strengthened or diminished as he confronts his failures and inadequacies?

1. Why does Prufrock fantasize about being a crab scuttling across the floors of "silent seas"? Why does he picture himself as a small, solitary, inhuman creature with "a pair of ragged claws"? (253)

2. Why does Prufrock identify himself with John the Baptist ("I have seen my head . . . brought in upon a platter"), only to insist that he is no prophet? Why does he think of himself as Lazarus, "come from the dead"? (254)

3. Why does Prufrock say, "I have seen the eternal Footman . . . snicker, / And in short, I was afraid"? (254) What is Prufrock afraid of?

4. Why does Prufrock insist that he is no "Prince Hamlet, nor was meant to be"? Why does he identify, instead, with the foolish Polonius, describing himself as "full of high sentence, but a bit obtuse; / At times, indeed, almost ridiculous"? (255)

5. Is Prufrock more self-aware, or just more self-conscious, than the average person?

6. What does Prufrock mean when he says that he has "heard the mermaids singing, each to each"? (255) Why does Prufrock conclude that the mermaids will not sing to him?

7. Who does the "we" refer to when Prufrock says, "We have lingered in the chambers of the sea / By sea-girls wreathed with seaweed red and brown"? (255) Is this image of underwater existence meant to be pleasing or disturbing?

8. Does Prufrock's monologue conclude with the suggestion that a dreamlike state is preferable to reality? Why does Prufrock equate waking with drowning?

9. Does the ending of the poem represent any kind of resolution for the conflicted Prufrock?

FOR FURTHER REFLECTION

1. Can a person who lives almost entirely in his or her own head be said to have a strong identity?

2. Given the increased permissiveness of contemporary society, would Prufrock find it any easier to integrate the cerebral and emotional aspects of his personality today?

3. Is Prufrock's malaise something that many of us should recognize in ourselves?

4. How is the expression of one's sexuality central to human identity?

5. When does coming to a clearer understanding of one's failures strengthen, rather than erode, identity?

Questions for

EMMA

Jane Austen

JANE AUSTEN (1775–1817) is one of the great masters of the English novel. Her works are renowned for their penetrating satire, innovative narrative style, and moral vision. Not many details are known of Austen's life, but the inscription above her tomb in Winchester Cathedral provides these particulars: "youngest daughter of the late Rev. George Austen, formerly Rector of Steventon in this County, she departed this Life on the 18th of July 1817, aged 41, after a long illness supported with the patience and the hopes of a Christian. The benevolence of her heart, the sweetness of her temper, and the extraordinary endowments of her mind obtained the regard of all who knew her, and the warmest love of her intimate connections." No mention is made of Austen's novels, because her name never appeared on the title page of the four books published during her lifetime—*Sense and Sensibility, Pride and Prejudice, Mansfield Park,* and *Emma,* which was dedicated to the flamboyant and prodigal Prince Regent at his request. Austen's two other completed novels, *Northanger Abbey* and *Persuasion,* were published posthumously in 1818.

NOTE: All page references are from the Bantam Classic edition of *Emma* (first printing 1981).

INTERPRETIVE QUESTIONS
FOR DISCUSSION

Why does the intelligent and observant Emma imagine everything wrong when it comes to love?

1. Why is Emma an "imaginist," who will not submit her fancy to her understanding? (91, 306)

2. Why does Emma insist that she has little intention of marrying and say that it is not in her nature to fall in love? (78–79) Why does Emma—a devoted daughter, sister, and friend—believe that she lacks the "tenderness of heart" possessed by her father, Isabella, and Harriet? (245)

3. Why does Emma call matchmaking "the greatest amusement in the world"? (9) Why does she want to be the first to plan the marriage between Harriet and Mr. Elton? (31)

4. Why can Emma imagine the kind of man she might marry, but not recognize him in Mr. Knightley until she thinks she has lost him to Harriet? (292, 365, 375)

5. Why does Emma take on Harriet as a friend if she knows that Harriet's nature is not "of that superior sort in which the feelings are most acute and retentive"? (127)

6. Why can Emma discern that the flirtations of Mr. Elton and Frank Churchill are not signs of real love, and yet not recognize that Mr. Knightley's steady, heartfelt conduct toward her is love? (125, 298, 337–338)

7. Why can Emma perceive Mr. Elton's lack of elegance, but not his social ambitions? Why does Emma rationalize away every indication of Mr. Elton's pursuit of her—even the fact that he pushes the "courtship" charade toward her instead of toward Harriet? (61–62, 72, 103–104, 124)

8. Why does Emma leap to the unseemly conclusion that Jane Fairfax is involved in a "reprehensible" attachment with Mr. Dixon, the husband of Jane's intimate friend? (144–145, 222)

9. Why does Emma "entertain no doubt" that she has fallen in love with Frank Churchill after his first two-week stay in the neighborhood? (239–240)

10. Is it Emma's vanity that leads her to believe that Frank Churchill is in love with her, or does Frank's delight in deceiving everyone make him overplay his attentions to Emma? (241, 289)

11. Why can't Emma, who loves romantic intrigues, perceive the secret attachment between Frank Churchill and Jane Fairfax? Why does Emma laugh at Mr. Knightley's hint at such an attachment and protest his observations so vehemently, even though she knows that he possesses "penetration" in such matters? (124, 321–322)

12. Why does Emma become fully convinced that Harriet is beloved by Mr. Knightley? Why is Emma more threatened by Harriet's avowal of love for Mr. Knightley, despite the improbability of its being requited, than she is by Mrs. Weston's reasonable suggestion that Mr. Knightley might love and marry Jane Fairfax? (205–206, 374–375)

Suggested textual analyses
Pages 55–62 (from Chapter 8): beginning, " 'Come,' she said, 'I will tell you something in return for what you have told me,' " and ending, "she was very sure did not belong to Mr. Elton."

Pages 123–127 (from Chapter 16): beginning, "The hair was curled, and the maid sent away," and ending, "the conviction of her having blundered most dreadfully."

Why does Emma come to recognize her faulty conduct only when Harriet confesses her attachment to Mr. Knightley?

1. Why does everyone in Emma's circle, with the exception of Mr. Knightley, think that Emma is "perfect"? (8)

2. Why is Emma "blind" to the abilities and social status of Harriet Smith? (55) Why is Emma so dismissive of the relative discrepancy between their positions in society when she is so particular in other instances?

3. Why is Emma so fixedly against Harriet's association with the Martins even though the family enjoys the good opinion of everyone—including Mr. Knightley—and Emma herself is impressed with their delicacy and warmth?

4. Why doesn't Emma learn from her error in promoting a match between Harriet and Mr. Elton? While understanding that her conduct was wrong, why is she unable to keep herself from "adventuring too far" with Harriet's future when Frank Churchill arrives on the scene? (126)

5. Why does Emma persist in her plan to make Harriet's visit to the Martins a short, formal one, even though her own heart doesn't approve and she is pained by her role in the "bad business"? (169–170)

6. Why can't Emma, despite all her good intentions, bring herself to befriend Jane Fairfax? Why doesn't Jane's interesting past and melancholy future ignite Emma's imagination and compassion? (81, 150–153, 185)

7. Why is Emma so quick to give Frank Churchill her honest opinion of Jane Fairfax—that Jane's reserve makes friendship with her impossible and suggests that Jane has something to conceal? (185) Why does Emma, who values elegance and propriety, confide in Frank her idea that Mr. Dixon is in love with Jane? (199)

8. When agonizing over how she had unknowingly encouraged Harriet to attach herself to Mr. Knightley, why does Emma conclude that "she had been imposing on herself"? (378)

9. Why does Emma mistake Mr. Knightley's remonstrance of her behavior toward Miss Bates as a sign of his indifference toward her? (381)

Suggested textual analysis
Pages 372–380 (from Chapter 47): from "She could not speak another word," to the end of the chapter.

Why does Emma violate her own principles of good behavior during the excursion to Box Hill?

1. Why is Emma's vanity flattered by Frank Churchill's false gallantry? Why does Emma find Frank Churchill "insufferable" when he is silent and unamusing? (337–338)

2. Why can Emma "not resist" telling Miss Bates that she will be limited to saying only three dull things? Why does Emma ignore the fact that she has caused pain to her grateful old friend? (340)

3. Why does Emma take pleasure in the idea of being coupled with Frank Churchill in her friends' imaginations? Why doesn't Emma allow herself to imagine marriage to Frank, thinking only "of finding him pleasant, of being liked by him to a certain degree"? (110)

4. Why does Emma participate in empty exchanges with Frank Churchill at Box Hill, even though she realizes that to others it appears that they are flirting excessively? Why does Emma's disappointment in the excursion make her act gay and thoughtless? (337)

5. Why does Frank Churchill make Emma appear to act without propriety, saying that she presides over the party and desires to know what everyone is thinking? Why does he make Emma the tool for affronting almost everyone in the party? (339)

6. Why does Emma find much to laugh at and enjoy in Mr. Weston's silly, flattering conundrum? (341)

7. Why doesn't Emma see anything odd in the exchange between Frank Churchill and Jane Fairfax about attachments formed in public places? (341–342)

8. Why does Emma need Mr. Knightley's reprimand to make her realize how cruelly she has treated Miss Bates? Why does Emma at first try to laugh off her insensitive conduct? (344–345)

9. Why does Mr. Knightley's remonstrance make Emma more upset and unhappy than at any other time in her life, even though she is used to his telling her "truths" about her obligations and judgment? (344–345) Why does Emma see her conduct at Box Hill as being more faulty than her other misdeeds?

10. Why does Emma conclude, after everything is resolved, that there is "a little likeness" between her and Frank Churchill? (440)

Suggested textual analysis
Pages 336–345 (Chapter 43)

FOR FURTHER REFLECTION

1. Is self-knowledge a requisite of healthy romantic love? Can one be in love without knowing oneself?

2. Do you find Emma "faultless in spite of all of her faults"? Why do some readers despise Emma, while others love and forgive her?

3. When do confidence and self-respect turn into vanity?

4. Are there elements of building a self-identity in a small village like Highbury that are missing in modern American urban life?

5. Is the reluctance to find fault in those dependent on us a serious flaw, undermining their ability to achieve self-knowledge?

Questions for

INVISIBLE MAN

Ralph Ellison

RALPH ELLISON (1914–1994), born in
Oklahoma a few years after the territory
became a state, grew up in social circumstances more akin to those of the frontier
than of the South with its rigid caste system.
A devoted follower of the jazz and blues
scene in Oklahoma City during his boyhood,
he studied music at Tuskegee Institute
from 1933 to 1936. From Alabama he went
to New York where he studied sculpture,
worked for the Federal Writers Project,
and met Richard Wright, who encouraged
him to write short stories and reviews. After
the publication of *Invisible Man* (1952),
which won the National Book Award,
Ellison taught at Bard College, the
University of Chicago, and Rutgers
University. From 1970 to 1980 he was
Albert Schweitzer Professor of Humanities
at New York University. He is the author of
two collections of essays, *Shadow and Act*
(1964) and *Going to the Territory* (1986).

NOTE: All page references are from the Second
Vintage International edition of *Invisible Man*
(first printing 1995).

Interpretive Questions
for Discussion

Why does his grandfather's disturbing advice to overcome the white man with "yeses" and "undermine 'em with grins" become a "constant puzzle" and "curse" to the narrator?

1. Why do the dehumanizing rites of the battle royal fail to shake the narrator's commitment to his formula for personal success—humility and hard work? (25, 32)

2. Why does the narrator dream that his grandfather tells him to open the briefcase and read the engraved document with the message, "To Whom It May Concern . . . Keep This Nigger-Boy Running"? (33)

3. Imagining himself back at school, why does the narrator wonder if the statue of the college Founder is lifting a veil from the face of a kneeling slave or lowering it more firmly in place? (36)

4. Why does Mr. Norton insist that the narrator, and the other students at the college, are his "fate"? (41–45)

5. Why do we learn that the source of Mr. Norton's fascination with Jim Trueblood's story is his own unacknowledged incestuous desires? (51)

6. After leaving the Golden Day, why is the narrator so shaken by Mr. Norton's anger that he feels he is losing the only identity he had ever known? (99)

7. Why does the narrator feel a numb, violent outrage when Dr. Bledsoe tells him, "This is a power set-up, son, and I'm at the controls"? (142)

8. Why does the revelation of Dr. Bledsoe's and the trustees' treachery cause the narrator, for the first time, to ask himself who he is? (194)

9. Why is Lucius Brockway the black father figure at whom the narrator finally strikes back? Why does "a wild flash of laughter" struggle to rise from beneath the narrator's anger at the old man? (225–227)

10. Are we meant to admire Lucius Brockway, the secret machine "inside the machine" of Liberty Paints, who enthusiastically allows himself to be exploited by the white industrial system? (216–217, 228)

11. Why does the author have the factory hospital doctors cure the narrator by means of an electric lobotomy machine? (236) Why are we told that inside the hospital machine the narrator feels utterly alone, and lost in a "vast whiteness"? (238)

12. Why is the narrator's release from the confinement of the machine described in terms that suggest a surreal birth? (243–244) Upon leaving the hospital, why does the narrator feel as if he is in the "grip of some alien personality lodged deep within" him? (249)

Suggested textual analyses
Pages 15–17: beginning, "It goes a long way back," and ending, "triumph for our whole community."

Pages 137–147: beginning, "When I went in he was wiping his neck," and ending, "I packed my bags."

Why does the narrator feel that working for the Brotherhood will save him from "disintegration"?

1. Why is the narrator's first real act of positive self-assertion to eat a yam while walking along the street? (264) Why does the narrator—declaring "I yam what I am"—resolve never to be ashamed again of the things he likes? (266)

2. Why does the narrator fear the rush of empathic feeling that draws him to the old couple evicted onto the street? Why is the narrator especially disturbed by the sight of the old man's free papers? (270, 272)

3. Staring at the old couple's belongings on the street, why does the narrator feel as if he himself "was being dispossessed of some painful yet precious thing" that he "could not bear to lose"? (273)

4. When recruiting the narrator for the Brotherhood movement, why does Brother Jack emphasize that the narrator is not like the old people, that he is emerging as "something new"? Why does he tell the narrator that he mustn't waste his emotions on individuals—"they don't count"? (291)

5. Why does the narrator decide to rely on the judgment of the Brotherhood when they demand that he leave Mary and live elsewhere in order to be a Harlem leader? (316) Why does he accept without questioning their providing him with a new name?

6. Why does the narrator feel compelled to hide from Mary the shattered bank with its grotesque caricature of a grinning Negro? (321) Why are we told about the narrator's unsuccessful attempts to get rid of the cast-iron bank and the coins that filled it? (328–329)

7. Why does the narrator tell the audience in the arena that *"something strange and miraculous and transforming"* was taking place in him—that he feels suddenly more human? Why does he tell the audience that he has found his "true family! . . . true people! . . . true country!"? (345–346)

8. Why does the narrator say that he felt as if he had awakened from a dream when Jack tells him he wasn't hired to think and he realizes that Jack doesn't "see" him? (469, 475–476)

9. Why does the "scientific objectivity" of the Brotherhood—its practice of sacrificing the weak—remind the narrator of being locked inside the hospital machine? (505)

10. Why is Hambro unable to convince the narrator of the correctness of the Brotherhood's methods? Why does the narrator insist that Hambro see him as an individual? (505)

11. Why must the narrator be disillusioned with the Brotherhood—and articulate his invisibility—before he is finally able to accept his past with all its humiliations? (507–508)

12. Why does the narrator determine to use his invisibility to destroy the Brotherhood by overcoming them with yeses? (508–509)

Suggested textual analyses
Pages 262–280: beginning, "I hurried on, suppressing a savage urge," and ending, "some of them laughing, some cursing, some intently silent."

Pages 500–511: beginning, "I was shown into a small, book-lined study," and ending, "until it exploded in their faces."

Why does Tod Clifton, a political activist, decide to fall out of history and sell Sambo dolls?

1. Why does Clifton knock Ras down when the black nationalist accuses him of being a "black traitor to the black people for the white people"? What is the silent question that Clifton seems to ask Ras as he looks gravely down at the black militant? (376)

2. Why does Clifton tell the narrator that "sometimes a man *has* to plunge outside history. . . . Otherwise he might kill somebody, go nuts"? (377)

3. Why is the Sambo doll described as having two faces, one that grinned back at Clifton while the other grinned forward at the crowd? Why are we told that Clifton "had been making it dance all the time and the black thread had been invisible"? (446)

4. After the narrator spits on the Sambo doll, why does the potbellied man point at the doll, then at him, and explode with laughter? (433)

5. Are we meant to view Clifton's final, violent act of self-assertion as deliberately suicidal? (436, 457)

6. Why does it suddenly occur to the narrator that it might be transitory ones like the zoot suiters—"men out of time" whose lives are too obscure to be recorded in history—who are the "true leaders, the bearers of something precious"? What does the narrator mean when he says, "What if history was a gambler, instead of a force in a laboratory experiment, and the boys his ace in the hole"? (441)

7. Why does the narrator conclude that it was his job to get inside the "groove of history" all of the black men and women who had previously been invisible to him? (443–444)

8. Why does the narrator's discovery that Rinehart inhabits a world of possibility—a "vast seething, hot world of fluidity"— profoundly shake his view of reality? (498–499)

9. Why does the narrator say that perhaps *"only Rine the rascal"* was at home in a world without boundaries? (498) Why are we told that Rinehart, the man of multiple identities, has a smooth tongue, a heartless heart, and is ready to do anything? (493)

10. What does the narrator mean when he says that "somewhere between Rinehart and invisibility there were great potentialities"? (510) Does Rinehart suggest a way out of the narrator's double bind—"Outside the Brotherhood we were outside history; but inside of it they didn't see us"? (499)

11. Why are we told that the narrator moves as one with the "black river" of rioters, his "personality blasted"? (550) Why does the author describe the rioters in language that recalls the fluid world of Rinehart? (550, 554–556)

12. Why does it turn out that by pretending to agree with the committee, the narrator made himself its tool just when he had thought himself most free? (553) Why does the reality of the riot—a mutual destruction of blacks engineered by and for the purposes of whites—recall the battle royal? (553)

Suggested textual analyses
Pages 368–377: beginning, "My Brothers, the time has come for action," and ending, "suddenly very glad I had found Brotherhood."

Pages 430–444: beginning, "A small fruit wagon," and ending, "I'd been asleep, dreaming."

Why is the narrator compelled to put his "invisibility down in black and white"—to exchange the role of orator and rabble-rouser for that of hibernating writer—in order to discover who he is?

1. Why does the narrator say that being imprisoned and invisible in the coal hole is a kind of living death? (566–567) Why does the narrator compare himself to Jim Trueblood's jaybird that "yellow jackets had paralyzed in every part but his eyes"? (63, 568)

2. Why does the narrator dream, in a state between sleeping and waking, that he is castrated by Jack, Bledsoe, Norton, Ras, and others from his past? (569) Why does he tell them that his testicles hanging from the bridge are their sun and moon, and that his seed wasting upon the water is all the history that they will make? (570)

3. Why does the narrator's dream end with the bridge striding off like *"an iron man, whose iron legs clanged doomfully,"* and the narrator screaming, *"No, no, we must stop him"*? (570)

4. While listening to the music of Louis Armstrong in his warm, bright basement hole, why does the narrator have a vision of an old woman who tells him that freedom *"ain't nothing but knowing how to say what I got up in my head"*? (11)

5. Why does the narrator have another storyteller, Jim Trueblood, resolve his feelings about how he's both guilty and not guilty by singing the blues? Why does Trueblood's resolution take the form of deciding "I ain't nobody but myself and ain't nothin' I can do but let whatever is gonna happen, happen"? (66)

6. Why does the narrator end his prologue with the threat of violence, asserting that all "dreamers and sleepwalkers must pay the price, and even the invisible victim is responsible for the fate of all"? (14)

7. Why does writing down his story show the narrator that at least half the blame for his invisibility, what he calls his "sickness," lay within himself? (575)

8. Having learned to view the world as possibility, why does the narrator see "imagination" as the alternative to "chaos" when a person opts to step outside the borders of reality? (576)

9. What does the narrator mean when he suggests that black people must "affirm the principle on which the country was built" because, given the circumstance of their origin, they "could only thus find transcendence"? (574)

10. Why does the narrator conclude that he has overstayed his hibernation—that "even an invisible man has a socially responsible role to play"? (581)

11. What does the narrator mean when he says that he wants more than simply "the freedom not to run"? (575) Are we meant to think that by the end of the novel he has found a way to rejoin society without being made to run? (579)

12. Why does the narrator end his epilogue with the suggestion that his listeners may also be invisible? Why does he say this idea frightens him? (581)

Suggested textual analyses
Pages 565–571: beginning, "I kept to the darker side of streets," and ending, "The end was in the beginning."

Pages 572–581 (Epilogue)

FOR FURTHER REFLECTION

1. Does the narrator in Ellison's novel speak for young black people today? Are blacks in the United States still required to conform to roles defined for them by whites?

2. Do you agree with Ellison's suggestion in *Invisible Man* that the strength of America as a democracy lies in its cultural diversity?

3. How can we best realize Ellison's vision of returning all Americans to a sense of personal moral responsibility for democracy?

4. Taking into account all of the images of failed leadership in *Invisible Man* (Bledsoe, Norton, Jack, Ras, Clifton, and the narrator), what might Ellison's definition be of a great American leader for the black community?

ACKNOWLEDGMENTS

All possible care has been taken to trace ownership and secure permission for each selection in this anthology. The Great Books Foundation wishes to thank the following authors, publishers, and representatives for permission to reprint copyrighted material.

The Fire Next Time, from THE FIRE NEXT TIME, by James Baldwin. Copyright 1962, 1963 by James Baldwin. "My Dungeon Shook" originally appeared in *The Progressive.* "Down at the Cross" originally appeared in *The New Yorker* as "Letter from a Region in My Mind." Reprinted by permission of The James Baldwin Estate.

Apology, by Plato, from SOCRATES AND LEGAL OBLIGATION, translated by R. E. Allen. Copyright 1980 by the University of Minnesota. Reprinted by permission of University of Minnesota Press.

A Real Life, from OPEN SECRETS, by Alice Munro. Copyright 1994 by Alice Munro. Reprinted by permission of Alfred A. Knopf, Inc.

A Room of One's Own, from A ROOM OF ONE'S OWN, by Virginia Woolf. Copyright 1929 by Harcourt Brace & Company; renewed 1957 by Leonard Woolf. Reprinted by permission of Harcourt Brace & Company.

A Dull Story, from WARD SIX AND OTHER STORIES, by Anton Chekhov. Translated by Ann Dunnigan. Translation copyright 1965 by Ann Dunnigan. Reprinted by permission of Penguin Books USA, Inc.

The Love Song of J. Alfred Prufrock, from COLLECTED POEMS 1909–1962, by T. S. Eliot. Copyright 1936 by Harcourt Brace Jovanovich, Inc. Copyright 1963, 1964 by T. S. Eliot. Reprinted by permission of Harcourt Brace & Company.

Cover photography: Robert Severi, Maryland

Cover and book design: William Seabright and Associates